THE LIBRARY
ST. MARY'S COLLEGE OF MARYLAND
ST. MARY'S CITY, MARYLAND 20686

D1710358

THE PRUSSIAN
BUREAUCRACY IN CRISIS
1840–1860

To learn how one can serve a system against one's conscience and conviction for an entire lifetime, one must be a Prussian official; to know how one covers the disgrace of abandoned conviction with a title or a decoration, one must know the secrets of the higher bureaucracy.   *Rudolf Gneist*

THE PRUSSIAN
BUREAUCRACY IN CRISIS
1840–1860

Origins of an Administrative Ethos

✻

JOHN R. GILLIS

STANFORD UNIVERSITY PRESS

STANFORD, CALIFORNIA

1971

Stanford University Press
Stanford, California
© 1971 by the Board of Trustees of the
Leland Stanford Junior University
Printed in the United States of America
ISBN 0-8047-0756-1
LC 70-130826

For Tina

Acknowledgments

First among those to whom I owe a debt of gratitude is Professor Gordon A. Craig of Stanford University. I also wish to thank James Sheehan, S. Frederick Starr, and John E. Talbott for their advice and, most of all, their criticism. The financial aid given by the Social Science Research Council, the Deutsche Akademische Austauschdienst, and the Princeton University Research Committee is much appreciated. Mention should be made of the efficient services of the *Bundesarchiv* at Koblenz, the Hauptarchiv at Berlin/Dahlem, and the *Staatsarchive* at Düsseldorf and Koblenz; the libraries of the Universities of Bonn, Köln, Princeton, and Oxford; and the Newspaper Library of the British Museum. I am grateful to Mrs. Nancy Donovan of Stanford Press for her editorial assistance, and to the editors of *Past and Present* for their kind permission to use material from my article "Aristocracy and Bureaucracy in Prussia." Finally, I want to thank David Flaherty for his moral support when this manuscript was in an earlier stage.

J.R.G.

Contents

Introduction

The importance of the study of the bureaucracy has always been apparent to those who have attempted to understand Prussian historical development; the bureaucracy has long been the focus of major studies by social scientists, and of the groups that were most influential in building Prussia politically, socially, and economically, only the army has attracted greater attention from historians. The approaches of the two disciplines have not been as different as one might think: although historians have generally devoted themselves to the institutional and political evolution of the bureaucracy, there have been those who have sought to understand the social dimensions of that process; and though many political scientists and sociologists have been content to theorize about the bureaucracy, a significant minority have remained loyal to the empirical tradition. In the cases where the methods of the historian have been combined with the insights of the sociologist, notable success has been achieved. Indeed, the founding father of German sociology, Max Weber, was a skilled practitioner of the historian's craft, and it was through his influence that Otto Hintze, perhaps the greatest of the historians of the Prussian bureaucracy, learned to appreciate the limitations of the conventional political and institutional approaches.[1]

The works of Hintze and of his close collaborator Gustav Schmoller, most of which were published before World War I, were unmatched in excellence until 1958, when Hans Rosenberg's study of the eighteenth-century bureaucracy appeared.[2] Since that time comparable works on other German bureaucracies have been written, and fresh studies of the Prussian civil service in the nineteenth and twentieth centuries have been made by Reinhard Koselleck and Wolfgang Runge.[3] Koselleck begins where Rosenberg leaves off, with the decline of bureaucratic absolutism after the reign of Frederick the Great and before the Revolution of 1848. Runge picks up the story in 1918, focusing on the part played by the civil service during the revolution and under the Weimar Republic. Rosenberg's theme was the transition from royal to bureaucratic absolutism; Koselleck's, the ripening and ultimate decay of bureaucratic absolutism; and Runge's, the change from monarchical constitutionalism to republican democracy. In every case the subject under investigation was the bureaucracy as both institution and social elite—an elite whose members were participants in a specific political context, acting in and being acted upon by the events of their times.

With the exception of the fragmentary work of Eckart Kehr, there is no study that treats the post-absolutist nineteenth-century bureaucracy in a comprehensive way.[4] I make no pretense of filling the chronological void with this book; I have made no attempt here to extend Koselleck's narrative into the period of national unification. Instead, I have chosen to describe the bureaucracy during the period roughly coinciding with the reign of Frederick William IV, which also encompasses an era of relatively rapid economic and demographic change. My study is concerned with the interaction of social and political events during these years, and takes into account long-term changes in social and political trends only insofar as they affected the transformation of the civil service in the 1840's and 1850's: the subject here is the origin and direction of certain changes, not their duration or completion.

These decades were a turning point in the history of the Prussian civil service—the formative time when patterns of social and political life very different from those of the earlier periods of absolutism began to crystallize. Bureaucratic attitudes and behavior originating in these years were to remain characteristic until the overthrow of the monarchy in 1918 and even beyond, well into the twentieth century. It is important to note, however, that this continuity embraced change as well as stability, for along with new rigidities in thought and action came the contradictions and tensions that were to provide the dynamic of later decades. In Koselleck's study the 1840's were viewed as the end of an epoch in the history of the bureaucracy; I have chosen, however, to treat the decades of revolution and reaction as a vantage point from which to see more clearly the process of the reshaping of one of modern Prussia's most important political and social institutions.

The new dimensions of the modern bureaucracy began to take shape during Prussia's transition from bureaucratic absolutism to constitutional monarchy. The members of the bureaucracy assumed important roles in these epochal events, and the bureaucracy itself was the major social body most affected by them. Before 1840 the civil service had occupied a dominant position in both the social and political spheres: with respect to the social prestige and political power of its individual members, it was probably the most influential group in Prussia at that time. This state of affairs began to undergo alteration during the 1840's, however, and with the Revolution of 1848, the supporting structure of the old bureaucracy was all but swept away. In order to salvage what was left of its political leadership, the civil service was forced to adapt to the unfamiliar demands of public opinion, representative bodies, and political parties. Furthermore, it was faced with the task of adjusting to the transition from a traditional corporate social order to a class-oriented society geared to the emerging urban industrial economy. Accompanying these changes was a cultural transformation characterized by increasingly rational and functional patterns of thought and behavior. The most striking change of all was that which took place in the politics of officials; the creation of parliamentary institutions, however weak, affected not only the formal functions of the bureaucracy but also the private lives of its members. In this case, modernization meant an increasing involvement of officials in party politics on both a voluntary and involuntary basis—a new experience for the members of this privileged body.

In speaking of the modernization of the bureaucracy, one must be careful to note that the process did not necessarily involve the cessation of all traditional habits and attitudes. On the contrary, one of the most striking characteristics of modernization in Prussia was the way in which apparently contradictory elements were combined, and many reformed institutions were dependent on traditional symbols and personnel for their authority. Nowhere was this more apparent than in the bureaucracy, a group that broke with the past in a rapid and dislocating manner, yet preserved many of the habits and attitudes associated with the earlier period. The bureaucracy was propelled toward its confrontation with economic, social, and political modernity by many traditional factors that were to prove sources of strength as well as weakness throughout the coming decades.[5]

The focus of my investigation is the higher state judicial and administrative bureaucracy—the sector of the civil service that by the 1840's had become closed to those without a university education. The subaltern bureaucracy, composed of men with lower academic qualifications, will be discussed only insofar as its history is related to that of the higher civil service. I have excluded from consideration the following as well: those technical officials, in many cases university-trained, who were not socially or functionally a part of the higher bureaucracy during the period under consideration; the patrimonial judiciary appointed by the owners of large estates in the eastern provinces in the pre-1849 period; and all other locally appointed officials, regardless of their educational qualifications. The *Landräte* from the eastern provinces, however, who were nominated by the estate owners but subject to final appointment by the state, are included, for although their legal status was something between that of a local official and a representative of the central bureaucracy, they were accepted socially as part of the higher bureaucratic elite.

From the materials in the archives of central ministries and provincial departments, as well as from published state papers and
other printed materials, I have attempted to piece together the
history of the entire elite, regardless of local differences. Because I
was unable to gain access to the East German archives, which con-
tain materials relating to the former eastern provinces, I have had
to rely heavily on the records of officials who worked at one time
or another in the western provinces, primarily in the Rhineland.
Although parts of the civil service in the Rhineland, notably the
Landräte and the judiciary, recruited extensively among the local
populations, by the 1840's most higher officials considered themselves part of a national rather than a local elite. Provincial pe-
culiarities were still apparent, particularly in the legal institutions
within which the bureaucracy operated in the Rhineland, but it
cannot be said that the officials who worked in the western provinces were any less representative of the bureaucracy as a whole
than those who were assigned to Brandenburg or Posen. It seems
safe to assume, then, with some qualifications, that the attitudes
and behavior of officials in the Rhineland were reasonably typical
of the bureaucracy as a whole.

A more serious problem of scholarship arises from the fact that
the Rhineland itself differed from the eastern parts of Prussia not
only in its legal system but also in its religious, social, and economic
composition. Nevertheless, by the 1840's the patterns of economic
development and social change in the eastern and western sectors
of Prussia were converging, and as the events of the Revolution
were to show, even differences in political tradition were less substantial than many contemporaries thought.[6] It is true that when
one takes the attitude and behavior of officials in the Rhineland as
examples of the bureaucracy as a whole, one must recognize that
conditions in the Rhineland were different from those in Pomerania or Silesia: the factor of local diversity in a state composed of
territories as different as those of Prussia is a problem that the historian cannot eliminate entirely. But it is in the interactions between officials and their environment that significant general pat-

terns are revealed, for no matter how diverse its various provincial settings, the bureaucracy responded in a unified way to the social, economic, and political challenges of the era of revolution and reaction. However different the origins of change in the various territories may have been, all were related to the general trend in Prussian society toward greater industrialization, urbanization, and political equality.

Part One

VORMÄRZ

Chapter One

Powers of Movement, Powers of Preservation

In 1840 Prussia stood unknowingly at one of the great turning points of political consciousness. Already men in other European countries were measuring the passage of time by general elections and industrial exhibitions rather than coronations; soon the Prussians' awareness of the past and sense of the future would be substantially altered, and by the time the next sovereign ascended the throne almost two decades later, their appreciation of the rate and direction of social change would be radically transformed. Although the Hohenzollern king crowned in 1840, Frederick William IV, encouraged his subjects to believe that his reign would usher in a new era, he was as unaware as they of the changes that were fated to take place. Since Frederick William gave the impression that he intended to initiate a break with the past, his first acts as ruler, such as the offer of political amnesty and easing of press censorship, were enthusiastically received by those most deeply committed to liberal reform. But neither the king nor his confidants, most of whom were advocates of rule by divine right, guessed that the next two decades would be among the most turbulent in Prussian history, and that future events would not only challenge the monarchy's ability to control the course of change but call into question its right to do so.

Those who lived through the *Vormärz* (pre-March) period cannot be blamed for lack of foresight. Historians, on the other hand, can be criticized for misusing hindsight and treating the events of the 1840's and 1850's as if they were part of a grand design—neglecting those aspects of change that left no lasting imprint on the society and ignoring the manner in which the old order and the new coexisted in an uneasy equilibrium.[1] Investigators would do well to adopt Wilhelm Heinrich Riehl's characterization of the events of those times as an unresolved struggle between the "powers of movement" and the "powers of preservation," the outcome of which was in doubt for most of the period.[2] As a contemporary observer, Riehl was not only aware of the surface manifestations of the conflict between the old and the new, but understood the underlying social, economic, and cultural dimensions as well. He saw in the events of these decades a crucial confrontation between what he called the "social-democratic" and the "corporative-aristocratic" value systems. Although he defined the period as a "turning point from old times to new," he did not oversimplify by pretending that this change meant simply the substitution of one set of institutions for another. Instead, he was careful to point out the interpenetration of the old and the new that was occurring in the 1840's and 1850's and to emphasize the unique transitional characteristics of the period, which were neither totally traditional nor totally modern.[3]

The changes that took place in the Prussian bureaucratic system during this decade were a reflection of the confrontation between the "powers" Riehl described. It is appropriate, then, to begin our study of the bureaucracy with a careful examination of the transitional aspects of the 1840's and the effects of social and economic change on the entrenched interests of monarchy, aristocracy, and civil service.

Legally and institutionally, Prussia was still an absolute monarchy in 1840, albeit a monarchy restrained by what amounted to a constitution. The General Code of 1794, somewhat revised and amended, served as Prussia's basic law. Like Prussia itself, the constitution was a complex of feudal and modern elements, of liberal principle and authoritarian practice; Alexis de Tocqueville characterized it as "a monstrous thing, which looks like a compromise between two creations."[4] The modernity of the constitution lay in the manner in which it regulated the relationship of the individual to the state; its feudal aspects were expressed in the way it safeguarded the traditional relationships among the members of Prussian society.

The modern tendency of the Code of 1794 was displayed in its proclamation of the equal responsibility of every inhabitant, regardless of birth, for the welfare of the state.[5] No one was exempt from this duty, which cut across all the traditional distinctions and divided society into legal units corresponding to the various forms that service to the state could take. The principle was established that rights and privileges were to be distributed according to the importance of the duties rendered, the highest rewards going to those who, like the monarch, first servant of the state, were directly concerned with defense and administration.

With respect to the mutual relationships of the citizens, the Code was thoroughly conservative. Social inequality was maintained, and a confused combination of hereditary and occupational distinctions was used to define a legal hierarchy that conformed in most respects to the structure of feudal society. In theory the relationships were regulated by the same considerations of utility that defined the individual's relationship to the state, but in practice the citizen derived his legal personality from his membership in one or more of the old estates of the realm—the aristocracy of birth, the burghers, or the peasantry—or from one of the recently established service estates, the most important of which were the civil and military services. Through his corporate identity he exercised his duty to the state; from it he obtained the rights and privileges accorded to it by law. In the case of one who was, for example, both an aristocrat and an officer in the army, there was a dual legal identity; but as we shall see, this complication affected only a small minority of this still relatively immobile society. Before 1848, the modern notion of citizenship, which involves both equal rights and equal duties, was alien to the Prussian concept.

The Code of 1794 had adapted the existing system of traditional hereditary estates (*Geburtsstände*) to the needs of the state; wherever they could not fulfill the necessary administrative and military functions, special professional estates (*Berufsstände*) were recognized.[6] Thus the older estates, the nobility, the burghers, and the peasantry were sustained by the new legal system. The nobility's agrarian and military services justified the retention of many of its ancient privileges; the townsmen and peasantry derived their traditional rights from similar functional considerations. At the same time, groups of more recent origin like the army, the bureaucracy, the clergy, and to a lesser extent the teaching profession, took their place alongside the established orders without seriously infringing upon areas of traditional privilege.

In many respects, however, the new legal recognition accorded the Berufsstände, was a major social innovation. Certain rights and duties that had been accumulated de facto by the corporate bodies during the preceding centuries were given a firm legal footing, and their members, who before had derived their legal personalities from one of the traditional estates, were now provided with independent standing. As Tocqueville put it, "Between the noble and burgher an intermediate class consisting of high functionaries who are not noble, ecclesiastics, and professors of learned schools, gymnasia, and universities, is placed."[7] As one of the most important of the new estates, the bureaucratic estate (*Beamtenstand*) occupied a position in the legal hierarchy only slightly inferior to that of the aristocracy of birth and far above the vast majority of the population.

The introduction of the new corporate bodies represented progress in Prussia's political modernization, for it meant a rationalization of the monarchical structure and a further step toward the integration of the state. At the same time, however, the social results were essentially conservative, adding more privileged groups to a society already rigidly stratified.[8] Even the legal and institutional innovations of the Reform Era (1806–1819) were aimed not at altering but at perfecting this aspect of the Prussian constitution. Although the monopoly of hereditary estates over certain occupations was ended in 1807, and all offices of the state were opened to competition on the basis of achievement, the social hierarchy remained intact: adoption of the principle of "careers open to talent" increased the individual's opportunities but did nothing to equalize the status of the existing regional and corporate groups.[9]

By the 1840's the effects of the Code's own contradictions were becoming evident. Equality in civic duty eventually produced the demand for equality in civic rights, and the Code's provision for individual mobility ultimately clashed with the strict enforcement of the legal and social barriers between groups. Furthermore, the modern principles embodied in other aspects of the law, particularly its integrating and centralizing tendencies, pointed in the direction of the realization of some more equalitarian idea of citizenship. Yet it is impossible to isolate the impact of these legal and institutional factors, for their effects were crucially connected with the cultural, economic, and social changes taking place during the same period.[10]

The new secular rationalism reflected in the Code was operating on every level of Prussian society during the first half of the nineteenth century. The ideals of the Enlightenment, once the monopoly of a small group of intellectuals, were now being given wide practical application. In literature and philosophy romanticism was still a powerful force, but in the economic, political, and educational sectors, the trend was mainly in the direction of rationalization. Both with respect to the functional and substantive meaning of that term, important steps toward modernization were taking place.

While it is difficult to measure precisely the rate of rationalization, the major breakthroughs are obvious. The Code of 1794 was itself a significant step, both with respect to the application of the concept of utility to political institutions and in the achievement of a relationship between the individual and the state that was more rational from the functional point of view. The Era of Reform also produced an administrative and military reorganization that facilitated a more efficient attainment of the goals of the state. The reforms encouraged the rationalization of the rural and urban economic structure, a process furthered by the creation of the *Zollverein* (Tariff Union) in the next decade. Aided by a new legal structure that emphasized equalitarian standards and universal norms, private individuals were better able to maximize the efficiency of their farms, businesses, and industries. The growth of capitalist enterprise in both the urban and rural sectors of the economy was but one of the features of the general modernization that was beginning to affect every aspect of Prussian life.[11]

By the time Frederick William IV came to the throne in 1840, the effects of this economic transformation were abundantly clear. Between 1815 and 1848 the amount of land under cultivation in Prussia rose from 7.3 million to 12.46 million hectares.[12] On the large estates, where most of this expansion took place, agrarian capitalism was already well advanced. Many landholding peasants had been able to persist in their traditional agricultural practices even against the advances of the market economy, but the situation of the landless segments of the rural population had been drastically transformed since their emancipation in 1807. What eventually came to be known as the rural proletariat had grown enormously during this period, tripling in size in some of the eastern provinces. Although the great exodus from the land did not begin until much later in the century, a significant proportion of the rural poor were already uprooted by the 1840's, wrenched from the customs of their native localities, and subjected to the harsh demands of the free labor market.[13]

It must be noted however that low status groups were not the only ones to suffer dislocation as a result of the capitalization of agriculture. The landed nobility, whose members had been experiencing economic difficulty since the last quarter of the eighteenth century, had not been able to take advantage of the general prosperity of large-scale agriculture that began in the late 1820's. Forced to sell land to reduce their debts, many noble families had lost their ties with agriculture entirely. By 1855, 45 percent of the privileged estates (*Rittergüter*) in the six eastern provinces had already been sold to nonnobles. The former owners either lived in relative poverty under the shadow of the new capitalist landowning class or turned to nonagricultural occupations.[14]

With 70 percent of the population still living in areas classified as rural, a good many aspects of the traditional agrarian society remained intact. Yet despite the relative stability of the rural-urban population ratio, many parts of Prussia, particularly the larger towns, were changing demographically by 1840. The population of Berlin had increased at twice the rate of Prussia as a whole, and many middle-sized towns had experienced even greater expansion. The still unreformed legal and institutional organization of the urban areas proved inadequate to deal with the problems of overcrowding that this growth occasioned. More importantly, economic development failed to keep pace with the need for employment. In 1846 the portion of the Prussian urban labor force actually employed in modern factories was only 4.2 percent. Large-scale industrial enterprise was extremely rare, and there were only about a thousand steam engines in operation.[15]

The problems of inadequate industrial growth, unemployment, and urban overcrowding were the subjects of an enormous pamphlet literature in the 1840's, most of which was concerned with the so-called social question. "The sickness for Germany," wrote one perceptive observer, "lies not in the excess of population, not in the machine system nor in the superfluity of industrial factories in general; rather it lies precisely in the lack of those machines which ought to create work and employment for our workers instead of the English."[16]

The flood of urban poor was fed by a steady immigration from nearby rural areas and by the demographic overflow of increasingly impoverished artisans and shopkeepers. After the abolition of guild restrictions in the Reform Era the number of artisans, including masters, journeymen, and apprentices, had almost doubled. At first this increase had not given cause for alarm, but after 1840 even the self-employed master craftsman in many trades found themselves without work. For the journeymen and apprentices the situation was much worse: their ranks had increased more rapidly than those of the masters, and they were less able to cope with rising prices and unemployment.[17]

The discontents of the artisan class, particularly its younger members, erupted in a series of incidents, the most famous of which were the uprisings of the Silesian weavers in 1844. Protests were directed against the freedom of entry into trade and various other steps toward economic modernization that had been taken earlier in the century; but the powers of movement were already too well entrenched to permit more than token restoration of traditional guild privileges. Eventually the employment opportunities created by the growth of heavy industry would bring relief from the conditions created by the contradictions within the economic system; but until this began to occur on a massive scale in the 1850's, the gains that Prussia made in such areas as railway construction and coal production brought little relief to the traditional working class, whose members were the chief but by no means the sole victims of transition.[18]

Some members of the traditional urban and rural groups rode out these economic crises and even improved their lot by taking advantage of the opportunities open to those capable of adjusting to the emerging capitalist economic order. A few artisans became minor industrial entrepreneurs, and there were landed nobles and even peasants who grew rich in large-scale production-oriented agriculture. In most cases, however, these advantages were purchased at great social cost, for Prussia was still overwhelmingly unreceptive to commercial values. Even in the western provinces, where entrepreneurial elites were most strongly developed, the social hierarchy was determined far more by birth and other traditional symbols of status than by wealth.[19] A rural-urban capitalist middle class was struggling for recognition in all parts of Prussia, but as far as the vast majority of the population was concerned, membership in one of the hereditary or service estates continued to be the desired goal. In 1849 census takers were still using traditional corporate categories to differentiate the various population groups. In official statistics published that year, the adult male population was still divided into three major corporate categories: the cultured estates, the middle estates, and the working class.[20] The term "class" was still being used only in connection with the lowest orders of society; this usage reflected popular consciousness of the fact that at the lower end of the social scale the corporate order was rapidly breaking down, while among the upper classes the emphasis on the importance of belonging to an established estate rooted in tradition was still relatively unchanged.

Long before 1840 members of the educated middle class had abandoned the feudal habits of deference to birth. Noble title unaccompanied by certain qualities associated with cultivation (*Bildung*) was no longer enough to gain their admiration; and while wealth or title alone could produce a certain amount of respect in some circles, it was only when these assets were combined with a cultivated manner and official rank that the highest social esteem was completely assured. Cultivation did not simply mean higher education, though it was often associated with a university degree; instead, it described a variety of traits—some assumed to be properties of birth, age, religion, or geographical origin, others viewed as the achievements of intellectual or artistic effort. Beginning in the late eighteenth century, Bildung became the hallmark of a greater part of Prussia's upper middle class. Earlier, birth alone had been sufficient to distinguish the higher from the lower orders; later, wealth and occupation would be the primary symbols of status; but in the interim, the style of life associated with the pursuit and enjoyment of cultural refinement marked an important social distinction.

Though Prussian society deferred to the cultivated individual regardless of birth, it often withheld its approval from those rustic Junkers whose uncouth habits were the subject of derision even among the more refined members of their own estate. The boundary between the landed and urban elites tended to be drawn by differences in culture; so too the distance between the older educated middle class and the newer business and industrial bourgeoisie. The merging of these two groups was only beginning, and it was still the members of the professions, especially those closely associated with the state, who were the objects of the greatest deference. The census takers were only reflecting the prevailing social consciousness when they placed many wealthy individuals engaged in trade a notch below the *Gebildeten* (cultivated classes).[21]

Since the end of the eighteenth century, the cultivated man had enjoyed unusually high status in urban society. Civil servants, doctors, professors, lawyers, and, to a lesser extent, clergymen and school teachers had come to occupy positions in the towns analogous to those of the larger landowners in the countryside. Indeed, the social standing of the professions had never been higher; even the least prestigious among them were a rung above other middle-income occupations in the social hierarchy. The economic position of the professions was exceptionally sound, for as incorporated bodies whose monopoly on certain services was protected by the laws of the state, they were normally free from the kind of economic competition that was harming the artisan and peasant classes.[22] The rate of expansion of the professions was to a large degree controlled by the state during the first half of the nineteenth century, and in almost every case it lagged behind the growth of the general population. Secondary school teachers, with 70 percent growth, exceeded this figure slightly, but their elementary school counterparts rose in numbers by only 40 percent during the same years, 1816–1846.[23] The rise in medical personnel also lagged behind population growth; and the clergy seems to have followed much the same pattern.[24] The civil service appears to have been increased by only about 10 percent, mostly at the lower levels,[25] and the law profession, which was still under state control in Prussia, remained constant in size throughout the same period.[26]

The combination of social prestige and economic security offered by the professions was doubly attractive at a time when a revolution in educational expectations was taking place among the lower orders. The educational reforms of the first decades of the century, which were capped by the founding of the new University of Berlin, had resulted in a great expansion of the numbers of students at all levels. From 1816 to 1846 the percentage of children between the ages of six and fourteen who were attending school rose from 61 to 82 percent. Added to the general increase in the population, this swelled the number of pupils in Prussian elementary schools by 108 percent.[27] On the Gymnasium level, the increase was 73 percent; and during the same thirty-year period the number of university students rose 40 percent.[28]

The effects of any educational reform are always delayed, particularly where university training is involved, and it was not until the 1830's and 1840's that the forces of movement in the educational field began to have an obvious effect on the size of the graduating classes. By that time Prussian educational institutions were serving as channels for individual upward mobility to a degree unprecedented in their history. From the 1820's through the 1840's, the universities experienced an influx of large numbers of lower- and middle-income group members—sons of peasants, artisans, lower-level officials, and elementary school teachers. At Halle University, the proportion of these groups to the total student population remained at about a third throughout this period; and only after 1850 did enrollment from the least affluent groups—the peasants and artisans—begin gradually to decline. The winds of academic change brought with them a new kind of student, less well-to-do but eager to grasp the great cultural, social, and economic rewards presumably offered by the professions to those with a university education. The appeal of education in these times of economic change and social dislocation was by no means limited to lower status groups. The landed nobility, which like the middle and lower orders, was experiencing some economic difficulty, was also sending its sons in larger numbers to the university. From 1830 on, the enrollment lists at Halle showed a steady rise in the number of sons of larger landowners.[29]

We have seen, however, that the rate of expansion of the professions themselves was not nearly so great as the growth of the student population. As one might expect, the result was an overabundance of qualified candidates in many professions, particularly the most prestigious; and by the 1840's, critics were commenting on the poor employment prospects of university graduates and lamenting the restrictions imposed on the size of most professions.[30] Why then did young men continue to stake their futures on training that offered such limited opportunities?

There were some university students who had no intention of going into one of the professions, did not complete their degree requirements, and were concerned only with obtaining a bit of social polish before entering business or agriculture. The vast majority, however, had their sights set on the professions. Because of the long years of training involved, many had taken this road long before the limitation on opportunities was fully apparent, and by the time the difficulties of their situation became clear, they had invested too much financially and emotionally to turn back.

An expanding industrial economy would have provided relief from these conditions by increasing the demand for services and thus requiring an expansion of almost all the professions. Before 1850, however, the professions found themselves in the dilemma of the artisans and laborers—the victims of a lag in economic development. The state itself was prevented from expanding professions like the civil service by political and financial considerations: still paying the debts incurred during the Wars of Liberation, it was extremely reluctant to extend anything more than the most necessary services. Furthermore, the professions themselves, many of them operating as self-governing corporations, were on the side of the powers of preservation, unable or unwilling to accede to demands that they expand to absorb the growing population of academically qualified candidates. Among those hardest hit by the contradictions of the transition period was the bureaucracy itself, which at that time was caught between an increasing number of candidates and a limited number of posts.[31]

By the 1840's, then, it was not only the lower orders that were experiencing the discomforts of transition. Prussia's most respected corporate groups, the professions and the landed aristocracy, were also in trouble—increasingly unable to produce the changes needed to uphold their privileged civil and social position. On one hand, they were challenged by representatives of the newer urban and rural entrepreneurial elites, who since the 1830's were claiming a share in the rights and powers previously reserved for the aristocracy and the service estates. On the other, they were faced with the dilemma posed by the internal tensions within the professions themselves—the discontents that had been growing in intensity during the same period. By the 1840's the call for reform within the professions had begun to be generalized into a demand for changes in the whole legal and political structure. Eventually this challenge to the existing system of corporate privilege merged with a broadly based movement calling for constitutional monarchy and modern representative institutions. From that point, social and political issues both specific and general were so much a part of the conflict between the powers of movement and the powers of preservation that only by drastic innovations could some form of disruption have been avoided.

The target of political agitation in the decade before 1848 was not the monarchy itself but the form that the monarchy had assumed since the late eighteenth century. Bureaucratic absolutism, not royal despotism, was the issue. The *Beamtenstaat* (bureaucratic state) had grown strong after the failure of the reform movement, taking advantage of the weak rule of Frederick William III (1797–1840) to gather into its own hands many of the powers formerly reserved for the king and the provincial estates.[32] If the liberal opponents of the bureaucratic state initially focused their hopes on Frederick William IV, it was not because they were in sympathy with the new king's concept of divine-right monarchy, but because they knew that he was a sworn enemy of the bureaucratic absolutism that his father had tolerated.

A new kind of criticism of the bureaucratic state was heard during the 1840's. Despite the attacks that Freiherr vom Stein and other reformers of the early nineteenth century had made on what they called the "mercenary, apathetic, propertyless bureaucrats," the system had been relatively popular.[33] The general economic and social backwardness of the country accounted in part for the situation. No group except the landed nobility thought of itself as a competitor for the power wielded by the officials; even the aristocracy was willing to trade political power for the economic advantages it enjoyed under bureaucratic rule.[34] Progressive forces also supported the Beamtenstaat during the period prior to 1840, however. The bureaucracy's record of liberalism during the Era of Reform and the leadership exercised by its members in the subsequent decades provided it with a favorable image that lasted well into the pre-March period. Until the 1840's Pope's dictum, "For forms of government let fools contest; whate'er is best administer'd is best" was an effective counterargument against both the liberal ideal of modern representative institutions and conservative dreams of a revival of feudal corporatism.[35]

Between the Reform Era and the 1840's, the bureaucracy occupied a position comparable to that of Plato's guardian class. This was the period when Prussia's highly placed civil servants believed their functions to include the entire range of governmental activity, including the responsibilities formerly delegated to the monarch and his personally selected ministers. This conception was reinforced by the weak reign of Frederick William III, the absence of strong leadership at the cabinet level, and the monopolization by career officials of the highest councils of state.[36] Officials saw themselves as Hegel described them, as "the class in which the consciousness of right and the developed intelligence of the mass of the people is found."[37] In turn, the general public accepted them as the guardians of the public interest rather than as narrow experts serving only specialized functions. To the high legal status that the Code of 1794 had accorded the civil service was added universal respect and social prestige. Surrounded by a mystique of omniscience and omnipotence, the bureaucracy was not only immune to criticism from above or below, but also from within its own ranks. In general, its members were blatantly paternalistic, stubborn, presumptuous, and complacently confident of their right to power.

Prior to the 1840's, bureaucratic absolutism had been looked upon, even by most liberals, as the embodiment of the highest principles of law and order. Legislation and administration were viewed as virtually identical processes; judicial and executive functions, though increasingly separate during this time, were still indistinguishable in many areas. The custom of giving administrators training in law seemed to confirm the compatibility of functions; the organization and procedures of the bureaucracy, recently rationalized and codified, seemed the greatest exemplar of the rational, efficient, and orderly world for which many liberals were struggling.[38] In this phase of Prussia's development, the powers of movement were more than willing to turn over the responsibilities of government to an elite whose sympathies appeared to be in the direction of what they defined as progress.

During the first three decades of the nineteenth century, Prussia's officials appeared to be firmly on the side of economic emancipation. Most officials of the Reform Era generation were trained in laissez-faire economics, which they combined with a more traditional mercantilistic pragmatism to facilitate economic growth in several important areas throughout the 1820's and 1830's.[39] Even in the Rhineland, where industrial development was most advanced and least in need of the tutelage of the state, the bureaucracy's economic policies did not come under serious criticism until the late 1830's and early 1840's.[40]

Achievements in other fields also reinforced the prestige of bureaucratic absolutism. Innovations in social welfare practices reflected favorably on the bureaucracy and increased its prestige among the neediest elements of the population.[41] Without parliamentary committees to gather vital information, the bureaus and the courtrooms were the primary research centers for demographic, social, and even medical problems; and in the absence of representative institutions, government officials performed the duties of deputies to whom grievances would ordinarily have been communicated. Prior to the 1840's, the state official was anything but an alien oppressor; on the contrary, in contrast to the ignorant and reactionary local notables, he appeared as a pillar of enlightenment and progress.

Because so much of the evidence concerning the character of government in the 1820's and 1830's is drawn of necessity from official sources, the historian cannot always be sure that he has isolated appearance from reality. Nevertheless, a comparison of the attitudes toward the bureaucracy before and after 1840 does reveal one undeniable fact: in the late 1830's and early 1840's, the prestige of bureaucratic absolutism suffered a number of serious setbacks. At least a decade before the Revolution of 1848 shook the entire system to its very foundations, the bureaucratic state was under attack from within and without. Not only in the eyes of the general public, but in the opinion of many officials themselves, the system had lost its legitimacy.

This change coincided with the accession of Frederick William IV, who by temperament and political conviction was hostile to the traditions of the Beamtenstaat. Unlike his father, who had been willing to allow the state apparatus to run itself, Frederick William IV had sworn to exercise fully the prerogative of divine-right monarchy. Determined to play an active part in decision-making, he resented any limitation that bureaucratic routine placed upon him. He longed for the freedom from officialdom that Frederick the Great had enjoyed through the device of the cabinet system, even though he rejected Frederick's concept of the role of the king as "first servant of the state." To Frederick William the very notion of the subordination of the monarch to the state was a Hegelian heresy—a direct contradiction of the vision of divine-right monarchy to which he and the religious romantics who were among his closest advisers were emotionally as well as intellectually committed.[42]

In theory Frederick William also rejected all eighteenth-century notions of royal absolutism, preferring instead a corporate system modeled along English lines; but in practice he adopted many of the means by which his predecessors had extended their personal power. In order to free himself from the advice of officials, he encouraged those around him to form a shadow cabinet, the so-called Kamarilla; for the most part, however, he himself assumed the major burden of the struggle against bureaucratic absolutism, trusting in his own infallibility and mobilizing his tremendous energies in order to intervene in almost every aspect of government.[43]

In the eighteenth century the Hohenzollerns had been successful in exercising this type of personal rule. By the 1840's, however, no one man could hope to successfully oversee a government with functions so diverse as Prussia's. Not only could the monarch no longer understand what was going on in all parts of the kingdom, but he could not be acquainted personally with more than a handful of the men involved in the day-to-day operations of the administration and judiciary.[44] Thus Frederick William's experiment in personal rule was largely a failure, and he was forced to seek other ways of restricting the powers of the bureaucracy.

Among the institutions that Frederick William sought to mobilize as counterweights to the bureaucracy were the provincial estates, which at that time were Prussia's most important representative bodies. Through these relatively conservative groups the king hoped for influence on public opinion without compromise to public sovereignty. They also offered him a way to seek advice and consent without passing through the bureaucratic channels of communication: since few members of the bureaucracy also took part in the provincial estate system, there was little risk in this venture.

The provincial estates proved reluctant allies, however, and the new reign had scarcely begun when the assemblies of East and West Prussia, meeting in joint session, embarrassed the king by calling for the fulfillment of an earlier royal promise to allow the establishment of national representative institutions. Frederick

William IV soon found himself in conflict with one of the monarchy's most respected public servants, Theodor von Schön, who despite his position as *Oberpräsident* of East Prussia, spoke out openly in support of this demand.[45] Schön's pamphlet, *Woher und Wohin?* (*Whence and Whither?*) caused a sensation when it was published in 1842, as much because of the author's identity as for the moderate liberalism of his proposals. In fact, Schön's thinking paralleled the king's almost exactly on the issue of representative bodies, for he too felt that their existence would strengthen the monarchy by freeing the ruler from dependence on the bureaucracy. Although he himself was a career official, Schön believed that the bureaucratic state had outlived its usefulness: earlier the bureaucracy had been the only body capable of responding to the needs of society; now it was a petrified *Schreiberkaste* (caste of clerks), caring only for its own well-being and insensitive to those whom it was supposed to serve.[46]

Despite the essentially conservative character of Schön's call for representative institutions, his demands soon became a rallying point for the powers of movement in all parts of Prussia. Frederick William encouraged the polarization of opinion still further when he interpreted the Schön pamphlet as a challenge to his own authority. Insisting that the reform of representative institutions could only come at the initiative of the crown itself, he abruptly turned away from his liberal program and unwisely postponed consideration of further changes for several more years. Consequently when the king finally moved in February 1847 to create the United Diet, Prussia's first national representative body, he found the mood of the country quite different from what it had been five years before.[47] The leadership of public opinion had passed from the hands of moderates to liberal and democratic elements who were satisfied neither with the corporate character of the United Diet nor with its limited powers. This time the threat to royal authority was real. The vocal opposition was no longer led by established senior officials like Theodor von Schön, but younger, less well-known men like the Breslau judicial official

Heinrich Simon and the Rhineland *Landrat* Georg Freiherr von Vincke.[48]

Ironically, an attempt by the monarch to limit bureaucratic absolutism had helped to encourage a popular movement that now threatened the entire political system. The protest against the objectionable aspects of the bureaucratic state was being led in part by men like Simon and von Vincke, who themselves were members of the bureaucracy. In both the east and the west, in Königsberg as well as Cologne, officials were by their criticism calling into question Prussia's basic civil and political constitution. This behavior, virtually unprecedented among members of the civil service, reflected not only widespread popular discontent with Frederick William's rule, but also the struggle between the powers of movement and the powers of preservation within the bureaucracy itself.

Chapter Two

The Bureaucracy in Transition

The political system inherited by Frederick William IV from his predecessors was to all outward appearances the same bureaucratic state that had emerged in the wake of the Reform Era. Otto Camphausen, an administrative official in the Rhineland, writing to his brother Ludolf in 1843, described it as a system of rulership by career bureaucrats peculiar to the Prussian state. "The king, who appears to be the top functionary, invariably selects his aides from the intellectual elite of the nation, recognized as such by means of truly or allegedly rigorous examinations. He allows them great independence, acknowledges thereby their co-rulership and, consequently, sanctions a sort of aristocracy of experts who purport to be the true representatives of the general interest." Yet at the same time there were those who detected signs of change. Karl Varnhagen von Ense was already writing in his notebooks of the "partisanship, conflict, and disintegration" that he encountered in the civil service; and he was not alone in predicting the collapse of the power and prestige of this "aristocracy of experts."[1]

The legal and institutional characteristics of the bureaucracy were inherited from the early nineteenth century, and the outlook of the senior officials reflected the values of previous decades. At the top of the ladder stood men committed to the ideas embodied in the Code of 1794 and the legislation of the Reform Era, who were not sympathetic toward the social and political transformations that had recently begun. In the context of the earlier period they had represented the powers of movement; confronted with an entirely new set of circumstances, they assumed the aspect of the powers of preservation. The powers of movement now were personified by the members of the younger generation within the ranks of the bureaucracy; and the distance between their ideas and those of their superiors was so great that conflict was virtually inevitable. To understand why the older men were unable to adjust to the new era and why the junior men were so unwilling to compromise with tradition, one must begin with the backgrounds of both groups, their respective styles of life, and their positions on important social and economic issues.

Under the provisions of the General Code of 1794 the bureaucracy was granted a legal status that reflected the compromise of modern and traditional occurring in the society as a whole. Prussia's basic law recognized the bureaucracy as a privileged corporation, subject to its own separate jurisdiction, distinct in title and rank, and exempt from many of the ordinary civil obligations.[2] Officials were free from local taxes, but as members of a "universal estate" who were answerable directly to the state, they were also discouraged from taking part in any form of municipal or provincial self-government. Representation was provided for the landed aristocracy, the burghers, and the peasantry in the provincial estates established in 1823, but there was no place for the bureaucratic estate as such. Individual officials could be elected through the other corporations, but this was a rare occurrence because of the difficulties caused by conflicting property and residence requirements.[3] Before 1840, however, the rights of citizenship were not at issue among Prussia's civil servants. To them, as to the members of the other corporations, freedom meant exemption from universal obligations. They were content, wrote Freiherr vom Stein, "to be left alone to scribble away in secret, well paid and comfortable, secure by virtue of their pensions."[4]

During the Reform Era the leading members of the bureaucracy were by no means indifferent to their official obligations, but they felt that these obligations exempted them from any responsibility for regional or local matters. The reforming ministers, Stein and Fürst von Hardenberg, gained widespread support among state officials, many of whom were harsh critics of professional apathy; yet both men were supporters of the corporate form of society, with its unequal distribution of civic responsibilities. They made no effort to eliminate the exempt status of the servants of the state, and were opposed to their admission to the regional institutions of self-government.[5] The post-reform governments did nothing to encourage officials to enter civic affairs; instead, steps were taken in the 1830's to further restrict their entry into the provincial estates.[6] As a result, the bureaucracy was a good deal more isolated from the rest of the community in 1840 than it had been at the beginning of the century.

Modern norms of equality and universality were applied only to the internal organization of the bureaucracy. The confused system of overlapping jurisdictions inherited from the eighteenth century was eliminated during the Reform Era, and a rationalized system of departmentalized government, in which each minister was responsible for a separate area of service, was established. After 1806 the connections between the various ministries and the provincial judicial and administrative agencies were also organized in an efficient hierarchical manner. The primary unit of provincial administration was the *Regierung*; the *Oberlandesgericht* handled judicial matters. Both these agencies were charged with overseeing activities at the lowest level of their respective jurisdictions, which for the administration was the *Landrat*, and for the judiciary, either the state *Kreis* court or the patrimonial bench.[7]

The efforts of the early nineteenth-century reformers resulted in a system that in its broadest outlines was fully modern. There remained, however, important remnants of traditional practice, particularly with regard to decision-making procedures and formal relationships between members of the profession. During the Reform Era every attempt to extend the principle of monocratic government to the bureaucratic hierarchy failed because of the resistence of the officials themselves. The principle of collegiate responsibility in decision-making was retained at both the ministerial and the district levels, where all matters of importance continued to require the deliberation of the entire membership of the particular unit concerned.[8] All members of the agency involved took part in the discussion of every major question to come before their college, and all shared legal responsibility for the collective decision.

The collegiate principle was the symbol of the corporate tradition of the bureaucracy. Though it was less efficient than monocratic organization, early nineteenth-century officials were strongly attached to it for reasons that were social as well as technical. Collegiate responsibility protected their profession against corruption and the threat of arbitrary intrusions from higher authorities,[9] and officials regarded it as a reinforcement to the corporate morale and professional solidarity they believed to be necessary to the preservation of the honor and prestige of the bureaucratic estate.

The college was much more than an administrative device: it was the very symbol of the traditional behavior pattern of the officials themselves, their deference to the wisdom of age, and their subordination of the individual to the group. The manner in which decisions were arrived at indicated the prevalence of collective over individual norms, for although personal initiative was encouraged, it was the will of the group that was decisive. The stability of the collegiate system was reinforced by the fact that the college was the officials' primary source of social identity. The authority of the senior members of the college was partially a function of the paternalistic social relationships between the younger and older members of the profession, which prevailed throughout the early nineteenth century. Procedures were cooperative but nondemocratic, and authoritarianism flourished, for age meant more than merit or achievement. This particular deference pattern was reflected in the seniority rules, under which age ordinarily determined the individual's rank in the hierarchy of authority.[10]

These patterns of behavior paralleled those of the other major

corporations and were consistent with the social code of the early
nineteenth century middle- and upper-class families. What the apprentice official did not learn from the law books and administrative manuals, he absorbed through the ritual of the *Rathskeller*
or during evenings at the homes of his senior colleagues. The social circles in which the state official moved were usually confined
to members of his own or other related professions. These informal
contacts were as important in helping him adapt to the conventions of his profession as the more formal aspects of his training
were.

During the early nineteenth century entry into the higher civil
service was not yet entirely dependent on formal education. The
judiciary required a university education in law for its members
(with the exception of the patrimonial judges), and the administration was moving in that direction, but in most instances training
still took the form of apprenticeship.[11] Those who did not pass
through the university entered upon their careers at an early age.
The transition from untrained youth to mature official was a gradual process, without the sharp discontinuities that we have come
to associate with the various stages of the modern educational process. For many, the socialization process was made even easier by
the fact that the bureaucracy was more or less self-perpetuating.
From the records of law students at Halle University in 1820 it
appears that at least half of those who came to the bureaucracy
through university study were from families with some previous
bureaucratic connection. Similar figures for the University of Berlin student body indicate that a majority of university-trained officials were recruited from the bureaucratic families themselves or
from their social equals in other professions.[12] Since it is likely that
a very large number of those who rose through the ranks without
higher education were also recruited from these circles, the degree
of continuity from generation to generation in the early nineteenth
century was probably even higher than the university figures would
indicate.

In such a situation it is little wonder that the values of the hierarchically organized, authoritarian family unit found expression within the profession. The General Code and subsequent adjustments during the Reform Era had made both the administration and judiciary self-governing with respect to recruitment, promotion, and discipline. The pressures of interference from above lessened sharply after the death of the conservative chancellor Fürst von Hardenberg in 1822, and for the remainder of the reign of Frederick William III the bureaucracy operated in a manner similar to that of any other traditional corporate body. In theory, decisions concerning the higher bureaucracy were acts of royal authority, but in reality Frederick William III rarely contradicted the recommendations of his senior officials. Appointment had become virtually a grant of tenure, for under the General Code officials who had taken the oath of office could only be dismissed through a series of elaborate proceedings. In principle, the king had the power to decide the fate of his officials; but in practice he merely passed on the decisions of the profession itself. First the judiciary and then the administration regularized their disciplinary procedures in such a way that offiicals were judged by their peers meeting in collegiate fashion.[13] This did not mean that the profession was any more lax in its discipline than the crown had been; rather, a powerful tool of social control was thus placed in the hands of the corporation as a whole and the senior members in particular.

Other institutional factors also reinforced traditional patterns of collective behavior. The secret personnel records, the so called *Konduitenlisten*, which had been used in the eighteenth century by the monarchs as a means of royal authority, had since come under the authority of the profession itself.[14] Because the less highly placed official had no access to these files and no right to correct their contents, he was virtually at the mercy of those senior members of the corporation who did have access to them.

Since the end of the eighteenth century, the principle of seniority had been rigorously applied in matters of reward and promotion—first as a means of eliminating the influence of corruption and royal favoritism, and later as a way of organizing the intraprofessional structure.[15] After 1807, recruitment was primarily on the basis of merit, regardless of birth, but age rather than achievement continued to determine promotion. Rank, age, and title were closely associated: salary and other types of reward were distributed in an unequal manner on the basis of them. The introduction of a fixed salary schedule was one of several interrelated steps toward modernization taken during the late eighteenth and early nineteenth centuries; the salary schedule was based, however, on a traditional corporate concept of highly differentiated standards of living rather than on the more modern ideal of equal reward for equal performance. Those at the highest ranks were thought to require a very high salary in order to meet their social obligations as heads of families belonging to Prussia's social elite. The lower ranks were provided with amounts thought appropriate to the much lower standards of expenditure expected of single men, with the result that their salaries were but a fraction of those of the senior officials.[16]

Similar inequalities existed with respect to the distribution of titles, decorations, and benefits such as housing and transportation expenses. With the highest positions went honorific titles that designated the bearer as acceptable at the royal court (*courfähig*). It was still the practice prior to the 1840's to endow many senior officials with titles of nobility; yet even those who did not receive this highest of all honors were richly rewarded with various types of royal decorations.[17] Many of these decorations seem to have been bestowed in a virtually automatic manner, rather than in return for distinguished achievement.

Years of service were rewarded by pensions according to a plan established in 1825—one of the first of its kind in Europe—under which officials contributed part of their salary to a fund that supported the disabled and retired. Although no fixed retirement age was set, the pension plan seems initially to have been successful in encouraging officials to retire at a reasonable age. The pensions were generally small, but they were adequate in view of the cost of living at the time. Only in periods of inflation were those on fixed salary and pensions seriously disadvantaged, and before the 1840's inflation was neither severe nor of long duration.[18]

Most of the characteristics of the bureaucratic estate reflected the qualities of the social groups from which the officials of the early nineteenth century were drawn. They were properties of the Gebildeten in general, and the generation of civil servants who began their careers in the first two or three decades of the nineteenth century shared them with professors, clergymen, and other professional men. These traits were not inaccessible to members of other groups, however: the values they represented were not so different from those of other corporate bodies that they prevented peasants and artisans from entering the profession. On the contrary, during the early nineteenth century the bureaucracy provided a carefully regulated opportunity for upward mobility through entrance into its ranks. The reformers had been successful in their attempt to sever the bureaucracy from the identification with the eastern aristocracy and the Protestant faith characteristic of the eighteenth century civil service, and had done so without the kind of social upheaval that had occurred in France. Actually, the "revolution from above," as manifested in the Declaration of October 1807, which declared all civil careers open to talent, was little more than a formal recognition of changes that had been occurring over a long period of time; even before the Reform Era, civil office had ceased to be the monopoly of the landed aristocracy and members of the Protestant faith, and men were being recruited from all parts of Prussia.[19] These legal and institutional changes were part of the social evolution of the bureaucracy itself. Paralleling the emergence of the bureaucracy as a legal entity was its evolution as a separate, self-conscious, and relatively homogeneous social group. "The stratification of the population along the lines of the old estates was not completely eliminated," wrote one nineteenth-century observer, "but the divisions became less pronounced and the differences between officials and nonofficials more accentuated than those between nobles and nonnobles. Civil service absorbed members of all three traditional estates and amalgamated them into a new estate that dominated the others."[20] At this time the assimilative capacities of the bureaucratic estate were so great that even though it served as an important channel of mobility for individual members of other groups, it remained relatively unaffected by the diverse backgrounds of those who entered it. Highborn or lower-middle-class, the recruits conformed to the standards set by the cultivated elites that formed the bureaucracy's primary reservoir of talent.

The bulk of the civil elite was made up of men of nonnoble origins, including a fair number from the lower and middle orders of the community, though men of title still predominated in the upper ranks. To all outward appearances, the old aristocracy reigned over the bureaucracy as it had in the eighteenth century. In 1820, 371 of the 893 higher administrative officials (including Landräte) were of noble title, and 88 of 347 state judges (excluding patrimonial judges) were also members of the same hereditary estate. The higher the rank, the greater the proportion of noble names: the cabinet itself was composed entirely of men of noble title; and only four out of twenty-four *Regierungspräsidenten* were nonnoble.[21] Yet these figures are deceptive, for "von" before a man's name no longer meant what it had in the eighteenth century, and a large part of those who used it were not direct descendants of the old landed aristocracy.

Over a third of the nobles who were members of the higher administration and judiciary during the period 1794–1806 can be categorized as "new nobility": men from families that had acquired their titles since 1700, primarily for services rendered to the state.[22]

Indeed, by the early nineteenth century it had become necessary to distinguish between two nobilities—an older one (*Landadel*) deriving its social and economic strength from agriculture, and a new "service" nobility (*Dienstadel*), an outgrowth of the expansion of the military and civil institutions of the state. The lines between the Landadel and the Dienstadel were often blurred; not all members of the former came from old families, nor were all the latter of recent origin. Nevertheless, in their social and cultural affiliations the differences between the two were reasonably clear. The Landadel remained attached to the traditions of the feudal estate, while the Dienstadel closely resembled the other service professions.[23]

Many of the Dienstadel were members of landed families who through service to the state had become accustomed to the lifestyle of the bureaucratic estate; others were products of the great increase in ennoblements during the late eighteenth and early nineteenth centuries, when Frederick William II and Frederick William III elevated a hundred and fifty civil servants to the nobility.[24] Because it is so difficult to obtain accurate biographical information on more than a handful of higher officials, evidence on this point is not decisive—but it appears from a sample of the highest ranks of the administrative bureaucracy that throughout the 1820's the numbers of the Dienstadel grew at the expense of the landed aristocracy. Two decades later the trend would be reversed, but not before other important social and economic changes had taken place.[25]

The percentage of titled officials who had no strong connections with the land was probably even greater on the lower levels, with the one exception of the Landräte, which remained the monopoly of the landed aristocracy throughout the first half of the nineteenth century. Records of student enrollments during this period show that the separation of the Dienstadel from the Landadel had proceeded to a point where the men of title in bureaucracy could no longer be considered socially a part of the old landowning class. Of the law students registered at Halle University in the 1820's, men who for the most part were preparing for some phase of civil service, only 8 percent were sons of larger landowners.[26] At Heidelberg University, where many Prussians studied, the rolls for the same decade show that of the titled individuals in law and mercantile economics there, only 20 percent were sons of landed nobility: a few were the sons of military officers, but most were from civil service families.[27]

Two decades later changes in recruitment were occurring that blurred the distinction between Dienstadel and Landadel, but these had not had time to affect the way most people still viewed the two groups. In 1840, when Frederick William IV proposed that the ennoblement policies of his predecessors that had so benefited the members of the civil and military services be altered in favor of the landowning classes, his ministers (most of whom were part of the service nobility) felt compelled to remind their king of the dual meaning of aristocracy in Prussia. "A great part of the Prussian nobility owes its position to the outstanding performance of its forbears in the civil and military service of the state," noted Heinrich von Mühler, Minister of Justice: the officials' "place in civil society, the orientation of their education and way of life, as well as the nature of their wealth, would prevent them from owning even a modest piece of land and therefore preclude their entry into the nobility."[28] In the words of another minister, Karl von Kamptz: "Since Prussia's greatness rests on intelligence and character, it should not be the first and only state to link the recognition of these qualities to material and incidental criteria like the mere ownership of land." Instead, wrote von Kamptz, the relationship should be reversed: outstanding service to the state should be rewarded with a grant of both land and title, thus preserving the integrity and security of this most important pillar of the monarchy, the "aristocracy of service."[29]

Over the years the shared life-style, legal privileges, and vocational concerns of the bureaucracy gave rise to a unique esprit de corps. Thus in 1809 the nobles serving on Prussia's highest court requested that the custom of seating titled and nontitled judges separately be abolished as an inappropriate distinction.[30] Such was the corporate solidarity that prevailed among the officials who entered the service in the first decades of the century, and such was the spirit they preserved as the changes of the 1840's began.

The bureaucratic estate of the early nineteenth century viewed itself as the rightful guardian of the public interest, and its attitude toward the rest of society was no less condescending than that of the landed nobility. The Junkers themselves were objects of considerable scorn among this new elite.[31] Officials felt superior not only to the landless nobility but also to the emerging urban entrepreneurial class, whose service to the state they viewed as infinitely inferior to their own.[32] For the lower orders of society, the bureaucrats had some sympathy but very little understanding. They were ready to educate them to their duties to the state and to encourage the ablest among them to aspire to official positions, but they were not willing to grant them either civil or social equality.[33]

The members of the civil service kept their distance from the rest of the urban and rural population, but stayed in close contact with the other service professions. In the smaller communities this exclusiveness was particularly noticeable, but even in the larger cities the officials kept apart from the local community. Rudolf von Delbrück, a junior member of the civil service in Berlin, observed that the members of the civil service rarely moved in aristocratic circles, yet did not feel at home among the bourgeoisie. "The bureaucratic circles," noted Delbrück, "finding themselves between the tightly closed court society on one hand and the bourgeois community on the other, led a life of their own."[34]

The profession's sense of distance from the rest of society was due in large part to its privileged status, but it also reflected the fact that prior to 1840 the economic situation of the profession was generally better than that of many other groups. At a time when the effects of rapid population growth and economic dislocation were causing considerable social misery, the civil service was enjoying the advantages of fixed salary and tenured position. Although the periodical strains on the state budget during the late eighteenth and early nineteenth centuries resulted in some reductions in salary and dismissals, most civil servants were better off than the rest of the population in those troubled times.[35] Their salaries were not high by the standards of the later nineteenth century, but if managed with care, were sufficient to sustain a respectable family life. Members of the profession were able to marry well, raise large families, and provide adequately for their sons and daughters through marriage or education.[36]

Cultivation continued to be the most highly prized attribute of the members of the bureaucratic estate; it was to the Prussian civil servant what the qualities of the gentleman were to his English counterpart.[37] This was particularly true of the older officials, for it can be estimated that of those who had been recruited through the universities in the 1820's, about 70 percent were members of the various groups that formed the core of the cultivated classes. Of these, more than half were sons of members of the civil service; the rest were from other professional backgrounds, and included a large number of clergymen's sons. Families of businessmen accounted for only 11 percent, and larger landowners, 9 percent; while sons of peasants and artisans together amounted to 12 percent of the total.[38]

As we have noted, in the 1820's only the judiciary was recruiting solely from among those who held university degrees; the administration had just begun to establish formal educational standards and until 1846 did not require university graduation as a prerequisite to entry.[39] The apprenticeship method still prevailed, and a large number of higher administrative officials were recruited from the subaltern ranks. Educational standards in this lower group usually included a secondary school degree, which meant that at the classical gymnasium the subalterns had been exposed to much the same cultural influences as the higher officials.

Among this generation of officials, recruits who came from groups outside the ranks of the cultivated elites were effectively assimilated. Schools and universities helped provide the acceptable qualities, but most important of all was the pressure for uniformity within the bureaucracy itself. The fact that the higher civil service was still relatively small in size (about 1,100 in 1840) contributed to the uniformity of its social codes, but what exercised the greatest pressure in the direction of conformity was the fact that success within the profession was still heavily dependent on proper social conduct. Until the ascriptive qualities associated with Bildung were replaced by new standards, the bureaucracy would remain a tight-knit social group.

In the early nineteenth century the bureaucracy's claim to be representative of the best elements of Prussian society also rested on its ability to attract and assimilate men from a wide range of religious and geographical backgrounds. It seems clear that the old religious prejudices that had favored the Protestant majority had receded enough to allow the recruitment of men from the cultured elite of the Catholic population as well as a representative sample of the Gebildeten from all the provinces. In 1815 when the question of staffing the newly acquired Catholic territories of the west arose, there was very little resistance within the previously heavily Protestant profession to the admission of Catholic members. Catholic judges and administrators were ordinarily assigned to provinces with large Catholic populations because they were more competent in handling the special problems of those areas.[40] If the proportion of Catholics in the bureaucracy fell short of the level of Catholics in the total population, it was not entirely attributable to religious discrimination, since the country's Catholics were primarily rural people, generally poorer and less cultivated than the Protestant majority. For the most part they were concentrated in recently acquired territories where the traditions of service to the Prussian state were not yet strong. Because their church was traditionalist in orientation and hostile to the ways of neo-humanistic culture, their chances of obtaining the prerequisites necessary for entry into the civil service were considerably less than those of the members of the Protestant faith. Nevertheless, the proportion of Catholics in civil service, particularly in the judiciary, increased in the early nineteenth century.[41]

The traditions that had worked against an equitable geographical distribution in the bureaucratic profession had been moderated in the course of the late eighteenth century. Earlier, the Prussian civil service had become a tool used by the Hohenzollerns in their efforts to unite their scattered territories, and as a result, its ranks were filled with men from the old provinces who regarded new regions in much the same way a colonial administrator views a backward land. Natives of these territories were discriminated against, and when they were permitted to enter state service at all, they were usually forced to serve outside their home provinces.

After 1815, however, it was clear that a new tolerance had triumphed. Instead of filling the positions in the newly acquired western territories with men from the old provinces, Berlin absorbed the qualified local officials and encouraged talented provincials to enter Prussian service. Except for certain appointive positions, by 1840 the regular bureaucracy of the new Rhine Province was largely made up of local men.[42] The Rhinelanders' earlier fears of domination by eastern officials proved to be largely unfounded; the inequalities that still existed were probably more the product of the native inhabitants' own prejudices against Prussian service than the result of a discriminatory policy on the part of Berlin.[43]

Naturally the same principle of recruitment that minimized provincial discrimination prevented the civil service in the new provinces from being staffed entirely by local men. The possibility that the new principle of selection by talent might strengthen the forces of provincial separatism was prevented by the gradual integration on the national level of men of differing geographical origins. In 1830 the members of the Rhineland's provincial assembly had complained of the exclusion of local men from the central bureaucracy in Berlin; fifteen years later, however, Prussia had its first western cabinet minister, and from all indications, there had already been a steady influx of natives of the new western provinces into the staffs of the various ministries.[44]

When Otto Camphausen wrote in the 1840's of an "aristocracy of experts" he was describing a generation of Prussian bureaucrats at the peak of a unique collective achievement—a generation that had claimed the respect of the general community, in part because they had opened their ranks to the talented at all levels of society. But the democratization of the profession was by no means complete. During the first three decades of the century a compromise between old and new seemed possible; then, as new utilitarian considerations made further modernization necessary, the equilibrium was upset. By the 1840's the powers of movement, represented by a new generation of officials different both in background and outlook from the old, were challenging the powers of preservation in a way unsettling to both the state and society.

The change came about subtly and gradually, in large measure as the product of earlier reforms. The introduction of a rationalized system of educational standards, culminating in 1846 with the introduction of a university requirement for administrative officials, was the extension of the earlier emphasis on merit. Instead of reinforcing the homogeneity of the profession, however, this requirement unexpectedly introduced division and conflict. We have already seen how Prussia's educational institutions had become major agents of social mobility, and how both in numbers and background the student body had changed since the 1820's. The standards of toleration of religious and regional differences established earlier in the century encouraged the entry of new groups, thereby contributing to the unprecedented increase in the numbers of students from lower and lower-middle income groups studying for all the professions, including the civil service. "In the towns there is not a baker, a shoemaker, or a tailor who does not send his son to school to prepare him for civil service," noted one observer.[45] The upper orders too were moving across the old barriers. For reasons of social and economic necessity, the landed nobility were showing a new interest in higher education. Their emancipation from the land was gradual and at first almost without effect on their social and economic relations with the bureaucracy. But by 1825 Karl Varnhagen von Ense detected the first signs of a realignment and wrote, "The aristocracy gains in strength daily: first at the court, then in the army and administration."[46] At first the flow of landed aristocrats into the higher civil service was merely a steady trickle; then, in the 1840's and 1850's, a significant increase began.

The same pattern, with a different set of causes, was to be seen in the influx into the civil service of members of the entrepreneurial middle class.[47] In the early part of the century, this group had little social or economic contact with the bureaucracy, but during the 1840's more and more sons of self-made men presented themselves at the universities.[48] Reaching for the symbols of status that wealth alone could not provide, Prussia's entrepreneurial class sought in the civil service a means of social mobility.[49] With reference to this phenomenon, wits would write of the German middle class: "The Frenchman wants the Order of the Legion of Honor; the Englishman wants MP beside his name; the German wants to become a *Kommerzienrat* or *Geheimrat*."[50]

Among the newcomers to the universities were the sons of lesser officials, who were turning to higher education as a means of attaining social and economic security. Before 1817 such men had been able to work their way up through the ranks, but now the few remaining opportunities for direct advancement from the subaltern to the higher ranks were closed, and there was no choice but to prepare for service careers through ever longer periods of higher education that forced the subalterns into direct competition with members of the other groups.[51]

The built-in advantages enjoyed by men of cultivation, even by those from bureaucratic families, were no longer of paramount importance for professional advancement: the mechanism of the academic marketplace was replacing the more traditional means of selection. In terms both of absolute numbers and percentages, the recruitment of men from groups previously outside the circle of the Gebildeten was increasing. Sons of professionals were also entering the university, but not in large enough numbers to sustain the earlier levels of generational continuity. The percentage of sons of higher officials studying for the bureaucracy remained at about 33 percent during the 1820's and 1830's, then began a steady slide downward, reaching 28 percent in the 1850's and 22 percent in the 1870's.[52] Replacing the Gebildeten were members of groups that had previously been much less closely associated with the bureaucracy—the landed aristocracy, the industrial bourgeoisie, and elements of the urban and rural lower-middle class. The coming generation of Prussian officials was much more heterogeneous in origin than previous generations had been: this was to be the cause of some tension between the older and younger members of the profession.

Under ordinary conditions, the bureaucracy might have been able to absorb the newcomers; it had been extraordinarily successful before in assimilating men of different backgrounds, and as long as its basic institutions remained intact, there was little reason why it could not continue to mold outsiders to its standards. There were additional problems connected with the unprecedented influx of university graduates, however, not the least of which was the great number of those seeking entry into the profession.

During the early nineteenth century the study of law was particularly popular among secondary school graduates, especially those from the eastern provinces. In 1821, 40 percent of those graduating from the gymnasia indicated a preference for law as their future field of concentration.[53] As a result, in the 1820's and early 1830's attendance at the Faculty of Law was second only to attendance at the Faculty of Theology. Although the numbers declined somewhat in the late 1830's, there was another surge of student interest in the late 1840's and early 1850's. In absolute figures, the amount of young men studying law at Prussian universities almost doubled between 1820 and 1830; their number had declined by 1840, but soon rose again to the previously high figure.[54]

In theory, the first state examination determined those who were qualified to begin training for civil service; in practice, however, it was so easy that very few who took it failed to pass. Instead of screening out the incompetents at an early stage, the system admitted most of the graduating class every year. As a result, the pressure of Prussia's growing student population was transmitted directly to the profession itself. Furthermore, the legal profession, which in other countries absorbed many law graduates, was strictly controlled in Prussia. Not only were its numbers limited, but available positions were reserved primarily for retired judicial officials.[55] As a result it was the bureaucracy itself that bore the burden of absorbing the university population.

An increase in the numbers of candidates would ordinarily have been welcomed as a sign of the good health of the civil service, but to a government still burdened by the debts incurred during the Wars of Liberation, the unprecedented number of candidates was hardly a blessing. As previously noted, the state made hardly any attempt to expand its services during the Vormärz period. The fear that an increase in expenditure might necessitate the calling of some form of representative assembly appears to have been partially responsible for the continuance of an austere personnel policy. As a matter of fact, Prussia's per capita expenditure on administration and justice actually declined during the Vormärz period, and when the King finally called the United Diet together in 1847 it was for the purpose of financing railway construction, not raising the salaries of state employees.[56] The pay schedule set in 1825 was adjusted in individual cases, but was not raised across the board until the late 1850's.[57] Despite contemporary charges that the Prussian taxpayer was supporting an ever-expanding horde of parasitical officials, Prussians were actually enjoying one of the least expensive governmental systems in Europe.[58] The burden of cheap government fell, of course, on the civil servants themselves—particularly on those in the lower ranks, whose salary was most seriously devalued by the prolonged inflation of the 1840's.[59]

When the universities began to deliver their burgeoning classes to the restricted bureaucratic marketplace, a crisis occurred. Throughout the 1820's the number of young men who passed the qualifying examination swiftly mounted, and by 1835 there were almost three thousand trainees in the three apprentice ranks of the judiciary alone.[60] The unprecedented overcrowding caused considerable concern, and the Minister of Justice, Heinrich von Mühler, felt compelled in 1839 to issue an appeal to the parents and guardians of prospective candidates, requesting their aid in preventing the further exacerbation of an already difficult situation. They should, he warned, encourage only those who "possess superior ability and those who are prepared to support themselves for ten additional years after the completion of university study." Because there were already more than a thousand *Assessoren* (those who had passed the three qualifying examinations and were awaiting tenure) ready for placement in salaried positions, no one should expect rapid promotion.[61]

Mühler's message had little effect; the number of candidates for the higher judiciary continued to grow at such a pace that in an average year during the 1850's there were almost fifteen times as many men taking the Third Examination as had taken it in a comparable period in the late eighteenth century, and five more than the number that had taken it in the first quarter of the nineteenth century.[62] Although this tide ebbed somewhat in the late 1840's, another increase followed, and not until the late 1860's did demand finally catch up with supply.[63]

Although the government went to great lengths to discourage candidates, the number of those who had passed the three qualifying examinations but had not yet received tenure continued to rise. From 1836 to 1848 the judiciary itself granted tenure to only twenty candidates per year, a figure only a little more than twice the number of trainees who died each year without attaining a permanent position.[64] The administrative branch managed to take another fifty-three per year and the legal profession thirty-nine, but even so the pressure continued to build.[65] During the 1840's the number of judicial Assessoren increased by twenty-five percent. Almost two thousand of these young men, plus an equal number of other types of trainees, were awaiting promotion when the Revolution of 1848 began.[66]

The administrative branch was no longer able to serve its old function as an alternative haven for those who found no place in the judiciary. It had felt the impact of the increase in university graduates later than the judiciary had, but by the 1840's it too was becoming overcrowded.[67] Earlier in the century the judiciary had the advantage of higher educational standards and was considered superior to the administration in terms of both social status and salary.[68] Gradually this situation had been reversed, however, and by mid-century it was the administration that offered higher pay and was attracting the greater number of upper-class applicants. Its educational requirements were now equal to those of the judiciary and its authority was rapidly expanding.[69] Now that it was more attractive to the higher status groups than the opposite branch, the administration was no longer dependent on the courts for its supply of talented young men.[70]

The influx of so many graduates in the 1820's and 1830's clogged the middle ranks of the bureaucracy. The problems in both branches were slowness of promotion and the aging of the higher echelons. From the seniority lists we know that by the 1850's the path to the top was a good deal more arduous than it had been twenty years earlier. During the 1830's men who had been named to responsible judicial positions had had an average of twenty-four years experience.[71] During the 1840's men with the same rank had had an average of twenty-seven years' experience, and in the 1850's, thirty-one years. This meant that although the talented jurists who had entered the bureaucracy early in the century could expect to reach a high post by the time they were fifty, many of those who followed were sixty before they finally reached a similar level.[72]

An analysis of the seniority lists of *Stadtgerichtsräte* (municipal judges) and *Kreisgerichtsdirektoren* (county court directors) shows that promotion had also slowed on the lower rungs of the judicial ladder. The municipal judge who became a Referendar in the 1820's had to wait on an average of two and a half years for his appointment to tenured position; those of similar rank who entered the service twenty years later had to wait an average of ten to twelve years for their first salaried position.[73]

Similar evidence for the administration is more difficult to obtain, but a survey of the various ranks does seem to indicate that promotions were slowing there also. Those who had entered the service during the 1830's took an average of 6.6 years to pass through the training period; in the 1840's, the time was 7.4 years. The time spent as an Assessor prior to attaining salaried position was also increasing. In the 1830's the young Assessor could expect to wait 6.6 years for his appointment; by the 1850's, the duration of the waiting period had stretched to 10.4 years.[74]

The overabundance of aged bureaucrats was the target of considerable criticism. One critic complained that most of the duties of the colleges were carried out by young unpaid Assessoren and that the performance of many superannuated senior officials no longer justified their privileged position.[75] Earlier, Freiherr vom Stein had suggested in jest that there be a periodical purge of all officials over fifty; now the problem to which Stein had referred was no jesting matter.[76] Since there was no compulsory retirement age, many officials preferred to die in office, rather than to retire on small pensions that would be rapidly devalued by the advancing inflation. The general increase in life expectancy probably contributed to the problem; as of January 1848, the average age of the fourteen officials of ministerial rank was sixty-one; the oldest, Karl Friedrich von Nagler, was seventy-eight, and the youngest, Friedrich von Rönne, was fifty.[77]

Senior members of the bureaucracy were not unaware of the problems affecting the younger generation, but they were prevented from attempting to relieve them by personal and professional considerations. The influx of candidates could not be restricted without violating the principle of open competition for state offices to which the profession and the state had officially committed themselves even before the Reform Era. This step toward the universalization and equalization of standards had been taken in the interests of the state and therefore could not be reversed without seriously compromising the whole course of modernization and calling the integrity of the political system into question. In fact, considerations of a purely utilitarian nature now demanded even higher standards of education for candidates, thus tying the profession even more closely to the university system. In addition, there were personal reasons why the older men did not move to improve the plight of their younger colleagues. Among these was the fact that the unprecedented supply of candidates, many of whom were superbly qualified, represented a challenge to their privileged position. Unable and perhaps also unwilling to expand the bureaucracy at such a cost, they did all they could to discourage new candidates by stiffening the standards of admission in the name of professional excellence.[78]

The tightening of standards was not, however, totally a manifestation of fear on the part of the entrenched officials. A general desire for improvement—the wish of those at the top for the most highly trained and efficient administrative and judicial personnel available—was in operation. The ancient Prussian tradition of *Staatsräson* was at work here, encouraging members of the civil service to demand in the name of the state the highest performance their colleagues could achieve. There had been cases of inefficiency and corruption in the 1840's, and many senior officials were sincere when they justified tightened controls with arguments for higher professional performance. At the same time, however, it served their own interests to do so, for those who suffered from the new austerity were primarily the younger and lower-ranking officials. Thus the requirements of further modernization dovetailed neatly with the instinct for self-preservation. While the measures that were enacted at this time were progressive to the degree that they furthered professionalization by enforcing academic and ethical standards, they were also socially conservative: they did not substantially alter the relations between the upper and lower ranks of the bureaucracy, nor did they change the bureaucracy's relationship to the society as a whole. Rather, their effect was to strengthen the hand of the senior officials, whose authoritarian habits and social conservatism were increasingly at odds with the norms of an influential part of the general population, including a large number of their younger colleagues.

When public appeals failed, more severe measures to limit entrance into the profession were instituted. The Third Examination, once virtually pro forma, was made so much more difficult that by the end of the 1840's, almost a third of those who took it failed. Local courts were urged to assist the government by weeding out incompetents and undesirables before they reached the final examinations. In addition to making the preparatory tests more difficult, superiors were supposed to review the records of those who showed insufficient dedication by appearing "lazy," either in the performance of their duties or in meeting the examination schedule. Furthermore, no candidate whose moral conduct was suspect or who was known to have substantial debts was to be allowed to continue candidacy. "The maintenance of regular and strict discipline among the Auskultatoren as well as the Referendarien cannot be too strongly recommended," warned the directive from the Ministry of Justice.[79]

In order to provide superiors with information about each official, the secret personnel files called Konduitenlisten were expanded to include reports on "moral behavior."[80] Knowledge that had previously been at the disposal only of the colleges was now transmitted at regular intervals to the appropriate ministries. Behavior both inside and outside the office was subject to review, a policy that brought bitter criticism from those who felt that the independence of the profession was being endangered. Throughout the 1840's the Konduitenlisten continued to be a cause of dissension within the bureaucracy.[81]

In March 1844, a new disciplinary code was promulgated that provided the government with a firm legal basis for closer regulation of the lives of its officials. "Dismissal from service shall follow," it read, "when the official is guilty of sustained neglect of his official duties or when he has prejudiced the respect and trust due his office by drunkenness, wastefulness, frivolous debt-making, or by religious or moral misbehavior."[82] With one major exception, this law did not go beyond previous regulations; only with regard to the transfer of judicial officials against their will did it depart from the rules that had governed the bureaucracy during the previous half-century.[83] But when interpreted in the light of the existing internal conditions of the profession, the 1844 law seemed to many to be a major departure from the previous guarantees of the rights of the individual against arbitrary actions.

Nontenured trainees had always been subject to dismissal without recourse to appeal, but prior to the mid-nineteenth century, the power to dismiss lay in the hands of their peers rather than with some higher authority. Candidates for higher office had been under surveillance in connection with the nationalist agitation of the decade following the Wars of Liberation, but few had been dismissed for political reasons.[84] In 1837, however, the local courts were ordered to oversee the private lives of their trainees with greater care. In the large cities, where young men were more difficult to keep track of, the police were asked to aid in this operation.[85]

The tendency on the part of superiors to interpret failure to meet the schedule of examinations or to fall into debt as grounds for dismissal was only one more step in the same direction. In the past, individual indebtedness had been a matter for corporate concern; the member was ordinarily protected by his colleagues against his creditors.[86] Now, though the debtor still had a certain immunity, he could no longer expect sympathy from his superiors. In the name of professional ethics, the Ministers declared that the financial situation of the individual was his own responsibility. In 1841 all departments were ordered to warn their subordinate members that excessive indebtedness would no longer be tolerated.[87] The administrative branch complied by declaring that it would no longer appoint persons owing "considerable" sums.[88] The judiciary followed suit and required candidates to disclose their financial situations before taking the first examination. Those who had not already settled their affairs were asked to guarantee that they would liquidate their debts within a year's time; otherwise, except in cases of extreme hardship, they would be automatically rejected.[89]

This order provoked unexpectedly strong opposition from those most directly affected. Members of the Trier judiciary were reported to have felt that the new regulations were "putting their estate in the shadows" by depriving it of the talents of the less fortunate.[90] It was not just the candidates from the poorest families who were affected: one superior court judge reported to his superiors that young men who incurred large debts before appointment were by no means exceptional. Apparently even the sons of more affluent households were impoverished by the expenses of education and the long period of unpaid apprenticeship they were forced to endure. "There are relatively few Assessoren ... who will not be in this position before they are finally appointed," wrote the judge. "Shall all these young men be forever robbed of the prospects of tenured position?"[91]

In reply, the Minister of Justice offered sympathy, but held out little hope for those in financial trouble. Special cases would be taken into account, and the regulations would not apply to sums owed to the university; but beyond this, there could be no relief except that provided by the individual's capacity for patience and self-denial.[92] In the service of both the profession and the state, it would be necessary to remove from the bureaucracy all those who could not meet the proper standards.[93]

It was with the same attitude that senior officials approached the problem of outside sources of income. A cabinet order of July 1839 forbade any state official to hold a second remunerative position without the prior permission of the authorities.[94] When the question arose of whether this rule should apply also to unpaid trainees, it was decided that they too fell under the ban.[95] Although conflict-of-interest laws were not new in Prussia, the timing of this regulation was particularly significant. Encouraged by the opportunities offered by the expanding economy, many officials were seeking outside sources of income. Even those with scant funds were taking advantage of investment opportunities. The younger officials did not feel constrained by the traditional mores that had inhibited their predecessors with respect to business operations: they were imbued by a new spirit more in tune with the first beginnings of industrialization in the 1840's. But what appeared to them as innocent essays at investment were to the older generation a threat to the moral fiber of the profession. From the conservative perspective, it was corrupt to speculate; and with the full weight of their powers, the older generation acted in the name of the honor of the profession to uphold a tradition that was becoming increasingly anachronistic. Their social bias was apparent in that the restrictions they imposed on speculation were directed at investment in business, not investment in land—restrictions on landowning would have seriously inconvenienced many of their own number.[96]

Those who made policy saw themselves as powers of movement serving the state by improving the bureaucracy. But such moves were bound to produce victims, and the men who were adversely affected by the new regulations saw them in a different light. From their perspective, many of the steps were not only unjust but incomplete, even hypocritical; and the bureaucracy's desire to maintain its high academic and ethical standards seemed only an excuse to prolong inequality. This caused them to question not only the integrity of their superiors but also the legitimacy of the existing political system. In a situation in which the powers of movement tended to reinforce the powers of preservation, it is not surprising that professional grievances ultimately became public concerns.

Chapter Three

Two Generations

During the last decades of the eighteenth century, the Prussian bureaucracy survived a serious crisis caused by a sharp rise in the
number of eligible candidates: although the problem continued
until the beginning of the Reform Era, it corrected itself without
extreme measures being taken.[1] Perhaps that is why senior officials
seemed relatively unconcerned when the same sort of crisis arose
in the 1840's. They resorted to time-honored methods of dealing
with the situation, relying on discipline rather than reform as a
means of control and making authoritarian pronouncements with
an assurance born of the conviction that loyalty and obedience
were "the natural habits" of the Prussian official.[2] In the past, mere
firmness had produced the desired results: subalterns had accepted
the decisions of their elders unquestioningly as necessary for the
good of the profession as a whole. But in the increasingly equalitarian political climate of the 1840's, highhanded methods on the
part of senior bureaucrats met with strong resistance from the
lower ranks. An unprecedented questioning of the very foundations of the bureaucratic tradition was beginning to take place.
The entrenched senior elements met this questioning not with
answers but with orders, and soon dialogue between the generations—the basis of the delicate equilibrium between tradition and
change—was in serious danger of breaking down completely.

Inequality between young and old had been one of the accepted
features of the profession in earlier decades—but not until the

introduction of new educational requirements began to divide the bureaucracy into an older generation, only part of whom had university educations, and a younger generation made up almost exclusively of university graduates did it become a source of conflict. The change lay not only in the amount of education but in the kind as well. Although the judiciary had required an advanced degree in law since the late eighteenth century, the administration, still partly under the influence of cameralism, emphasized practical knowledge until well after the end of the Reform Era.[3] Even among the reformers, who as a group embodied the highest ideals of the administrative bureaucracy, there was still a deep distrust of pedantry. Although many of the older generation had been advocates of the educational reforms advanced by Wilhelm von Humboldt and embodied in the new University of Berlin, they did not always understand the spirit of the new learning.[4]

The introduction of new educational requirements had been dictated primarily by the needs of the Prussian political system. Because the General Code of 1794 covered almost every area within the competence of the bureaucracy, administrators as well as judges had to know something of law; and even those officials to whom practice was more important than academic training could not deny the utility of a higher education. The elevation of standards was also a response to the growing prestige of education itself. Law, then closely associated with the other scholarly disciplines, was queen of the faculties at the University of Berlin for much of the early nineteenth century; and its intellectual appeal was reinforced by the popularity of the ideal of the *Rechtsstaat* (constitutional state) among a growing segment of the public. The achievements of the Reform Era, insofar as they were directed at the integration and rationalization of Prussian institutions, further increased the need for administrators trained in law.[5]

The utilitarian reasons for the emphasis on legal knowledge must not be overestimated, however. Legal studies in the early nineteenth century were a relatively theoretical, highly academic affair, both with respect to the content of the university curriculum and to the method of instruction. In contrast to the heavily dogmatic curriculum of the pre-Reform days, the new knowledge, defined now as "the science of law," was abstract and nonauthoritarian. Students no longer learned by rote; the seminar method of education stressed research on scholarly rather than practical subjects, and the professors, freed from their earlier responsibility for both academic and social discipline, taught whatever suited their own interests, however unrelated it might be to the entrance requirements of the various professions.[6]

For those students who took their newly acquired academic freedom seriously, the scholarly approach to learning was enormously stimulating; in the long run all the professions felt the benefits of the self-discipline demanded of the student trained in independent inquiry. The young men who passed through the reformed universities tended to have a much broader perspective than their predecessors, and conceived of themselves as true intellectuals, well qualified to deal with a wide range of social, political, and cultural problems. Many of the first wave of graduates entered the civil service during the 1820's and 1830's, bringing with them a new breadth of vision and commitment to progress.[7]

In the short run, the positive effects of the new learning were not always so obvious. To many students the new freedom meant no more than a release from the authority of parents and secondary school. Among the law students laxness was particularly noticeable; of all the faculties, law was the one most closely associated with the licentious side of early nineteenth-century student life. Many future jurists were members of the hard-drinking student fraternities and ranked among the most energetic of the duelers.[8] Yet like the more serious students many were different from those of earlier generations insofar as they were quick to defend their personal freedom and to resist what they considered the unjust exercise of authority.

The most eloquent testimony to the results of early nineteenth-century education is found in the memoirs of the graduates themselves, some of whom came to regret not having prepared more conscientiously for the harsh realities of the professions. Even the most diligent among them found the gap between their learning and the demands of day-to-day practice difficult to bridge, for service to the state demanded not only an unaccustomed personal discipline but also practical knowledge that the university had not provided.[9] This disparity between the aims of education and the realities of the professions seems to have been growing throughout the 1840's. The gradual tightening of standards that had culminated in the regulations of 1846 demanded a higher level of education, but not necessarily the kind that the universities were providing. Those who took the administrative and judicial examinations found their legal training of only minimal value and were forced to resort to private cram courses in order to master the additional material. Candidates for the administration were particularly hard-pressed, for they had to master the fine points of both law and the administrative sciences, with which most were unfamiliar.[10] The first examination was notoriously easy; the second and third examinations, taken at intervals in the candidate's training, were extremely difficult. A large number of students did not pass—an average of 20 percent for the judiciary's third (final) examination during the period 1841–1848. The likelihood of failure gave rise to an almost compulsive concern with examinations among the senior students.[11]

There had always been a certain tension between the universities and the bureaucracy: the interests of the university and the profession had always been, by virtue of their different functions, in opposition to some degree. But rarely had the disparity of aims been as marked as it was in the early nineteenth century, for at this time changes in the educational system were out of phase with those within the profession. Prior to the Reform Era, the state had virtually dictated educational policy, and the universities had in turn assisted with the administration of entrance exams for the various professions. One of the major achievements of the early nineteenth-century reform was to separate the processes of preparation and qualification. Attempts were made to coordinate them, but this task was difficult because of the differing points of view of those who controlled the universities and the topmost bureaucratic officials.[12] Here it is important to keep in mind that the men who set policy for the bureaucracy in the 1830's and 1840's were of the pre-reform generation. Though most of them were convinced of the utility of higher educational standards, they had little understanding of or sympathy with the results of the new learning. In examinations on practical matters therefore, they did not always do justice to the qualifications of the candidate, or at least so it appeared to those who were undergoing the difficult transformation from student to state official.[13]

Many young bureaucrats were resentful of professional requirements that seeemed to contradict the previous direction of their education, many older officials reacted strongly to what seemed to be a challenge to the wisdom and authority of seniority, and the generations began to withdraw from dialogue. The tension over professional requirements was only the occasion, however, for the expression of widespread generational differences, which were also reflected in the student unrest of the 1840's.[14] On the surface, student activism of the late Vormärz period seemed to be a revival of the earlier *Burschenschaft* movement—but beneath the superficial similarities in symbols and rhetoric there lay profound differences. The members of the Burschenschaft movement, which had flourished in the years after the Wars of Liberation and then been driven underground during the 1820's, had been idealistic in attitude and individualistic in behavior. The leaders had devoted themselves to moral and cultural reform and only rarely engaged in direct political action. Most believed in the regenerative powers of youth itself, and implied in their theory of generational change was the notion that the students, as the nation's creative elite, could accomplish their aims by joining the established institutions and working from within.[15] They saw no necessity for a more broadly based political coalition with less privileged groups. Thus those who passed through the universities immediately after the Wars of Liberation were generally willing to accept the rules of a society in which privilege and power were distributed according to a highly stratified age and social structure. They placed their hopes

for change on the ability of the university graduate to put his idealism into practice when he had achieved high office or prestigious
position within the community.[16] Thus they remained elitist in
orientation, keeping their faith in transformation from above.

The generation of students that emerged in the 1840's was of a
different character. To be sure, there were many, probably a majority, who remained conservative, happy in the good life of the
university and complacent about the future. But a significant minority became politically awakened and as a result changed both
their personal goals and their political tactics. This active core
emphasized the role of youth in the transformation of Prussian society—but unlike their predecessors of the Burschenschaft movement, they did not view themselves as a group apart, a youthful
elite working within established institutions. Rather, these students believed that if they were to be effective agents of change
they must integrate their efforts with other groups, merging with
the movement toward civil equality outside the university. Thus,
while their politics symbolized the profound difference between
themselves and the earlier generation of students who now occupied the ranks above them, they felt no need to elaborate an ideology of generational change like that of their predecessors. Paradoxi-
cally, this generation expressed its protest against an older elite by
denying its own status as the leaders of Prussian youth, preferring
instead to remain free to form alliances with the members of other
groups, regardless of age, whose grievances against the established
order complemented their own.[17]

To this generation the student years were no longer merely a
period of preparation for the rights and responsibilities of adult-
hood. Most of these men were several years older than their counterparts of earlier decades, for since 1834, when the *Abitur* (sec-
ondary-school-leaving certificate) was made compulsory for university entrance, all shortcuts had been closed,[18] and the average
age of students attending the university rose as a result. Young
men were entering the university later and staying there longer
because of the gradually lengthening course of study. The day

when the young man could begin his career was thus postponed; and by the 1840's the average candidate did not take his first state examination until he was twenty-two or twenty-three years of age, considerably later than the earlier generations.[19]

The effect of all this was a change in the notion of student status. Arriving at the university with greater maturity, these young men took themselves very seriously. They had been taught to look upon themselves as adults, and from what evidence there is of their attitudes toward their elders, it seems safe to say that many felt themselves to be their equals by virtue of education, if not experience. This made it difficult for them to accept those traditional institutions that put seniority above merit, and it probably inclined them toward systems more consistent with their ideals and previous training—systems based on recognition of individual achievement.

The men of the older generation, who had risen through the ranks during the first three decades of the century, were unable to understand why anyone would challenge the seniority system. Many of them had also gone through a rebellious youth, and some had been members of the Burschenschaft movement, but their very presence in the bureaucracy attested to their belief that change could be brought about from within the system. They considered themselves fairminded men—and indeed, many were "modern" by the standards of their generation. For this reason they resented the charge made by junior officials that they were using discipline to protect their own positions, thereby discriminating against the talented and hurting the reputation of the profession.[20] While they acknowledged the inconveniences of a long and unremunerative apprentice period, they were ill-equipped to understand the point of view of the younger men. As far as they were concerned, the only system that could guarantee just treatment was one based on seniority. All others were bound to lead to corruption and favoritism, ending in what they termed the "disruption and deterioration of the character of the bureaucracy."[21] Ultimately they fell back on the argument that the younger officials had no right to criticize the existing system, for "officials exist for the state and not the state for the officials."[22]

While senior officials argued that the seniority system was essential to the independence and integrity of their profession, junior officials claimed that the overly strict enforcement of the system was harmful to professionalism because it discriminated against merit. By the late 1840's it was clear that neither side was willing to see the other's point of view. The question of seniority had become a symbol of all that divided the two generations—a point of honor for the older men, an example of injustice to the younger. In such a situation every action that involved the relationship between the junior and senior ranks produced controversy.

In 1830 the right of advanced trainees (Assessoren) to vote in the colleges had been suspended indefinitely. The reason given at the time was that the growing number of trainees threatened to outvote the tenured members—a situation that might disrupt the proceedings of the colleges. The government declared that so long as these "emergency conditions" continued, the Assessoren were to have no voice in the decisions of their colleges. This ruling does not appear to have been challenged until a decade later, when the new generation demanded a return of their traditional rights. Their attitude was described by one Assessor as a "feeling of injured honor." During the 1840's a number of younger officials took issue publicly as well as privately with the policies of their superiors.[23] Inequality in salary and privilege, and several other issues connected with seniority were openly discussed. This so disturbed the higher authorities that they took steps to monitor the press and to counter any criticisms that appeared in print with arguments of their own.[24]

The conflict between young and old was exacerbated by a number of factors peculiar to the profession itself. We have already seen how the ferment at the universities was directly transmitted to the professions by the graduates. The same equalitarian ideals held by the students were fostered by an increasingly active political press and supported by the growing body of liberal public opinion. However isolated the bureaucracy had been in the past, it was no longer immune to these influences, for among the most active proponents of the new spirit were members of the cultured middle class from whose ranks the profession still drew the majority of its candidates.[25]

But what of the weakening of social barriers that was occurring during this period? We have seen how changes in recruitment patterns had brought the profession into closer contact with members of groups previously outside the circle of the Gebildeten. Just how much effect this individual mobility had on the transformation of the attitudes of the profession is difficult to measure. The results of the simultaneous influx of larger numbers of sons from the landed aristocracy and industrial middle class as well as from the artisan and peasant classes were bound to be somewhat contradictory. Furthermore, as long as the assimilative capacity of the universities and the bureaucracy remained as strong as it had in the past, the values that these outsiders brought with them had relatively limited impact.[26] Still, the new mobility could not but open up the bureaucracy to new ideas and patterns of behavior.

This is not to say that all university graduates of the 1830's and 1840's were cut to exactly the same radical pattern, or that the young candidates were uniformly critical of their elders. Still, they did belong to a group that shared a common experience of education and apprenticeship. Trainees were encouraged to think and act alike. In the past this had been the very basis of professional solidarity; now it became a major source of division. Working and living together, they could not but absorb one another's ideas—in this case, ideas that on the whole were antithetical to those of the senior members.

Changes in education and training were not the only factors troubling the profession: the economic situation of the bureaucracy, particularly its inequities, added to the general unrest among officials. Earlier in the century the profession had enjoyed a relatively favorable position among the upper income groups; now a number of factors were working to place it at a distinct economic disadvantage. While the wealth of the rural and urban entrepreneurial groups grew with the expansion of the economy, that of the bureaucracy was closely tied to a salary scale that had remained stationary since 1825. Apparently many officials did attempt to implement their salaries by taking advantage of opportunities for investment and ownership—some with considerable success—but the profession as a whole was restrained from this kind of activity both by its traditional distaste for business and by the increasingly strict enforcement of conflict-of-interest rules.[27]

The 10,000 *Thaler* yearly income of a *Staatsminister* or the 3,500 Thaler salary earned by a Regierungspräsident certainly provided sufficient income for a suitable way of life, but the men in the middle and lower ranks were much less fortunate, since they did not ordinarily have the advantage of the nonmonetary benefits, including housing, that were the perquisites of their superiors. The standard of living had changed, and incomes that had once appeared ample seemed less so when compared to those of the entrepreneurial classes. Moreover, inflation had gradually diminished the benefits that professional privileges such as exemption from local taxes could provide.

For the subaltern official, whose income might be a fortieth of the Staatsminister's, the situation was extremely serious by the middle of the 1840's. In the two decades since the salary level had been fixed, the price of some food items had doubled.[28] The cost of housing, particularly in the cities, was up, as were the costs of clothing, heat, and other essentials.[29] The official who earned only 240–360 Thaler per year was spending two-thirds to four-fifths of his earnings on these necessities. To live in the way to which they had been accustomed, many of the lesser officials were forced into debt early on in their careers.[30]

The subalterns escaped the worst effects of these economic conditions, because since the 1820's these officials had as a group become increasingly separated from higher officialdom, both legally ize4_

and socially. Not only were the educational standards for the subaltern and higher bureaucracies now quite different and mobility between the two unlikely, but the subaltern service was no longer attracting as many members of the upper ranks of society as it had before. Whereas earlier the institutional and social lines had been blurred, now they were becoming quite distinct; subaltern rank was generally considered beneath the dignity of both the nobility and the wealthier burghers, and the standard of living expected of a subaltern was therefore much more modest than that expected of a higher official.[31] The pattern of consumption characteristic of the subalterns was austere in comparison to that of the upper ranks, with more being spent on necessities and less on conspicuous items such as fashionable clothing and expensive furnishings. To what degree this separation of lifestyles was the result of inflation is difficult to determine, but what is clear is that the economic burdens of the subalterns did not include social competition with the better-paid upper ranks of the higher bureaucracy.

The trainees for the higher bureaucracy enjoyed no such dispensation from the social demands of the profession. It was an unwritten rule that all higher officials, regardless of rank, were responsible for "keeping up appearances." As stated in the regulations, all apprentice officials were to "conduct themselves in such a manner as to deserve public esteem"[32]: this referred not only to morals and manners but to dress and life style as well. Admission to the profession might be dependent on academic qualifications, but acceptance by one's colleagues still involved conformity to social convention. In the past, trainees had been expected to live frugally during their unpaid apprenticeship on funds provided by family or relatives.[33] Since many of the trainees had come straight from secondary schools into the profession, this had been a reasonable expectation. Now as the average age rose the tradition of apprenticeship without pay worked a hardship on the prospective officials, particularly those who were married or who wished to marry.

At the beginning of the century, education in Germany had been

relatively inexpensive; now many trainees were in debt even before they took the first examination, and few could finish the long
pull to tenure without owing large amounts.[34] Their position was
complicated by the fact that a young man often became engaged
on the condition that he would not marry until he had attained a
secure salaried rank. Earlier, a young man could expect to be able
to marry in his middle twenties, but no longer was this the case.[35]
The difficulties that this state of affairs caused for parents as well
as young couples were enormous. Once married, the pair might
draw on the wife's dowry during the first difficult months, but
when this was used up, there was no way short of borrowing from
family that a respectable woman of the educated middle class
could supplement her husband's income. When young Otto von
Bismarck set out upon his administrative career in 1836, he was
warned by his close friend Ernst von Bülow-Cummerow that the
demands of the profession could make marriage difficult for men
of modest means;[36] and it was the same difficulties that Assessor
Loos was referring to when he asked, "Shall Prussia's judges be
condemned to the celibate condition?"[37]

The support that the young man expected from his own family
was not always forthcoming. Such a large proportion of the recruits were drawn from professional families living on fixed incomes that many fathers who had expected to be able to provide
support when their sons began their training in the 1830's could
no longer afford to do so a decade later. Men learn to adjust to
restrictive financial situations, but they cannot easily anticipate
them: one of the reasons why applications for the bureaucracy remained at such a high level even during the 1830's was that many
of the young men had started their training so long before that
they were in no position to turn to other career possibilities. Advantage was turned to disadvantage when being the son of an
official no longer helped a young man to achieve his professional
goals.

Young men from other backgrounds often had a greater freedom
of choice: sons of landowners or businessmen could return to their

father's occupations. This is what Otto von Bismarck did when he became exasperated by the bureaucratic career in 1838.[38] Peter August de Weerth, a young man from a wealthy Rhenish industrial family, wrote when he gave up the judiciary in the 1850's: "Nothing that can still entice men, be it wealth, be it social prominence, can be won through this career."[39]

Bismarck and de Weerth were fortunate in having secure positions to fall back on. For men like Heinrich Simon, whose father was a high court judge, the alternatives were limited. During the mid-1830's this talented jurist had thought of giving up the judiciary for the administration, where the salary was somewhat higher and the chances of promotion greater. "I am not willing to work myself to death for the necessary minimum of existence," he wrote during the darkest part of this period. Eventually a promotion and raise in salary were secured, but it was more the absence of attractive alternatives and his devotion to service than the small raise that determined Simon's decision to continue.[40]

Little wonder that by the 1840's many observers detected what they described as a growing spirit of materialism that reached down even into the professions. Society was now judging occupations on the basis of financial reward. Occupations like those in the bureaucracy, which offered a great deal in the way of public esteem but relatively little in the way of salary, were less and less sought after. Simon noted this, and Clemens Theodor Perthes warned in 1838 that soon entry into the bureaucracy would no longer be viewed as "a sacrifice which the individual makes to the whole. . . . Service to the state will be seen as just another occupation, chosen as a way of making a living."[41]

By the 1840's the traditional distinctions between what were then called the "public" occupations—those involving service to the state —and the "private" occupations—those directed exclusively toward individual gain—were considerably blurred. The old distaste of the Gebildeten for the private occupation was gradually disappearing, and many sacrosanct public occupations were being subjected to the ultimate test of financial viability and social utility. Rhineland industrialists like David Hansemann argued that free enterprise could better serve the common good than bureaucratic traditions could.[42] His arguments were taken up by leaders of the landowning community, who were now also stressing the value of individual initiative.[43] Their case could not but appeal to those within the bureaucracy itself who had found their personal efforts stifled by outmoded procedures and paternalistic leadership: appeals to patience in the name of the honor of the profession sounded hollow and hypocritical to those who felt themselves both powerless and overburdened.

Idealism was by no means extinguished among the younger generation of the 1840's. Indeed, the desire for effective service to the state and society were perhaps stronger in them than in any generation since the Wars of Liberation. The fact that many were turning away from state service did not reflect a diminution of civic spirit but rather a recognition that the highest ideals of service to state and society could be achieved outside the bureaucratic profession. As the prestige of business began to grow, more and more young men began to see it as a way of expressing their altruism while at the same time satisfying their financial needs. Under these conditions it was little wonder that senior officials were seriously concerned about the loss of talented men to occupations that were considerably more lucrative than their own.[44]

Unfortunately, the senior men did not respond to this situation with much insight or understanding. Their response was to condemn their younger colleagues as careerists who put their own interests ahead of those of the profession.[45] In doing so they ignored the fact that the growing concern over salary and promotion was the product of prevailing conditions, and that younger officials were virtually compelled to use every means at their disposal to get ahead. Membership in the best student fraternities, apprenticeship at certain elite courts and agencies, and exposure in the proper circles were widely recognized as necessary for those who wished to rise in the profession.[46] The career of Rudolf von Delbrück, a man of great ability but small means, was probably typical in many respects. During his university years, Delbrück had come to know the lot of the poor student and was determined to ensure his own financial security. Initially he aspired to the prestigious Foreign Office, but on the good advice of a family friend entered the less crowded internal administration. Eventually he was fortunate enough to be assigned to one of the so-called *Garde-Regierung* (elite posts), from which speedy promotion was almost assured.[47] But even a rapid rise within the provincial government had only limited appeal for the ambitious young man; he had his sights set on a place in the more prestigious and better paid central ministries, where rules of seniority were not so strictly applied.[48] His funds were limited; his plan was simple. It would be better, he calculated, "to live in circles from which I could expect promotion, than to go along trying to preserve this small capital." Investing his funds in his future, the young Assessor began to dine at one of Berlin's most elegant restaurants, the favorite meeting place of the highest government officials. Before long Delbrück was a regular member of their table and it was through one of their number that he soon found a place in the Ministry of Finance.[49]

Delbrück's talents were beyond question, but there were others of equal worth who were passed over. Rudolf Gneist, a young jurist who had already made a name for himself as one of Prussia's most brilliant legal minds, was denied salary and tenure for eight years during this same period.[50] Little wonder, then, that when Gneist wrote about the conditions of the judiciary he was particularly bitter about the malfunctioning of the seniority system, which, as he pointed out, opened the door to personal favoritism and political manipulation.[51] Gneist became acutely aware of the pauperization of the lower ranks of his profession. He compared their fate to that of the laboring poor during the same period and wrote of the emergence of a "proletariat" composed of subaltern officials and young interns, which would threaten the stability of the entire society.[52]

Heinrich Simon, who like Gneist had been poorly compensated for his contributions to the judiciary, also complained of the excessive burdens placed on younger officials.[53] These complaints were echoed by Loos, who spoke for many of the younger officials when he wrote: "While the majority of this generation who chose other careers have already established a family or are at least in sight of salaried position, the Prussian jurist is the only one who, though he has already reached maturity, has not been able to achieve what he set out to do."[54]

One more problem contributing to discontent was the deprivation felt by the younger men when they considered the success of those of their own age who had chosen other careers. In the past, a stronger continuity of generations as well as greater corporate solidarity had discouraged such comparisons: the frame of reference for the younger official had been narrower, extending only to the bureaucratic estate itself or, at its broadest dimension, to the circles formed by the other groups that comprised Prussia's cultured elite. By the 1840's, however, there were the first faint signs that this previously cloistered few were beginning to recognize the existence and legitimacy of other groups whose social backgrounds were different from their own. Prussia's version of a modern upper class was just beginning to come into existence and affecting the awareness as well as the habits of the major segments of society that were to be its constituents—the landed aristocracy, the wealthy industrialists and businessmen, and the members of the higher military and civil services. The change was a gradual and subtle one involving an accommodation of various value systems rather than the abrupt substitution of one set of attitudes for another. Each of the major groups involved influenced the habits of the others; and it is this change that we see reflected in the growing awareness of the importance of material well-being among the bureaucracy in the late prerevolutionary period.

One of the ways that social accommodation with the urban and rural entrepreneurial groups affected the civil service was in the reordering of priorities. The desire for material well-being and external display, more characteristic in business circles, had never been entirely absent among civil servants, but previously it had been subordinated to other corporate goals. Expensive tailoring or lavish entertainment had not been considered comparable to spiritual refinement. Without necessarily abandoning culture as a desirable attribute, the bureaucracy began to add more conspicuous items of consumption to its repertoire of social necessities. Now more than ever before appearances counted and, as all the various estates competed on the basis of "the lustre and brilliance of externals," the burdens on all ranks increased correspondingly.[55] A fashionable address, expensive clothes, and lavish entertainment were required of the aspiring bureaucrat; wives of high officials were seen more frequently in court circles; and in the major cities, the life of all the senior officials was noticeably more luxurious.[56]

Because of this shift in standards, the bureaucrat was faced with new demands that often strained his resources. Previously each rank had been characterized by its own standard of living, to which the salaries of its members were roughly adequate. The replacement of this kind of stratification with a more uniform style of upper-class life required a kind of social conformity that strained the budgets of all but the most affluent officials.[57] Attaining a salaried position did not solve the dilemma: as one young lawyer noted, "Even a judge cannot remain socially acceptable unless he has an independent source of income." The tension between salary and social position was such, he reported, that few officials high or low could live without worries and frustrations.[58]

The breakdown of the bureaucracy's former social isolation brought with it tensions that were unknown in the old corporate order. Officials were forced to participate in a new set of social roles for which they were poorly prepared both financially and psychologically. It was difficult to adjust to the expectations of a society that demanded evidence of wealth and occupation in addition to and even at the expense of the old qualities of cultivation and refinement. Yet it was a good deal easier for the senior officials, with their salaries and security of tenure, to make the transition than it was for the younger men, who ran the risk of a complete loss of social identity.

Both Rudolf Gneist and Wilhelm Heinrich Riehl compared the plight of the lower-ranking officials to that of the proletariat. Gneist saw the parallels in the pauperization of the officials; Riehl went beyond the economic analogy to compare the anxiety of the officials to that of the skilled worker faced with the loss of personal identity. He argued that like the pauperized artisan or the landless peasant, the lower-ranking official was having difficulty maintaining his particular social position on the limited means available to him. The elementary and secondary school teachers, the parish clergymen, and the small-town lawyers were less acutely affected. Their discontents were the product of frustrated desires for upward social mobility; and though there were some among the bureaucracy, notably men from lower-class backgrounds, whose frustrations were attributable to the same cause, the fear and despair of most was of a different origin. For the vast majority of young officials, attendance at a university and the experience of apprenticeship had erased any inherited sense of social inferiority. Their problem was not so much attaining social prestige as maintaining it. Their inability to protect themselves against the effects of inflation on an already inadequate salary base was the cause of their discontent.[59]

Riehl observed that in this situation frustrations quickly turned into a generalized resentment toward all the established institutions of society. Typical of those affected by status anxiety was the young official "who wanted to reform society because he had no way to improve his meager salary." His fears became diffuse, his aggression was diverted from specific grievances toward those very things that he found it so difficult to attain; his struggle was "with family, with status, with a historically given place in society." Out of despair he turned to social and political radicalism as the only solution to his personal problems. From among such members of the "intellectual proletariat," as Riehl called it, came the leadership for those groups that were to constitute the powers of movement.[60] From the desire to conserve was born the desire to change.

Chapter Four

Prerevolutionary Politics

The almost imperceptible but steady breakdown of barriers between the bureaucracy and other groups was nowhere more evident than in the involvement of state officials in new forms of civic activity, including the expanding political press. Organizations like the Casino in Aachen and the Free Trade Association in Berlin, whose membership included elements of both the professional and the industrial middle classes, as well as the many cultural associations that fostered contact between the educated elites and the working classes, reflected the variety of the social and political interchange characteristic of the decade prior to the Revolution.[1] Men of differing professions and regional backgrounds exchanged ideas at the many academic and scientific conferences held during the 1840's. The rapidly expanding popular press attracted to its editorial boards men from many occupations, and publishers' lists featured titles by men who were not full-time authors, including a large number of civil servants. The various political factions, though still loosely organized, brought together men previously separated by corporate or regional distinctions. Most officials who were active politically were connected only with organizations that were acceptable to their social peers and to the authorities. A small minority, however, forged contacts with political groups and ideological movements of a more questionable sort. The radical Karl Brüggemann boasted that the bureaucracy's "lower circles" already tended toward "a coalition with the radical press and the 'Proletariat.' "[2]

Most of the new alignments and alliances were scarcely recognizable as political, however, centering as they did around cultural, religious, and professional interests that were only vaguely connected to political questions. The absence of modern representative institutions prevented the growth of party organization; restrictions on the rights of press and association had similar inhibiting effects. Concern for political issues tended to be derived either from narrow social and economic interests or from extremely broad intellectual commitments that were equally devoid of political relevance. The practical reformers and the theorists did have some common interests, but not until the Revolution of 1848 were there any broadly based political organizations similar to those already established in other German states and throughout Europe.[3]

The bureaucracy accurately reflected the rest of Prussian society in this respect. Its members were involved in the same range of apparently unrelated activities, from protest over concrete conditions to involvement in movements almost purely intellectual or esthetic in nature. A radical philosophical or religious position was not always accompanied by an equally strong radical political tendency, nor did humanitarian sympathies guarantee a progressive commitment on political questions. Few Prussians had thought through crucial issues such as what form the state should take, or what the extent of the franchise should be—the answers to which were later to mark the divisions between the political parties.

The distinctions among conservatives, liberals, and radicals were still blurred at this time, and the stereotypes connected with the various political positions had not yet come into sharp focus. In view of this, it is difficult to fit the civil servants of the 1840's into the categories that historians have created for them. Within their ranks they encompassed a range of positions as broad as that found among the educated elite in general, which spanned the entire spectrum from the unyielding defender of the status quo to the alienated intellectual. Most fell somewhere between these two extremes, their position a compromise of the liberal and conservative, the traditional and the modern. Even the most radical among Prussia's officials were unmistakably marked by their professional status, particularly when this was the cause of their discontent. And by the same token, a certain critical detachment was found among even the most reactionary, for this too was a product of their training and occupation.

Once again we are confronted with the transitional character of the period. If the positions taken by the actors seem ambiguous, it is because the times were exceptional. The absence of clearly defined political divisions makes it difficult to provide anything more than an impressionistic survey of the diverse ideological tendencies within the civil service at this period. Nevertheless, some attempt must be made to establish a background against which to examine the behavior of officials during later periods when clear-cut ideological positions and party affiliations became both possible and, to a certain extent, necessary.

Among the first signs of a quasi-political consciousness were the attempts made by officials to form themselves into professional organizations along the lines previously established by the scientists, doctors, and teachers. Prussian officials from both the administrative and judicial branches of service were present at the congresses of the *Germanisten*, professional men and students of law interested in restoring a Germanic legal tradition, whose meetings at Frankfurt am Main in 1846 and Lübeck in 1847 can be seen as harbingers of a nationalistic awakening. The delegates, who discussed both the practical and the academic problems connected with the formulation of a national body of law, saw in these meetings not only a chance to improve themselves professionally, but also a means of advancing the cause of national unity.[4]

Certain professional conferences held in Prussia itself followed a similar pattern. At a convention of Rhenish and Westphalian jurists held at Soest in 1843, the delegates confined themselves largely to the technical aspects of law and court procedure, but the recommendations that they produced had distinctly liberal political overtones. They called for the strengthening of the independence of the judiciary, the abolition of patrimonial justice, and the improvement of the conditions of the legal profession—all issues currently being debated in the larger arena of public opinion.[5]

The government was noticeably concerned about such conferences and tolerated them only so long as their political overtones remained muted. When in early 1844 the call for a national conference of lawyers was issued, the Ministry of Justice forbade attendance to members of the Prussian bar on the grounds that the meeting represented a form of nationalist agitation.[6] A number of Königsberg lawyers protested, but the ministry remained unmoved and merely reiterated its previous position, this time extending the ban to all those associated with the judiciary, including the professors of the faculties of law.[7]

Attempts to force reform of the professions through organization and appeals to public opinion could make little headway before 1848. The Soest conference of 1843 set up a permanent executive committee, but there were no further general meetings. The leading journal of the legal profession, *Central Blatt für preussische Juristen*, argued timidly for the formation of an association of jurists, but nothing came of the suggestion. The failure was not surprising, however, for the upper echelons were opposed to new organizations they could not easily control; and even the lower ranks were still looking to the bureaucratic estate as constituted to solve their predicament.[8] Few officials could make the connection between their struggle for rights within their profession and the rising national demand for civic and political equality. They anticipated no confrontation with the existing political and social order over what they considered to be purely a corporate problem; liberal on specific issues connected with the bureaucratic procedure and working conditions, they nevertheless remained relatively conservative on larger political questions. Even the most discontented still felt that there was something undignified about appealing to the public on matters concerning one's own estate.

Even activities that were eventually to have immense political repercussions often originated in concerns of a purely corporate nature. One example was the protest movement that began in opposition to the 1844 regulations concerning the disciplinary procedures of the judiciary. The government's claim to the right to transfer judges from one court to another against their will was initially interpreted as an infringement on the traditional independence of the courts from political control. Under the leadership of a young Breslau jurist, Heinrich Simon, officials of both the junior and senior ranks fought the regulations through the press and by means of petitions to the provincial estates. Attempts by the Minister of Justice to have Simon removed from office only increased their distrust of the government's motives, and the refusal of Simon's colleagues at the Breslau court to prosecute the charges against him stiffened their resolve.

Harassment continued until Simon voluntarily left the service in 1845, but by then the issue had become one of civil rights as well as professional independence. Forty petitions containing the signatures of many junior officials and some senior men had been presented to the provincial estates, and by 1847 the assemblies of the Rhineland, East Prussia, Silesia, Westphalia, and Posen had endorsed the demand for the repeal of the regulations on the grounds that they violated the integrity of the judiciary. By then the struggle had become part of the broad movement against absolutism; and in 1848 the platforms of both the liberal and the democratic factions contained promises to repeal the 1844 regulations.[9]

The campaign against the 1844 regulations could not have remained confined to the purely institutional issue of judicial independence—Simon himself had tied it to a much broader program of civil rights and constitutional reform. Formal protection of the independence of judges would no longer suffice; only the addition of effective representative government, a jury system, public-oral courtroom procedure, and complete freedom of the press would provide the necessary framework for effective justice.[10] Simon and his followers remained conservative to the extent that they believed in the necessity of maintaining a large professional bureaucracy, but they were determined to minimize the arbitrary aspects of bureaucratic rule by transforming Prussia into a constitutional monarchy. In taking this position, they departed from the previous liberal concept of the bureaucratic state, which had placed so much emphasis on a self-regulating body of professional officials. For these men nothing short of an overhaul of the entire political system would suffice to eliminate the threat to individual liberty and social progress posed by absolutism.

Many of those, however, who supported the repeal of the 1844 regulations did so for reasons quite unrelated to a desire for governmental reform. The issue of the independence of the judiciary could mobilize even the most conservative members of the profession because it involved a threat to cherished privileges. Their sense of independence was well established; their honor was challenged by any interference, whether from above or below, in matters reserved to corporate decision. While they supported Simon on the specific issue of repeal, they rejected his attempt to tie it to a general liberalization of the state.

The banding together of diverse forces in support of Simon's petition campaign did not signal the politicization of the country's educated elites, nor was it indicative of the political progressiveness of Prussia's bureaucracy. Bureaucratic liberalism remained for the most part unchanged, embracing economic laissez-faire and public welfare measures but excluding political individualism and social equality. The child labor laws of 1839 and the new trade ordinance of 1845 showed that the old progressive instinct was not entirely moribund; yet Rudolf von Delbrück could describe his colleagues of the 1840's as being "by an overwhelming majority liberal, but still in no way constitutionally minded." What they wanted to achieve, said Delbrück, was "the development of law and government along lines of civil and religious freedom," and their discontent with the system was based on this desire.[11] Concern for the elimination of arbitrary practices rarely went beyond adjustments in the existing system: the majority supported the principle of equal opportunity, but when it came to actually giving every inhabitant the opportunity to become socially and economically mobile, they dissented. They desired the abolition of the remaining feudal aspects of the legal system and were disturbed by the revival of royal absolutism under Frederick William IV, but they did not believe that modern parliamentary government was necessary for the protection of the rights of the individual. Most continued to think in terms of the restoration of the glories of the old bureaucratic state, ruled by the strong, independent hand of the educated elite.

Even the few officials who were advocates of representative institutions rarely questioned the need for a powerful bureaucracy. Their arguments for the addition of separate legislative institutions were based on the desirability of the separation of powers—a separation that would free the civil service from tasks that conflicted with its basic functions and thus permit it to carry out its administrative duties more effectively.[12] Furthermore, modern centralized representative institutions suited their purposes better than the provincial estate system did. The estates were resented not only because officials were virtually excluded from them, but also because it was thought, rightly enough, that Frederick William IV intended to use them to strengthen his personal powers. Before 1848 many officials conceived of a modern legislature as an ally in bureaucracy's long struggle against royal absolutism.[13] They not only hoped that representative institutions would place a further check on the king's authority, but they intended to use the legislature as a means to their own ends: in the German states that already had legislatures, men of their rank were in a position to influence or even to dominate legislative proceedings. Liberal factions in the constitutional states of southern and western Germany had welcomed officials as prestigious and influential allies in their struggle against absolutism; and Prussian officials could reasonably expect the existence of a legislature to enhance their own power.

Officials of various political persuasions, though viewing the possibility of modern representative institutions with favor, were wary of taking a position on this or any other political question. Most prerevolutionary political life was confined to local issues, and it was there that the kind of divisions that we associate with modern political and ideological conflict were visible. In the pre-revolutionary debates over the Rhineland's municipal suffrage law, there were indications that officials tended to be somewhat more liberal than businessmen on the issue of franchise, but even there it was not altogether clear that the civil service was, as David Hansemann charged, "democratically minded."[14] Many who favored an extended franchise were quite conservative and simply preferred an equally exclusive educational requirement to the existing property qualification. The few officials who were ready to advocate universal male suffrage were, for the most part, young men already at odds with the corporate system.[15]

The slightest political stirring among the civil servants was sufficient to arouse the suspicions of the higher authorities, and Frederick William used every occasion of dissent to interfere in the profession's internal affairs. He acted on the precedents established by his predecessor during the third decade of the century, when the Prussian government, under the authority of the Carlsbad Decrees, had forbidden its civil servants to join the Burschenschaften groups that were gaining a large following among university students. Members of these organizations were refused admission to public office, and those already in the service were suspended when identified.[16] In what one young official was later to call "the era of repression," even the wearing of folk costumes was forbidden to off-duty civil employees.[17]

The attention of the government had again been focused on the public behavior of the bureaucracy in 1830, at a time when revolution in states on Prussia's eastern and western borders revived fears of internal disorder. On this occasion, orders were passed to superiors to be particularly observant of the political activity of the younger officials.[18] In the 1840's the problem took on new dimensions. Not only was Frederick William IV more determined than ever to assert his personal authority, but what interest in politics there was among the bureaucracy was considerably more obvious.

"The interest of the educated circles in public matters in the 1820's had been very slight," wrote Delbrück, but now these same groups "made day-to-day events the topic of conversation."[19] In 1843 the Oberpräsident of the Rhine Province felt compelled to walk out of a banquet when speeches in favor of constitutional reform became embarrassing. Many of his fellow officials did the same, but apparently enough stayed to arouse the king's concern.[20] He instructed his ministers to issue directives forbidding civil servants to participate in any demonstration of protest, and vowed to see to it personally that those officials who were guilty of opposition were punished by denial of promotion.[21]

Officials were not only restrained from joining controversial groups, they were warned as well against membership in even the most moderate civic organizations.[22] They were given to understand that the king disapproved of all public activity on the part of his loyal servants, except in those cases where it was a matter of royal command. The monarch ordered surveillance of organized contacts between the bureaucracy and other social groups, particularly those in which members of the laboring poor were involved, and which were therefore considered potential agencies of subversion. The *Bildungsvereine* (cultural clubs), the major points of contact between the educated bourgeoisie and the working men, were particularly suspect. Although the radicalism of these groups was more often philosophical than political, they were viewed by the cabinet ministers with increasing alarm.[23] In Elberfeld, near Düsseldorf, one such cultural association attracted the authorities' attention in 1845 by inviting two well-known radicals, Moses Hess and Friedrich Engels, to address one of its regular Friday evening meetings.[24] Most of those present, including a number of state officials, seem to have been intellectually curious rather than politically motivated, but nevertheless the police, who had previously ferreted out at least one radical from among the ranks of the local bureaucracy, henceforth kept a close watch on that particular group.[25]

In most cases the government was satisfied if it could keep this

type of organization out of contact with the lower orders of society
—a relatively easy task, since the professional middle class who
made up the bulk of the cultural club membership had little contact with other social strata.[26] But in a few of the larger cities, the
old social barriers had already been destroyed to such an extent that
members of the civil service were in close contact with the politically active elements of the middle and lower classes. The first
bonds were usually formed in an informal manner, at someone's
home or at the popular meeting places of the time—the restaurants
and confectionary shops.[27] Stephan Born, a skilled artisan who
was to become a leader of the Berlin workers' movement, first came
into contact with the intellectuals, including a number of officials,
through his brother, a student at the University of Berlin. He extended his contacts through his association with the Berlin Artisans
Association, a group founded in 1844 to "further the popular development of the spiritual, moral, social, industrial, and civil life
of the workers," which soon became a major nucleus of radicalism.[28] In Breslau, membership in reading circles of thirty to forty
people brought officials into contact with a broad spectrum of like-
minded colleagues and townspeople.[29] And in other Prussian
cities, from Königsberg to Cologne, similar small groups served
the same purpose, bringing people together in philosophical and
religious discussions that often turned to political speculation.

Although it was uncommon for professional men to associate
with working men on a social basis, there were now some official
institutions that fostered such informal association. The government itself sponsored the Association for the Well-being of the
Working Classes, the purpose of which was to educate the workers
against subversive influences.[30] In this and similar organizations,
young doctors, lawyers, and civil servants, acting as teachers, came
to know the more articulate and politically conscious laboring men
and women. Some, like the young intern Rudolf Virchow, were
already sympathetic to the problems of the poor, for in the course
of their official duties they had been confronted with overwhelming
evidence of the poverty existing at virtually every level of working-

class Prussian society. The injustices of their own situation too were more evident in the light of their new knowledge of wage-scale inequities: Virchow, for instance, was shocked to find that a young man of his own age working on the railroad earned the same amount in a day that a medical intern did in a month. After trying to understand the extraordinary proletarization of the medical profession, Virchow found himself launched in 1848 on a crusade for social improvement and soon stood in the vanguard of the radical movement.[31] Routine investigations of local matters opened the eyes of many a young official to the dimensions of Prussia's social and economic problems.[32]

Senior officials were less likely to be directly confronted with the truth about social conditions, for their time was spent with matters of a more abstract nature, and the reports that they received from underlings often told them what they wanted to hear rather than what was actually happening.[33] Little wonder then that the upper echelons soon began to question the wisdom of bringing younger officials into contact with workers in the government-sponsored self-help organizations. In Cologne it was found that certain young jurists were using the local branch of an officially sponsored workers' club to spread "communist" ideas.[34] Similar instances were reported in the Rhineland town of Cleve; and in Berlin radicals infiltrated the Artisans Association.[35] When the authorities purged the Berlin radicals, the workers and political activists went underground, thus solidifying the radical social and political coalition that was to appear in full force during the first days of the March revolution.[36]

Instances of the participation of officials in radical journalism also excited the government's suspicions of disloyalty within its own ranks; but attempts to suppress dissent only served to alienate the dissenters and to intensify opposition to the regime itself. Members of the bureaucracy were subjected to the same censorship as other members of society, and in a number of cases resorted to publication outside the borders of Prussia in order to put their views in print.[37] When officials became too closely associated with radicals, they were transferred to other locations.[38] There were even cases in which the higher ranks of the bureaucracy suppressed the publication of official reports that might have proven embarrassing to the profession. This was one of the reasons why Heinrich Simon, a victim of censorship himself, believed firmly that "publicity is the only protection against all that is rotten in Denmark."[39]

The demand for publicity was not always an indication of political liberalization. Simon advocated an end to censorship not because it would limit government activity, but because it would strengthen it. Others demanded freedom of expression not as a civil right, but as a corporate right due to men of their status. Repression of the printed word galled them only insofar as it interfered with the traditional prerogatives of their office; in short, they wanted more freedom of communication for reasons that were essentially conservative.

The development that disturbed the government most at this time and had the greatest significance for the future was the change in the role of state officials in the provincial estates and the United Diet of 1847. Before 1848 the franchise was so restricted that only officials who owned substantial property and had been resident in the province for a considerable length of time were eligible to become members of the Diet. These were qualifications that few of the younger men, with the exception of the Landräte, possessed; and therefore it is not surprising that only 17 percent of the members of the United Diet of 1847 were state officials and that most of these were senior men.[40] Yet in 1847 when four Landräte became leaders of the liberal opposition in the new assembly, the king felt compelled to apply the 1844 discipline regulations in order to silence the offenders.[41] The king wanted to remove them from office, but his ministers were less willing—partly because they realized that the provisions of the 1844 law did not cover such political activities and partly because the dismissal of the four was sure to cause public opposition. Instead, they worked for conciliation: the four Landräte were permitted to remain in office on the condition that they pledge loyalty to the king and his edicts.[42] All were willing to do so, but they argued that such an oath was made unnecessary by the fact that they had acted as private citizens, and that what they had done in no way contradicted their professional duties to the crown. Florenz von Bochum-Dolffs, one of those under investigation, testified that he had never considered himself disobedient simply because his views conflicted with those of the king.[43] The best known of the defendants, Georg Freiherr von Vincke, admitted that overt political opposition might be incompatible with his office, but denied that he had been disloyal in his role as a leader of the liberal opposition. Although Vincke stated that he was ready to resign if his views were truly incompatible with those of his sovereign, he felt that his actions in the United Diet had in no way contradicted his oath of office.[44]

The testimony of all four men reflects the ambiguities characteristic of this period. While it is clear that these moderate liberals had no intention of challenging the existing system, each seems to have stepped to some extent out of the traditional role of state official in civic affairs. All felt that some distinction should be made between their status as members of the bureaucratic estate and as citizens; they continued to recognize certain rights and duties peculiar to their profession, but at the same time they demanded civil rights held in common with the other members of the state. At this stage they were only dimly conscious of the possibility of conflict between corporate privilege and civil equality, and hardly aware of the complications that would arise from the full exercise of the right of political participation. It should be noted that they did not argue that the bureaucracy should be granted complete civil and political equality. Instead they took a middle position similar to that taken by Heinrich Simon in 1845 when he resigned from the bureaucracy. Simon had been quoting Frederick William III when he wrote: "Every civil servant has a double duty: to the king and to the country. Situations may occur when the two are incompatible; in that case, the duty to country comes first."[45]

A similar concept of dual responsibility had long been accepted within the bureaucratic profession. There was nothing radical about the notion of the preeminence of loyalty to one's country, for the bureaucrats had ceased to view themselves as the personal servants of the king a century earlier. What was new, however, was the concept of country as something more comprehensive than the state itself. Previously the official's responsibility had been solely to the policies and institutions of the state; now as other groups and institutions began to challenge the bureaucratic state's position as sole representative of society's interests, the bureaucrat's role became far more complicated and the tension among his plural loyalties far less easily reconciled.

In the eyes of the king and his more conservative advisers, any attempt to put the interests of the country before that of the monarchy was tantamount to dereliction of duty. Even when the four Landräte reaffirmed their loyalty in writing in January 1848, Frederick William IV made it clear that it would take more than mere passive obedience to win back the benefits of full royal favor; and from the tenor of his response it was evident that he was by no means satisfied with the cabinet's compromise solution.[46] A clearer definition of the political rights of officials was needed; but it did not come until the events of the revolution forced the Prussian government to look more closely at the issue of the compatibility of public service with the rights and duties of the modern citizen.

Central to all of the sociopolitical problems faced by Prussia in the 1840's was the challenge of finding a way to reintegrate the social and legal orders and rectify the growing imbalance between economic and political power that had become evident during the late Vormärz period. It was obvious to all concerned that the bureaucracy would play an important role in this process, for whether its members realized it or not, pressures were at work that involved the civil service in these changes in the deepest way. Forces within that previously close-knit profession were turning many of its members outward in search of contacts with other groups, while at the same time most of the emerging political factions were actively recruiting officials for their own goals.

Only the extreme right and extreme left had no place for a strong professional civil service in their conceptions of the ideal state and society. Except for a minority who believed that the clock could be turned back on the achievements of the previous centuries, most conservatives viewed a highly trained civil service as a necessary part of the powers of preservation. Even those close to Frederick William IV, who were so devoted to the ideal of divine-right monarchy, argued the necessity of a body of efficient administrators and able judges. Their criticism of the bureaucratic state was directed primarily at what they considered its encroachment on the monarch's prerogatives. They wanted the king to possess full political authority and the members of the bureaucracy to reassume their roles as the loyal servants of the royal will.[47]

Prussian liberals also viewed a professional bureaucracy free from external interference in its executive capacity and neutral in political matters as a desirable component of a modernized political system. The majority on the left rejected as dangerously utopian the notion that a professional civil service could be replaced by a system of self-government. The programs of the radical fringe included the demand for the "abolition of the existing army of bureaucrats and their replacement with economical government consisting of the freely elected men of the people," but this vision of participatory democracy was as alien to the mainstream of Prussian liberalism as it was to conservative thought.[48] Most liberals were reluctant to invoke the principle of the sovereignty of the people against institutions that they had once regarded as the guarantors of law and progress. They continued to believe in the need for a strong civil service for a state that was a patchwork of so many disparate territories, religions, and customs.[49] Although the authors of the liberal programs of the pre-March period called for the replacement of corporate and territorial privilege by a system of equality before the law, they were generally unclear on what the status of the bureaucracy should be in the new social and political order. The relationship of the official's rights as a private citizen to his special status as a servant of the state had already been worked out in the German states to the south and west, and the variety of solutions there showed how little consensus existed on this issue. In most cases the exigencies of politics had more to do with the final result than ideology did; and in 1848, when Prussian liberals were forced to confront and decide this issue, similar uncertainties and divisions would also be in evidence.

Characteristic of the still ill-defined political programs of the left and the right was the distinction they made between efficient, honest, neutral bureaucracy and what they called *Bureaukratie*: corrupt, arbitrary rule by a politically incompetent body of officials. They could agree with the position articulated by Ernst von Bülow-Cummerow that the "chief principle of government must be that the governing officers do not administer and the actual administrators do not rule."[50] There was also a general feeling that the bureaucracy had disqualified itself by selfish attention to its own material concerns. The liberals worried that red tape would block economic development; the democrats saw the bureaucratic mentality as hostile to social and political progress; the conservatives argued that bureaucratic absolutism ran counter to Prussian tradition.[51] Opposition to the bureaucratic state, which had begun in regions where resistance to things Prussian was already strong, namely in the western provinces and in East Prussia, developed by the 1840's into a broad social and political movement that knew neither provincial nor ideological boundaries.[52]

The desire of both the left and the right to exclude bureaucracy from the executive political decision-making process by restricting its competence to matters purely administrative or judicial did not preclude encouragement of the political activism on the part of individual officials. As a group, the bureaucracy continued to exercise great influence even during that period when its legal and institutional status was under attack. During the late Vormärz period, when organized political parties were still unknown, the influence of the local notables was paramount and in most communities it was still the state official who was looked to as the primary source of wisdom and guidance. Even among those factions most deeply engaged in the campaign against Bureaukratie, the bulk of the leaders were men in the service of the state or members of related professions. In the countryside it was the Landräte and the local judges, in the towns, members of the courts and *Regierungsräte*; but in almost every case the authority and experience of the officials had propelled them even before 1848 into positions of enormous influence and power.[53]

The influence exercised by the officials among various political groups differed according to the way the individual bureaucrat viewed his role in the state. Many civil servants, particularly those of the older generation, were accustomed to thinking of themselves as members of a political elite even though they had no practical experience in civic affairs. They approached popular politics with a condescension bred of this sense of superiority and interpreted civic duty as little more than an extension of their traditional roles as guardians of the state. Senior officials were proud enough of their profession and their long tradition of resistance to arbitrary royal authority that when Felix Eberty took his oath of office in 1834, the head of the court to which he had been assigned reminded him of the famous Müller Arnold case, only one of the many instances in the previous hundred years when officials had risked royal displeasure in order to uphold the law.[54] Many older bureaucrats could still remember the constructive role of their profession in the Reform Era, and most continued to think of themselves as heirs to the tradition of progressive administration and independent justice established during that period. Because these men did not see themselves as reactionaries, it made it all the more difficult for them to understand the challenge to their authority that the popular movements of the 1840's represented. Accustomed to thinking of themselves as responsible for the well-being of the state, they found it difficult to imagine the benefits of representative government; and thus they were caught between a monarch who viewed it as his duty to interfere in every aspect of administration and a reform movement also determined to curb their power.[55]

The misguided confidence with which many senior officials faced the difficulties of the 1840's may account for the absence of real innovation on their part, a condition on which so many contemporaries commented in the decade before 1848. With the exception of a few officials like East Prussia's Oberpräsident Theodor von Schön, Prussia's senior bureaucrats showed little of the vitality that had been their hallmark in earlier decades. Part of the reason was simply the lack of strong, steady leadership from above. The king's anti-bureaucratic biases made it difficult for Berlin to cooperate with the provincial bureaucracies from which so much of the reform impulse had originated in the past.[56] But not all the blame rests with Frederick William and his ministers, for there was also general agreement among those close to the provincial bureaucracies that stagnation had set in there as well. Some blamed this on the advanced age of many in high posts; others believed the bureaucracy to be so concerned with its own internal divisions as to be incapable of dealing with broader issues.[57] Both these factors probably contributed to the paralysis noticeable on all levels in the 1840's, though it must be admitted that the problems facing the bureaucracy at that time were such that even if it had displayed its previous energy and initiative it is doubtful that it could have solved them with the means available. But whatever the cause, the apparent loss of purpose at the top had the effect of forcing many younger officials to look elsewhere for ways to solve Prussia's problems. Whereas the older men were generally content with the institutions of the bureaucratic state, the rising generation sought new ways to solve Prussia's social and political dilemmas.

The younger generation seems to have been somewhat better prepared than the older to adapt to the new politics of participation, both because it was less committed to the old corporate notions and because it viewed its role as extending beyond the well-defined limits of service to the state to service to society in general. Experience had convinced many young officials of the desirability of reforms that would allow greater individual freedom and equality. They tended to reject the concept of the guardian bureaucracy as a hypocritical projection of a selfish and essentially unrepresentative caste, and they were ready to cooperate with members of outside groups to achieve the reform of the state and society. Gradually they abandoned the spirit of corporatism that had so long characterized their profession in favor of a civic consciousness more appropriate to the values of a modernizing society.

Without fully realizing what they were doing, many young officials had begun to grapple with the problems created by the inability of absolutism to adjust to the needs of a rapidly changing society. A few, once they realized the proportions of these problems and the bureaucracy's inability to solve them, found it necessary to abandon their profession and to press for radical changes from outside the system. The vast majority, however, were attempting to do the best they could from within their occupational and social confines. They attempted to hold a balance between their loyalties to the existing social and political system and their desire to see reforms in particular aspects of that system. The philosophical and religious discussions of the 1840's had awakened a new social consciousness in the young bureaucrats, and their own unfavorable social and economic position and the desperate condition of the laboring poor had aroused their compassion—but full political awareness was still rare. Before 1848 few realized fully the contradictions of attempting to work from within the system, and when the events of March caught up with them, they were every bit as unprepared as their fellow citizens for the difficult choices that were to be required of all Prussians in the months to come.

Part Two

REVOLUTION

Chapter Five

From the March Days to
the November Coup

An accidental clash between a peaceful crowd and units of the royal cavalry at the gates of the Berlin palace on March 18 abruptly brought to an end the ambiguity that had heretofore characterized Prussian politics. In the violent days that followed, amorphous ideologies crystallized into concrete political programs, and public opinion was polarized. The issues were no longer aesthetic, theological, or philosophical. Cultural improvement associations became political caucuses, and self-help organizations turned into cells in a growing network of political organizations; movements of social and economic protest that had been concerned mainly with theory rapidly became politicized, as each level of society began to view its particular problems in the broader context of constitutional change.

The behavior of the bureaucracy in the first days of the revolution differed from that of the rest of society only in degree. The same polarization occurred in its ranks, as divisions scarcely perceptible months before were widened by partisan politics. The vortex of frantic political activity drew in much of the civil service, and for a few short months officials played roles in civic affairs totally unprecedented for men of their position. That the revolution proved to be a brief and unusual interlude in Prussia's history does not minimize its importance in the history of the bureaucracy, for the actions of bureaucrats in the months between the March Days and the conservative coup in November left an indelible mark on both the structure of the civil service and the lives of its members. The internal divisions within the Prussian bureau-cracy during the years before 1848 not only help account for the origins of the revolution, but also explain much about its course and outcome.[1] The part played by the bureaucrats in revolution and reaction was highly important in the shaping of both parlia-mentary and extraparliamentary politics and permanently changed the position of the bureaucracy vis-à-vis society as a whole.

The March Days were as much of a surprise to Prussia's civil servants as they were to the rest of the population, and in most cases just as unwelcome. This was a revolution without revolution-aries, in which even the most radical elements looked upon the bloody events of March 18 and 19 as unfortunate occurrences never to be repeated. But the fact that most Prussians were not prepared for revolution did not prevent them from participating in the course of events initiated by the Berlin upheaval. Indeed, in the absence of organized political parties and an established press, the sudden, apparently successful challenge to monarchical authority created a vacuum into which a large part of the population, par-ticularly in the urban areas, was drawn regardless of previous political experience.

Among those most directly affected were the servants of the state, who by virtue of their official capacity were already close to the vortex of public activity. Even those officials who before 1848 had had little or no contact with groups or movements out-side their own corporation now found themselves drawn into un-accustomed civic participation. "The more strictly the correct bu-reaucrat had conducted himself before," noted Peter Reichen-sperger, "the more he now strove, through word and deed, to erase his past."[2] Opportunism was undoubtedly involved, as Reichen-sperger implied, but any explanation of the behavior of the civil service in those terms alone misses significant aspects of the revolu-tionary situation. The confusion of the period and individual un-certainty about new roles in the changing social and political sys-tem, must also be kept in mind. When called upon at a later date to explain his actions during the first days of the revolution, one administrative official named Scherer replied that like most of his acquaintances, he had been swept up almost involuntarily by the political events. "Before 1848 I did not concern myself with political things," he recalled; then, with the coming of the revolution, everything, even administrative matters, suddenly took on political significance.[3]

The king's March promise of a constitutional assembly elected by universal male suffrage and his subsequent announcement on April 6 of every citizen's right to freedom of speech and association in effect suspended the General Code of 1794 and terminated the corporate legal order. Pending the creation of a new constitution, Prussia entered a period of unprecedented uncertainty, during which men were thrown largely on their own judgment in matters both large and small. Stripped of the formal aspects of its traditional corporate identity, the bureaucracy was left with the choice of acting out of habit or adopting a new role more consistent with the conditions of civil and political equality. Some officials continued to act as if nothing had happened, going about their duties, avoiding involvement, resentful of the changes around them. Others were swept up totally into the new politics and resigned from the profession to become full-time politicians. Most, however, became involved in the new duties of citizenship without abandoning their occupation and the concerns appropriate to it. Their attitudes during the next few hectic and trying months combined the desire to protect their position as servants of the state with a readiness to take advantage of the opportunities that civic activity offered. This was true in different degrees of both generations of officials, with the younger men taking a more active part initially. In their own ways, all were attempting to adjust to what they recognized to be a new era; and the divisions between their various conceptions of what the future should be cut much deeper than any of the issues of the prerevolutionary period.

Few had anticipated the rising in Berlin and the demonstrations in other parts of the country, but when the first shots were fired and violence swirled through the boulevards and back alleys, some members of the civil service found themselves joining journeymen and shopkeepers in building barricades and sniping at government soldiers. A number of younger officials are known to have taken part in the Berlin uprising. One administrative trainee, Gustav von Lensky, was killed on the barricades, and a candidate for the judiciary, Gustav Rasch, distinguished himself in the street fighting.[4] In Cologne Hermann Becker, another young official, was a leader of the demonstrations, and in other provinces officials participated actively in the events of the first days of the revolution.[5] In Westphalia, one observer noted that the supporters of the revolution were representatives of various discontented elements and included "several young officials who, just out of the university, had entered their training full of ideas of equality and in a frenzy for freedom"; and in Koblenz, Peter Reichensperger was present at a rally where a young judicial official climbed atop a table to denounce the House of Hohenzollern and its symbol of reaction, the Prince of Prussia.[6]

The number of officials who actually participated in street fighting and the initial round of public demonstrations was probably very small. Most officials seem to have taken a wait-and-see attitude during the March Days. Even those highly placed and close to the king were not sure what course to follow. Their advice to the monarch was often indecisive and contradictory and thus reinforced Frederick William's tendency toward vacillation and contributed to the general paralysis of will that characterized the government at this most decisive moment. "From the lowest to the highest classes, there was no confidence in the bureaucracy, nor did the bureaucracy have confidence in itself," recalled Rudolf Gneist.[7] Civil servants in the Rhineland were so severely shaken by events that some, like the Regierungspräsident of the Cologne district, Karl von Raumer, begged to be relieved of their posts.[8] The same thing occurred in other provinces, where at the first signs of trouble officials either abdicated their responsibility or were replaced by men thought by the government to be more popular with the inhabitants.[9] In early April the government moved to replace its Oberpräsident in Silesia with a more popular official, Julius Pinder;

while in Cologne the pre-March administrator was so discredited that the government gave in to the popular demand that the respected city councilor Heinrich von Wittgenstein be appointed as Regierungspräsident, a position usually reserved for members of the regular civil service. The appointment of someone from outside the professional ranks was exceptional, but the fact that a large number of officials signed the petitions in favor of Wittgenstein's appointment was an event completely without precedent.[10]

A few highly placed officials worked feverishly behind the scenes, encouraging the king to take a stronger stand against the rebels in the hope that he would use the unimpaired strength of the army to restore the old order. Understandably, they reacted with anger when Frederick William conceded most of the opposition's demands and appointed a liberal ministry composed mainly of men from outside the ranks of the profession. But their resentment soon turned to pessimistic resignation as they found themselves helpless to reverse his decisions. A number of the most conservative had to be persuaded not to resign their offices in protest; a few left the service, but most stayed on, passively obedient to the new liberal government. No doubt many of them felt as Otto von Manteuffel did, that they would eventually be able to work quietly from within to influence the new liberal government in a conservative direction.[11] Long association with the bureaucratic state had accustomed them to the idea that the king and his cabinet could be manipulated by their subordinates; their strong sense of corporate honor kept them aloof from popular politics, and their contempt for modern representative institutions reinforced their preference for more subtle forms of intrigue. For the time being, they adopted a cautious attitude consistent with the mood of debilitating pessimism that pervaded conservative circles during the first months of the revolution.

After March, the field of public activity was left initially to those members of the younger generation of officials who were more eager and somewhat better prepared than their seniors to experiment with the newly created rights of free speech and association. These men were less likely to use official channels to influence policy, not only because their position within the hierarchy prevented it, but also because many of them felt much more at home in the world of the press, public meetings, and political parties. In March and April of 1848 a fury of organizational activity swept Prussia and hundreds of political, economic, and social bodies came into being virtually overnight. Almost every profession and interest group established some form of club or league through which to express its common will. The subaltern ranks of the civil service were particularly active in this respect. On April 18 the General Assembly of Secretaries, Clerks, Helpers, and Chancery Scribes met to name a committee to create a permanent Chancery Institute. On the following day an association of *Justizkommissarien* was announced, and shortly thereafter an organization for subaltern officials of all branches of government was created. Railroad officials united to create a pension fund and to defend themselves against arbitrary dismissal, and in the capital city the mailmen, bitter over poor employment conditions, organized the League of Berlin Postal Officials.[12] In their declaration of purpose the postmen gave expression to the motives behind the formation of all these organizations: "Was it to be expected that the corporation of postal officials (*Postbeamtenstand*), who have for so long suffered under the yoke of intolerable conditions, should fail to raise their voices loud and clear at a time when all over Germany greedy political systems are being overthrown?"[13]

The language of estates and corporations betrayed the origins of the subaltern officials' solidarity. Yet if their sense of common interest was not new, its expression in the form of voluntary associations formed outside the legal framework of the traditional corporate institutions represented a major break with the past. The emergence of this type of organization, free from the control of superiors and directed toward immediate economic and social goals, represented a direct challenge to both the traditional system of authority and the corporate ideal. It was the first sign of a new, more modern spirit on the part of the subaltern officials, for not only was the pretense of solidarity with the higher bureaucracy abandoned but the corporate sense of honor that had previously inhibited separate organization was replaced by a more aggressive self-interest.

The subaltern ranks were drawn to new forms of organization much more readily than the higher bureaucracy was. During the first half of the century differences in the educational standards of the two levels had evolved into tangible social distinctions. "In the world of the Prussian administration and judiciary the Assessor examination creates an unbridgeable gulf between those who have passed and those who have not," wrote one official who had experienced this change.[14] As part of the modernization process, the university-trained officials had cut themselves off from the less highly educated state employees in much the same way that doctors had divorced themselves from the practitioners of folk medicine and members of the bar from street-corner lawyers. For the subalterns this was the cause of considerable frustration. At the same time, however, it was an advantage, freeing them from corporate honor and its modern counterpart, the desire for professional respectability, and enabling them to adopt methods of organization that many higher officials still felt beneath their dignity.

Although some members of the higher bureaucracy participated in the various national academic and professional conferences held during 1848, there was no concerted effort to hold similar meetings in Prussia itself. The conservative upper ranks would have opposed it, and the government, which on July 8 initiated a formal ban on the establishment of self-help organizations by public employees, was also hostile.[15] Not until almost a decade later did Prussian jurists form their first professional association, and then only after their internal differences had diminished and the political situation had become considerably more stable.

There were, however, those in the higher bureaucracy, particularly among the younger men, who were uninhibited by the corporate tradition and unawed by the government warnings. Younger members of the Berlin *Kammergericht* met informally beginning in March to discuss matters of professional and political interest, and other officials were working individually or in small groups to make their grievances public.[16] A journal, *Der Publicist*, was the arena for the most radical segment of the profession, who presented plans for institutional reforms and demanded improvements in the conditions of the profession. Other less specialized organs of opinion were also used to reach the government through public opinion, yet one of the major reasons why no professional organization emerged from these scattered efforts was that those who were sufficiently emancipated from the corporate tradition to challenge authority on these issues were also so detached from purely professional concerns as to have little time for such effort. Younger officials now viewed their professional discontents as a subordinate aspect of the broader political and social situation. Corporate interests had been displaced by civic concerns, and recently organized pressure groups and political parties, which were composed of a much wider spectrum of society, absorbed the ideas and eneries of the most progressive members of the bureaucracy.

Now the contacts established in the pre-March period began to take on a new significance. The informal associations of liberal officials with members of the industrial and business groups had evolved into organizations like the Civil Guard (*Bürgerwehr*), which in almost every city became a symbol of the civic responsibilities of the propertied classes. Even as the first units were formed, it was apparent that the Civil Guard would serve as a major organization of middle-class interests and as a focal point for moderate liberal opinion. Its ranks were filled mainly with property owners and members of the professions; a minority of the Guards were of lower-class background, but the officers were invariably of higher social rank.[17] In Berlin the well-known liberal judge Heinrich von Grolmann was the chief of the Guard, and other members of the bureaucracy led local units.[18] As one of his last acts in office, the conservative Minister of the Interior Graf Arnim had ordered that administrative officials be encouraged to join the Civil Guard whenever it was compatible with their official duties.[19] While this helped ensure the Guards' loyalty to the regime, it did not deprive them of their importance as arbiters of liberal opinion throughout the country.

The more radical members of the bureaucracy were less inclined to take part in organizations that were so closely associated with the government and the propertied classes. Even before March their contacts had been with different strata of society, and from the first informal meetings of professional men and the laboring poor had grown a political alliance aimed at the abolition of social and economic injustice and the establishment of a democratic Prussia. In a number of the working-class organizations that sprang up shortly after the events of March, the cooperation between the workers and radical officials was striking. According to the statutes of the Berlin Central Committee of Workers, that organization was open to "trade and workers groups in the broadest sense"; and the committee's president, Stephan Born, was a man with many contacts among the professions and the laboring classes.[20] The officers of this organization included Dr. Wöniger, the representative of the organization of government office clerks, and Dr. Ries, of the employees of the state mint.[21] The Berlin branch of the *Arbeiter-Verbrüderung*, the most important of the new workers' organizations, listed an association of subaltern officials and even an artists' union among its twenty-nine affiliated groups.[22] It is significant that while members of the professions were readily admitted to this organization, owners of larger businesses and industries were specifically excluded.[23]

The educated men who allied themselves with the popular pressure groups did so for a variety of reasons, not the least of which was a sense of shared injustice and deprivation. It was not uncommon in 1848 for the radical intellectuals to refer to themselves as members of the proletariat, thus drawing attention to the parallels between their situation and that of the workers.[24] Although the story of an official who in the heated election campaign of May

1848 appealed to the voters by shouting, "I too am a worker," may
be apocryphal, it nevertheless gives expression to the feeling of
solidarity that existed during this period.[25] According to one anony-
mous intellectual, the concept of the working class was broad
enough to include students, writers, artists, and propertyless professionals as well as unemployed journeymen and factory workers. "I call us the Fourth Estate—the estate of intelligence and
work," he wrote. "We are one and the same."[26]

The membership of professional men in the workers' organizations was not simply a symbolic demonstration of solidarity; it
was also an expression of active political cooperation designed to
improve the position of all concerned by bringing pressure to bear
on both the government and the parliament. The working-class
paper *Deutsche Arbeiter-Zeitung* published notices of professional
organizations and editorialized on the conditions of state employees. In turn the organ of the radical jurists, *Der Publicist*, dealt not
only with the democratization of the legal system but also with
the social and economic implications of a system of free and equal
justice.[27] Working-class leaders like Stephan Born emphasized the
equality of men regardless of occupation and advocated alliances
with other underprivileged groups as part of a program to achieve
a democratic state and society.[28] The newspapers most frequently
read by the Berlin laboring poor reiterated the theme of brother-
hood and showed sympathy for the members of other occupations
who were the victims of exploitation. The grievances of exploited
officials as well as the complaints of unemployed artisans found
voice in this press. Articles that appeared in such journals as *Feuerbrände* demanded relief for what they called the "hungry *Assessoren*" as well as equality for members of the working class.[29]

This unprecedented use of the rights of free speech and association was a reflection of the bureaucracy's deep involvement
with the participatory politics of the revolution. Beginning with
the March Days, when members of the profession proudly carried
a banner reading "Freedom and Law" in the massive funeral pro-
cession for the heroes of the Berlin barricades, officials played a

prominent role in the political clubs that were organized in anticipation of the first popular elections in Prussian history.[30] In these first months of hectic activity it was officials with liberal or democratic leanings who tended to exercise their rights of citizenship to the fullest extent. Their previous experience had prepared them to some degree for the new politics, and although few had ever been elected to public office, they possessed aptitudes for organization and public relations that gave them an immediate advantage over their more conservative colleagues. The latter, who were slow to accept the necessity of participation in mass politics, were restrained by an ideological distrust of parliamentarianism and inhibited by habits of an authoritarian corporate tradition that had little relevance in the new setting. Many older officials who had initially refused to participate in any kind of public activity became involved in the wake of the May elections, but only after a conservative party began to emerge.

Except in those parts of Prussia where religious or ethnic questions assumed an overriding importance, the clubs and press of the liberal and democratic factions had the political field virtually to themselves during the first months of the revolution. In Berlin the Political Club (later known as the Democratic Club) and the Central Committee for Workers were the main strength of the democratic movement. Opposed in doctrine, though overlapping with the Democratic Club in membership, was the more moderate Berlin Constitutional Club. Similar divisions were found in most other Prussian cities: Düsseldorf, for instance, had its democratic People's Club and Democratic League, which were opposed by the liberal Citizens and Constitutional Leagues. The same pattern, repeated in other major towns and some rural areas in the western provinces, held for other parts of Prussia as well. In some cases men of different localities were linked by personal acquaintance or correspondence, but in general it may be said that no true statewide parties existed, and that political factions grew originally from local concern with basic social, economic, and political issues.[31]

The liberal and democratic factions were now not only better organized but much more sharply divided ideologically than before the revolution. Confrontation with political questions such as the form of the state and the extent of the franchise had cleared away earlier ambiguities. The liberals emphasized the importance of establishing a legislative body, but stopped short of the democratic principle of universal manhood suffrage. They favored equality before the law and the abolition of all restrictions on individual opportunity, but would not go so far as to advocate the creation of conditions for economic and social equality. While the democrats wished to implement the principle of popular sovereignty, the liberals wished to limit rather than displace royal authority.[32]

The social lines between the two factions were also more clearly drawn. Liberalism, with its insistence on the property qualification for voting, mainly attracted men of the propertied classes and senior members of the professions, while the democratic clubs had broader support among the poor and the younger educated people. Berlin's democratic Political Club, for instance, included low-ranking members of the professions, artisans, small shopkeepers, and day laborers.[33] A similar spectrum was represented in the democratic organizations in Düsseldorf, Koblenz, Wetzlar, and other areas about which there is detailed information. Wetzlar's democratic Citizens League mixed doctors and teachers with tradesmen and artisans; and at Trier, the Democratic League had on its rolls laborers as well as a number of young civil officials.[34] In Düsseldorf the pattern was the same, while in Cologne, where members of the professions including some judicial and administrative officials were active in democratic politics, similar cooperation had been established before the revolution.[35] It was also reported that Aachen's Citizens League "followed a democratic tendency, which attracted especially young doctors, candidates for the bureaucracy, and tradesmen."[36]

As might have been expected, in most cases it was the young intellectuals who took command of the leadership of the democratic clubs. Two candidates for the judiciary, Georg Jung and Rudolf Schramm, served as presidents of the Berlin Political Club, and another young jurist, Lothar Bucher, was the mainstay of the democratic movement in Pomerania.[37] In the small Rhineland village of Wetzlar a medical doctor and two teachers formed the executive board of the local democratic club; and in the university town of Bonn the popular young professor Gottfried Kinkel was the leader of the radical faction, which also included some officials.[38] An administrative trainee named von Steinacker served as vice-president of the Democratic League in Trier, while in Cologne another bureaucrat, Hermann Becker, earned the title of "Red Becker" through his service to the radical cause.[39] A number of officials at the Düsseldorf Regierung were close to that city's democratic movement; and in Breslau the leader of the pre-March protest, Heinrich Simon, continued to be a leading figure in the city's radical movement.[40]

By contrast, liberal organizations tended to attract members of the propertied classes as well as the senior members of the professions. Those higher-ranking officials who had not withdrawn from politics entirely were usually to be found among the moderate liberals during these first months. There were a few notable exceptions like the radical Supreme Court Judge Benedikt Waldeck, but the overall picture was one of division along the lines of age and rank. Stephan Born's description of the politics of the working class as a struggle between "two age groups, not two classes" also describes the prevailing situation within the bureaucracy.[41] Liberalism represented, as one observer put it, the "moderate elements of the bourgeoisie and the bureaucracy," for it was the liberal faction to which the politically active among the middle and upper ranks of both branches gravitated during the first months of the revolution.[42] For those who had "too much money to be democratic, but too little to think autocratically" there were clubs like the Citizens League in Bonn, the Constitutional Club in Berlin, and the Political Club in Koblenz.[43] In most cases their membership was made up of the same people who joined the Civil Guard, namely advocates of constitutionalism who were at the same time determined enemies of social or political equality.

Many of those officials who in the first months sided with the moderates eventually shifted to more conservative organizations. For the large number of officials whose political ideas were relatively fluid and who had not been strongly attached to the idea of popular sovereignty, the growing conflict between what seemed to them to be the defenders of order and the advocates of anarchy offered no other choice. Those, like the bureaucrat Scherer, who had originally viewed liberalism as a "safe" position, now turned increasingly to the conservative factions.[44] As the democrats' demands became more insistent and the prospect of popular sovereignty loomed ever nearer, the fence-sitters were forced to make a choice between further commitment to revolution and acceptance of reaction. At that point, many of those who had been mouthing liberal phrases while holding themselves aloof from direct involvement opted for the conservative solution.

The liberal Political Club in Koblenz, which had originally counted some number of civil servants and military officers from the local garrison in its membership, lost many members during the summer of 1848, when a split occurred over the issue of the democratization of the Prussian army.[45] A similar schism took place in the Berlin Constitutional Club when many of the officers and civil servants shifted their loyalties to the newly formed conservative clubs like the League for King and Fatherland and the Patriotic League.[46] The image of the Geheimrat gradually moving to the right was understandably a popular target of the radical press throughout the summer and fall of 1848.[47] By the time of the military coup against the constitutional assembly in November, the politics of the bureaucracy were almost completely polarized between supporters and opponents of the government's counterrevolutionary action.

A strong conservative movement, willing and able to use the modern instruments of press and party to gain its ends, had not yet cut into the strength of the left factions when the elections to the Berlin and Frankfurt constitutional assemblies were held in the spring of 1848. In May, when communities met to choose their candidates, members of the civil service had been prominent in their nominating meetings, often exercising influence far out of proportion to their small numbers.[48] When the candidate lists in the various localities were finally completed, a significant number of officials had been put forward by the parties. Senior officials were heavily represented on the liberal lists, while the democrats had nominated an even larger number of younger men from both branches of service.

Both generations owed a good deal of their success to their high social position and the enormous prestige conferred on them by public office. They also benefited from the general political immaturity of the Prussian people and the infant state of the political parties. But the influence that they wielded was not due entirely to ascribed qualities or to the fluid condition of preelection politics. Officials were generally inexperienced in civic affairs but their education in law and training in office had provided them with a level of knowledge of state and society superior to that of most of their fellow citizens. The older men were capitalizing on a reputation for experience accumulated in long years of public service; their younger colleagues relied more on their skill on the speaker's platform and the ability to convince the party members of the sincerity of their democratic sympathies.

It was natural that the senior members should appeal largely to the respectable propertied burghers, who may have detested the bureaucratic absolutism of the Vormärz period, but who feared the recurrence of disorder. They subscribed to the liberal notion of rule by law under a limited monarchy and were attracted to the experienced civil servant who fit their image of the kind of person capable of assuming the responsibilities of government. The high-ranking official with liberal tendencies suited their requirements: a man of property or education or both, someone they could feel comfortable with in a social setting and trust with the duties that they themselves neither wanted nor had time for. Rather than investing their own energies in politics, the Prussian business classes preferred to select others to represent their interests. The Hansemann-Camphausen ministry, appointed in March, had established a precedent in bringing together representatives from among the ranks of businessmen and moderately liberal bureaucrats.[49] Subsequent liberal governments relied on the same mixture, and when the conservatives regained power in November, they followed the same pattern by including business and bureaucratic elements in their cabinets.

Radicalized junior members of the civil service appealed to quite a different constituency, which was unprepared and unwilling to act directly, but was on the lookout for representatives with sympathy for the needs of the poor and the oppressed. The younger officials who offered themselves as candidates appealed to the lower classes by emphasizing those aspects of their own existence that most closely paralleled the condition of the laboring poor. When they campaigned they presented themselves as members of another exploited group. Georg Jung, the young jurist who became the leader of the Berlin democratic faction, took care when he appealed to the need for political democracy in all areas of national life to point out the relationship between his profession's demand for "the nomination of judges independent of executive control" and the guarantees of individual liberty and social justice sought by the working classes, and to make clear the connection between the elimination of corruption and interference within the bureaucracy and the achievement of a democratic society.[50] His professional and political colleague Gustav Bergenroth was even more explicit in linking the achievement of justice and equality in state employment to the realization of democracy in the society at large. Using the civil service as an example, he argued that equal opportunity was impossible under the old system. "Even now and then, when the son of a poor man becomes a Minister of State, he too often forgets his humble origins," he argued. Together with other partisans of the democratic ideal he campaigned for equal educational and economic opportunities and stressed the need for reformed taxation in the interests of the poor.[51]

By associating themselves directly with the aspirations of the poor, candidates like Jung and Bergenroth were able to persuade the voters that they would be represented by men whose ideas were the product of experiences not unlike their own. Even before March the younger officials had been in closer contact with the mass of the population. In May, their personal association with the needs of the poor and the contrast between their social programs and the essentially laissez-faire doctrines offered by their superiors assured them of victory in the elections. Lower-class voters, particularly in the urban areas, proved more sophisticated in their choices than might have been expected. Their hostility toward the bureaucratic state was great, but they were able to distinguish between the officials who sympathized with their feelings and those who did not.[52] "The hatred of the bureaucracy was so powerful that those bureaucrats who were elected owed their success to special circumstances," recalled Rudolf Gneist. "Only the *Juristen-proletariat,* the young Assessoren, were exempt, because they, as a result of the peculiar conditions of the jurists in Prussia, were in a position analogous to that of lawyers in other countries."[53]

Gneist was referring to the fact that while the lower-class voters in other German states tended to elect members of the law profession, Prussians often preferred bureaucrats to represent their interests in local and national affairs. When they chose the members of the Frankfurt Assembly they may have been somewhat swayed by the appeals of men of more established national reputation, among them a number of noted professors, high administrative officials, and former leaders of the opposition of the United Diet of 1847. There was a higher percentage of somewhat older high-ranking administrators among those elected to Frankfurt than among the Berlin deputies, but in both delegations there were cores of younger men of liberal and even radical political persuasion. Gneist undoubtedly exaggerated the popular distrust of the higher bureaucracy, but the emergence of the younger men, elected in numbers far larger than in any of the previous Prussian assemblies, reinforced his impression that in both the national and state elections voters had swung in large numbers to men of lesser position. Thirty-three percent of those elected to Berlin were members of the university-trained bureaucracy: 24 percent from the judiciary and 9.5 percent from the administration. Of the bureaucrats present, 31 percent and 13 percent can be counted as belonging to the lowest ranks of the higher judiciary and the administration, respectively.[54] Observers were immediately struck by the youth of many of those who arrived in Berlin that June to debate and resolve the future of their country.[55] "Young and undistinguished in appearance" was the way one conservative observer described them, "with the mawkish sophomoric expressions typical of young jurists."[56]

The traditionally conservative eastern regions tended to send more higher-ranking bureaucrats to Berlin than the western provinces did. Although both sections of the country elected a large number of officials, the Rhineland and Westphalia accounted for the majority of those from the lower ranks. One hesitates, however, to make generalizations based on east-west differences. The pattern in the eastern province of Silesia was much like that of the Rhineland, and in the larger cities of old Prussia, particularly Berlin and Breslau, the results were also much like those in the western towns.[57] A more important distinction can be made, then, between the urban and rural areas. With a few exceptions, like the victory of Lothar Bucher over his conservative opponent Landrat von Gottberg in the Pomeranian district of Stolp, the radicals had little success in the countryside, except where religious or ethnic issues aided their cause.[58] Traditional deference patterns, combined with the political apathy of the peasantry, favored the defenders of the status quo in these regions and made it difficult for those who challenged established authority to gain electoral victory. Nevertheless, with the dyed-in-the-wool conservatives still largely inactive at the time of the elections, the countryside did elect a number of moderately liberal senior officials.

In the towns a more radical alliance was already well established.

There existed a greater concentration of officials in the urban areas, where the economic conditions were more difficult, than there did in the countryside.[59] The urban poor were noticeably more politically conscious than the peasantry and had better means of communication at hand. State officials who had been largely excluded from civil affairs before 1848 now began to dominate urban politics. In Berlin, where in previous decades civil servants had only rarely been elected to the city council, the voters now elected a delegation to the Prussian Assembly that included one industrialist, two former members of the city council, an Oberbürgermeister, a pastor, one doctor (Johann Jacoby), a Geheimrat named Bauer, and three members of the judiciary: Assessor Georg Jung, State Prosecutor Julius von Kirchmann, and Supreme Court Justice Benedikt Waldeck. All of those elected were of a liberal or democratic tendency, and Kirchmann, Jung, Jacoby, and Waldeck were all leaders of the democratic opposition.[60]

The politics of 1848 were still the politics of the notables: disciplined parties with organized bases of mass support were not yet even within the realm of possibility. Those elected to Frankfurt and Berlin viewed themselves as holding a mandate from the people, yet they did not consider themselves bound by their constituents on every detail. The democrats felt the most responsibility to the wishes of the electorate, but even they considered themselves free agents. The voting habits of the deputies did not conform to distinct party divisions, and members passed from one faction to another as their moods and ideas changed with time and circumstance. The four factions that can be identified in the Berlin Assembly never included all the deputies, nor were they able to maintain tight discipline over those who were their nominal members. The Left and Left Center factions, both of which were committed to democratic programs, had a combined membership of just over a hundred supporters, or about 30 percent of the Assembly. The Right and Right Center, the factions with liberal tendencies, claimed a slightly larger total.[61] There were no formal conservative or socialist factions, though a few individual deputies might be described as adherents of one or the other of these positions.

Since 1847 the political spectrum in Prussia had shifted so far to the left that the members of the former opposition in the United Diet formed the Right bloc in the new assembly. They were for the most part members of the higher bureaucracy, the industrial-commercial bourgeoisie, or the liberal aristocracy—men like David Hansemann, Ludolf Camphausen, Karl Milde, Geheimrat Kette, and the von Auerswald brothers, Rudolf and Hans. All were certainly liberal in attitude, but all feared the results of universal suffrage and shied away from any reforms involving political or social rights for the propertyless classes. Frederick William had chosen his March and June ministries from these ranks, and they justified his trust by remaining loyal to royal command throughout the months of the revolution. Immediately to their left were men like railroad official Hans Victor von Unruh and Berlin city councilman Hermann Duncker, deputies who, though liberal rather than democratic in inclination, were ready to resist the King when he threatened to destroy the constitution.[62]

The Left and Center Left were of different ideologies and social composition. Led by men who generally stood lower on the occupational hierarchy, the membership of the democratic factions was made up mainly of members of what Riehl called the "Fourth Estate"—the radical members of the artisan class and their intellectual allies. Young officials like Georg Jung, Lothar Bucher, Jodocus Temme, Hermann Schulze-Delitzsch, and Julius von Kirchmann provided the leadership of these factions; Benedikt Waldeck was one of the few higher-ups who joined them.[63] Of those who are believed to have belonged to the two Left factions, almost half were members of the academically trained professions, and most of them were just beginning their careers.[64] The judiciary was most heavily represented, with nine of the thirteen jurists coming from the lowest ranks; representation from the administration was much smaller, but the pattern of rank was the same.[65] The other half of the membership of the Left and Center Left were members of the artisan and peasant class, but as in the case of the democratic clubs, it was young professionals who provided most of the leadership.[66]

The roll-call votes on specific issues provide an even more concrete demonstration of party alignments. When in June Julius Berends moved that the Assembly unequivocally "recognize the revolution," the younger officials supported him but their seniors did not.[67] Again, in the case of the important Stein motion of August 9, which called on the government to discipline reactionary elements within the officer corps, the junior ranks took the more radical position. Of twenty Assessoren and Referendarien who voted, only four were in opposition to this measure; among the higher ranks, however, a majority voted against it.[68] In October, when the Assembly voted on a number of constitutional amendments involving corporate rights, the younger men again demonstrated their democratic convictions. In almost direct contradiction to the position taken by their superiors, they voted solidly for the abolition of the legal status of the nobility.[69] Although in almost every case the higher echelons of the judiciary showed themselves to be somewhat to the left of their administrative counterparts, the division was primarily between ranks rather than branches.[70]

The decisive division occurred in November when the new reactionary government of Count Brandenburg disbanded the Civil Guard, placed the capital under military rule, and ordered the National Assembly to move its deliberations from Berlin.[71] The liberals, who feared that even passive resistance to the king's orders might provoke renewed violence, urged compliance, and their deputies quickly left the city. The deputies of the Left and Left Center, on the other hand, defiantly stayed in Berlin to organize a rump parliament in opposition to the government's orders. Forty percent of those who defended the National Assembly's right to determine the place and duration of its sessions were members of the professions—most of them young men who had not yet established their economic and social positions. Of the 35 civil servants involved in the passive resistance, 26 were from the lower ranks; and of these 26, most were members of the judiciary.[72]

The reluctance of the liberals to support even passive resistance meant that more forceful demonstrations were out of the question. Few radicals even suggested the possibility. Instead, they passed a resolution on November 15 advocating that the citizens protest the government's coup against the constitutional assembly by with-holding taxes.[73] No provisions for the actual implementation of the tax strike were voted, and although copies of the resolution were distributed throughout Prussia the opposition deputies relied main-ly on the moral force of their resolution to bring the protest move-ment into being. Success was heavily dependent, of course, on the support of those who collected the taxes and distributed govern-ment funds, so once again the bureaucracy found itself at the center of political controversy. In Bonn, for example, the issue split the population along the familiar social lines. The propertied bour-geoisie and most of the full professors at the University sent a mes-sage of support to the government; the workers and their leaders among the students, junior faculty, and other young professionals backed the rump parliament's decision. In Berlin and other parts of the country the situation seems to have been much the same.[74]

The Brandenburg ministry had made it abundantly clear that it would deal harshly with any official who disobeyed its orders. Acting on the command of Minister of Interior Otto von Manteuf-fel, the Oberpräsident of the Rhineland issued explicit commands concerning the conduct of his officials toward the tax strike: "I ex-pect all the provincial and local bureaus to fulfill their duties un-waveringly and to use all the power that the law provides to hold the debtors to their tax payments."[75] While most officials obeyed, a minority placed loyalty to the elected parliament ahead of obedi-ence to their superiors. On November 19 six Düsseldorf adminis-trators confronted Regierungspräsident von Spiegel with the dec-laration that they would no longer comply with orders to collect taxes or transfer funds to the central administration. Although it is not clear that the six attempted to stop others from fulfilling their duties, this action was considered serious enough to warrant their immediate suspension.[76]

In Silesia the highest ranking state official, Oberpräsident Julius

Pinder, was suspended when he refused to order the release of tax monies for transfer to Berlin. One of those whose reputation for progressive sympathies had gained him his appointment during the March Days, Pinder remained true to his ideals. He begged the government not to force an open break with the Assembly: "The mistrust of the government is so great among the mass of the people that the whole country may go up in flames." But this attempt at reconciliation only reinforced his superiors' suspicions; and when he was suspended from office on November 20, the tax strike in Silesia was at an end.[77]

The Brandenburg ministry had been able to act so decisively partly because of the lack of preparation by its opponents, partly because the propertied classes and the upper echelons of the army and bureaucracy had moved gradually toward the conservative side since the May elections. This shift of opinion had not been apparent in the Assembly, but it had been registered in the attitudes of the Civil Guard and in the defections from the liberal to the conservative factions outside parliament. The radical deputies were still firm in their democratic convictions, but they lacked the mass base outside parliament that well-organized political parties would have provided, and therefore were virtually isolated. By late November their weaknesses were so obvious and the government so confident of the support of the most influential elements of the civil service, the military, and the general population that it was ready to impose a unilateral resolution of the constitutional crisis that had existed since March.[78] On December 5 the second stage of the coup was completed: the Constitutional Assembly was terminated and a new constitution, liberal in character but free of all association with the principle of the sovereignty of the people, was enacted by royal edict. Two days later, Minister of the Interior Manteuffel ordered the various government agencies to begin investigating the activities of all those officials who had been associated with the Constitutional Assembly, in order to determine whether disciplinary proceedings should be brought against them. This directive was followed in twenty-four hours by the announcement of the State Prosecutor in Berlin of proceedings against those deputies present at the passage of the November 15 tax strike resoluion.[79] The first of a series of actions against officials who had dared to place their duties as citizens ahead of their loyalty to their superiors was about to begin.

This was neither the first time since March that the problem of the compatibility of political opposition and public office had been raised nor the first instance of the limitation of the rights of civil servants in the name of executive authority. For those in power as well as those in opposition, for the general public as well as the officials themselves, for every segment of the political spectrum, this had been one of the major unresolved questions of the revolution. Ever since the suspension of the corporate legal system, the constitutional rights of state officials had been in a state of limbo, undefined by law and subject directly to the conflicting political forces that filled the political vacuum. By December the issue was still formally unresolved, but out of the confusion was emerging a de facto resolution that served as a basis for the actions of the Brandenburg-Manteuffel government.

The one constant factor in this long struggle over the role of officials in politics, which had begun even before the revolution, was Frederick William's steadfast insistence that civil servants remain loyal to royal command, even if this deprived them of the rights of citizenship. The king's opinion had provided a mandate for the liberal ministries and for their conservative successors to impose restrictions on the freedom of individual officials. Faced with the practical problem of defending their programs in parliament and implementing administrative directives even the liberal ministers David Hansemann and Ludolf Camphausen were soon ready to undertake the disciplining of politically recalcitrant officials. Hansemann had entered office with the intention of dealing severely with subordinates who might try to sabotage the liberal program. He seems to have expected the most serious opposition to come from conservative officials, and he apparently contemplated little difficulty with those bureaucrats who were elected to the Constitutional Assembly.[80] But as time went on both he and Camphausen were forced to reevaluate their positions in order to take into account the opposition to the government from officials on both left and right. Both men eventually abandoned their original intention not to interfere directly with the political rights of the bureaucracy, though they were at first very cautious about moving against those radicals who disagreed actively with their regime.

The first public pressure on the government to restrict the rights of civil servants seems to have come from the left rather than the right. In June members of the democratic opposition in parliament demanded that the government curb the activity of certain conservative officials who were using their influence in the countryside to encourage counterrevolution. On July 15 the Hansemann-Auerswald government issued a circular aimed at establishing guidelines for action against political opposition: those who "straightforwardly" refused to recognize the present system of government and "intentionally" opposed it would be removed from office by available legal means.[81] With the suspension in April of the 1844 disciplinary regulations, it had become unclear on what legal basis the government could act, but its will to eliminate overt opposition was now public record. The ministers justified the new regulations by pointing to the existence of the legislative branch of government, which they claimed required tight control by the executive over subordinates. According to the dualistic concept of constitutional monarchy held by these liberals, a legislature was by its very nature a threat to the discipline of the executive. The possibility of conflict between the official's responsibilities as an elected member of the parliament and his duties to the state were inherent in such a situation, so that in order to protect itself against subversion the state was required to limit the rights of its civil servants.[82]

Ironically, the first manifestation of the liberal government's determination to keep order in its own house was the disciplinary action taken in July against two deputies of the democratic left, Julius von Kirchmann and Jodocus Temme, both of whom were members of the judiciary. The action against them took the form of involuntary transfers from their Berlin posts to provincial positions, a move which not only revived the issue of the 1844 discipline regulations but called the integrity of the government into question.[83] To the democratic opposition these moves were more than just violations of the professional privileges of judiciary: they constituted direct interference with the basic rights of the official as a citizen. Under the rules of the Constitutional Assembly, those deputies who were transferred or promoted in civil office were required to seek reelection. This regulation, originally supported by the left as a means of protecting the legislature against interference from the executive, was now turned against them as a means of harassment.

Despite the fact that both Temme and von Kirchmann won reelection easily, considerable inconvenience was caused both to them and to the democratic factions. Temme, who only weeks before had been told by Ludolf Camphausen himself that the government envisioned no conflict between the official's full exercise of his rights of citizenship and his duties in civil office, fought in vain against the transfer decision. He and his more radical colleagues rejected outright the government's argument that the existence of a legislative branch required that the executive assume tighter controls over its subordinates. According to their conception of popular sovereignty, there should be no conflict between the branches of government; with both the legislature and the executive subject to the will of the people, such limitations on the rights of the civil servant should be unnecessary.[84]

But this view of the citizenship of the bureaucracy was held by only a few, even among the radical democrats. The majority of the democrats and liberals had already committed themselves to restrictions on the freedom of officials, for in practice they opposed the government's right of disciplinary power only when it was directed against their own power. In August when the same sanctions were imposed on the conservative Landrat Hans von Kleist-Retzow for conspicuous participation in the politics of the right opposition, the Left applauded the liberal ministers.[85] The Stein motion of August, which encouraged the government to control the political activities of reactionary elements within the army, was another reflection of the same flexible attitude on the part of the Left.

Conservatives had worked out their position on the rights of state officials in the same pragmatic manner. Their original tendency had been to reject the concept of equal citizenship entirely and to hope for a revival of the corporate system. By the middle of the summer, however, the more realistic among them had begun to work within the framework of the new politics, still upholding the principle of monarchical authority but seeking ways to adjust it to what seemed to be an irrevocable reality. They did so reluctantly, even pessimistically, but with a certain willingness to learn from their opponents those skills appropriate to the modernized political system.

When the conservative Brandenburg ministry came to power in early November, it quickly demonstrated how much it had learned from its liberal predecessors. Graf Brandenburg himself was a consummate realist, desirous of lifting the threat of popular sovereignty posed by the Constitutional Assembly, yet unwilling to risk a second revolution by abruptly restoring pre-March civil and political institutions. His Minister of the Interior, Otto von Manteuffel, was an experienced senior bureaucrat who had stayed at his post in the personnel division of the department during the first months of the revolution, and was therefore thoroughly aware of the extent of the politicization within the profession. Although he personally favored a return to a corporate system, Manteuffel was willing to go along with Graf Brandenburg in attempting to steer a course between revolution and restoration. One of his first official acts was to issue an order reminding administrative officials of their duty to uphold law and order, but also extending the promise of the protection of the profession against arbitrary violation of its traditional rights: "The state expects that all its agencies, especially the officials whose duty it is to firmly and loyally uphold, develop, and promote legal order, will respond with courage and restraint.

The agencies may be assured that they will have the fullest protection of the government; the government sees itself obligated, however, to dismiss immediately, and in a legal manner, those officials who cannot or will not fulfill their obligations."[86] Just what legal order the government was referring to was left vague so as not to commit the regime to any particular course of action. On the other hand, the government's intention not to permit overt acts of opposition was made abundantly clear in this and other directives issued during the first days of the November coup.

The constitution promulgated by the Brandenburg-Manteuffel government on December 5 guaranteed the civil servant full rights of citizenship, subject to further definition by future detailed legislation.[87] The door was thus left open to practical restrictions if and when the conservative government saw fit to press the issue. For the time being, it seemed content to warn its officials to respect the provisions of the new constitution and to refrain from overt acts of opposition to the government. Again, the rights of officials to the protection of tenure and due process in matters of discipline was upheld, and the government went out of its way to denounce those who would subvert the morale of the bureaucracy by a campaign of secret denunciations.[88] It appeared that the conservatives were willing to accept the "double-duty" concept of the official as long as the ultimate loyalty was to the state rather than to the people. But it was also clear that the Brandenburg-Manteuffel ministry had not yet decided the exact form the rights of officials were to take. That would have to wait upon the events of coming months, a period of constitutional revision and ratification.

Political options had narrowed considerably since March, and there was already a kind of rough consensus as to how the bureaucracy should be integrated into the new political system. Almost all factions, both Left and Right, were now committed to some kind of compromise between the rights of the official as private citizen and his special obligations as a servant of the state. None but a tiny minority on the extreme left demanded complete freedom for the civil servant; and few outside the reactionary circles close to the king advocated the restoration of a corporate system that would exclude the official from civic affairs. All the major political factions were too dependent on members of the bureaucracy to be able to dispense with them entirely, but at the same time they were too deeply committed to a dualistic concept of constitutional monarchy, which supposed an antagonism between state and society, to believe that the government could afford to allow complete freedom to its officials.

Almost all the political factions believed that since order had been restored, a balance could be struck between private right and public duty, and that the individual official should be left to coordinate his double duty to state and society without undue interference by those in power. Even the conservatives, who by this time were very suspicious of the radical tendencies among the lower ranks, were apparently ready to wait and see how the bureaucracy would react to the November coup and the December constitution. Moderate liberals were eager to see some type of equilibrium established, for they too were unwilling to continue the conditions that had existed since the March Days. Only the extremes at both ends of the spectrum wanted to bring the issue of the bureaucracy to the boiling point.

This consensus on compromise was the product of both the forces of movement and the forces of preservation operating within the revolutionary situation. The corporate tradition of the bureaucracy worked against the concept of equal rights for civil officials; the high status customarily accorded to the profession and its deep involvement with public affairs worked in the opposite direction, making the participation of its members indispensable to all the political parties. The memory of the pre-March bureaucratic state may have influenced many against the participation of officials, yet despite the contempt for political democracy displayed by many older members, the general public was still prone to look to the bureaucracy for leadership in public affairs. Thus while the memory of bureaucratic absolutism exerted pressure in one direction, the record of the civil service in the Constitutional Assembly worked the opposite way. The existence of new institutions had similar contradictory effects, for while in principle the constitutional monarchy involved the concept of equal citizenship, it also presented the practical question of the compatibility of the political and professional roles of civil servants in ways that the previous absolutism had not. The government supposedly endorsed the principle of individual freedom, but in practice it worked for greater centralization and more direct control of the bureaucracy by the cabinet ministers. While tending in one direction toward greater liberty, the new system fostered stricter authority, thus further complicating the question of the participation of civil servants in the affairs of the body politic.[89]

To the contending pressures of old and new political institutions must also be added the contradictory social and economic forces at work within the bureaucracy itself. The effect of the experiences of the 1840's had been to push many officials toward an embrace with individual liberty and social equality. But the same tensions that fostered democratization strengthened the possibility of authoritarianism by arousing the enmity of the older generation against the younger and by destroying some of the restraints on the use of arbitrary authority that had been a part of the old corporate ethos. In the Vormärz decades and during the revolution itself, there had occurred a progressive weakening of the collegiate principle and the tradition of professional solidarity. The old rights of professional self-government were already endangered, and a severe form of hierarchical control under a monocratic system of organization was now much more probable than it had been before March.

The tendency of the older generation of Prussian officials had been toward what Karl Mannheim was later to describe as one of the basic tendencies of bureaucratic thought: "To turn all problems of politics into problems of administration."[90] The younger generation had reversed this to the extent that they turned administrative questions into political questions. They had been the first to enter into the public arena and the first to use that forum for their own ends. Initially, therefore, the politicization of the bureaucracy had primarily benefited the liberal and democratic forces of movement, but with the emergence of a more up-to-date form of conservatism, freed from the inhibitions of the corporate tradition and ready to take advantage of the instruments offered to the powers of preservation by the new constitutional system, the politics of the bureaucracy began to serve a new cause. In the next decade, matters of politics and administration would become even more closely fused, not, however, to the advantage of greater liberty and equality for the society in general and the bureaucracy in particular, but rather in the service of an authoritarian state and a highly stratified class society.

Chapter Six

Restoring Order

The absence of strong resistance to the November coup had surprised the Brandenburg-Manteuffel government, and the generally favorable response to the constitution of December 5 surpassed even the most optimistic expectations of the conservatives. Nevertheless, so abrupt a restoration of political order left many with the uneasy feeling that they could not subdue revolution without making the attempt to deal with the causes as well as the symptoms of the discontents that had led to the March upheaval. For the next two years the official policy remained one of attempting to steer a course between revolution and restoration. Operating according to Graf Brandenburg's principle that in troubled times "it is not a matter of doing what is best but of doing what is possible," the government made every effort to avoid provoking a resurgence of disorder.[1] Until December 1850, when in the showdown at Olmütz Prussia abandoned all pretensions of leading a liberal unified Germany, the main thread of its policy on both the foreign and domestic fronts was one of adjusting new institutions to the purposes of old elites—of adapting the available democratic instruments to suit monarchical requirements.

From the start, the Brandenburg-Manteuffel government met resistance from the king and the advocates of the restoration of the corporate system, the Kreuzzeitungspartei. Men on the extreme right were not equipped to understand either the tactics or the strategy behind the promulgation of the new constitution and the series of liberal reforms that followed. Their ideological attachment to the past prevented them from comprehending the nature of the accommodation that this government was willing to make with modern institutions in order to secure the power of the old elites.[2] They were also slow to understand that 1848 had been a turning point not only for German liberalism and nationalism, but also for German conservatism.

"The old times are gone and cannot return," Otto von Manteuffel told a gathering in 1849. "To return to the decaying conditions of the past is like scooping water with a sieve."[3] He meant this to apply to every aspect of Prussian life, including the bureaucracy. We have seen how the government moved swiftly against those officials who had been involved in the November tax strike, yet took care not to arouse the kind of opposition that might precipitate further resistance and possibly trigger a second revolution. In early December the cabinet had decided to bring charges against those who had voted for the original resolution, but this was done through the regular courts, and no widespread purge was initiated.[4] Furthermore, the government let it be known that officials would be protected against arbitrary persecution and that anonymous denunciations of its members would be ignored by superiors.[5] Coming as it did after the proclamation of a constitution that contained provisions for the independence of the judiciary and civil rights for officials, these actions were part of the broader program of calculated concessions to liberal and democratic demands.[6] In the months that followed, the government used the same tactics with regard to judicial reform and the establishment of new regulations concerning intra-bureaucratic discipline that it applied to the larger political problems. The overall strategy was essentially that practiced in the past by Prussian governments in times of crisis—the strategy of "revolution from above," aimed at the conservation of the substance of the traditional social and political order at the expense of antiquated ideas and institutions.

The day after the promulgation of the December 5 constitution, which differed only in minor respects from the one drawn up by the Constitutional Assembly, the Brandenburg-Manteuffel government announced elections for a new bicameral legislature that would have the right to revise and ratify the new document. High age and property requirements were set for the upper house, but for the lower chamber there was to be suffrage for all males over twenty-four who could fulfill certain minimal residence requirements and were not recipients of public welfare.[7] In its statement of December 28, 1848, the government pledged free elections, and promised that its officials would not "exercise a direct influence on the outcome of the elections," or even demonstrate an "unfair" zealousness. "It is the task of the bureaucrats to avoid every intimidation, every seduction of voters, to oppose every dishonest means, every kind of corruption, and all that which in form or essence seems to offer ephemeral success." Officials were told in no uncertain terms that it would be their duty to uphold the constitution and its "liberal spirit."[8] In turn, the bureaucracy was reminded that its civic rights would not be interfered with—a promise that the government apparently managed to keep during the January campaign.[9]

The second major conciliatory step taken by the government was to announce judicial reforms. This it did on January 2 and 3, 1849. The universal norms and equalizing tendencies inherent in the new constitution were extended to the judicial branch of government. The abolition of the last vestiges of the feudal practices of patrimonial justice, the introduction of jury trials, the reform of the law profession, and other changes that constituted a major rationalization of Prussia's court system were all steps aimed at satisfying long-standing criticisms. Almost all the demands for judicial reform that had been voiced in the pre-March period were encompassed in the new laws, which, like the new constitution itself, were subject to ratification by parliament. Included in the elimination of the feudal forms of justice were the abolition of some 970 patrimonial courts and their replacement with state courts staffed by professional officials. In the six eastern provinces and in Westphalia over two hundred municipal and county courts

(*Stadtgerichte* and *Kreisgerichte*) were established at the local level. A large number of one-judge commissions and three-judge deputations were also created to serve the judicial needs of the remoter areas where patrimonial justice was no longer available. The judicial hierarchy was rationalized by establishing twenty-one courts of appeals (*Appellationsgerichte*) to replace the old higher district courts (*Oberlandesgerichte*); and at the top of this heirarchy was placed a new Supreme Court, the *Obertribunal*. The Rhine Province, whose judicial system provided the model for many of these changes, was permitted to retain its original structure.[10]

Not only was the framework of justice revised, but the qualifications for judicial offices were standardized and professionalized. Formerly there had existed two distinct levels of judiciary: state office had been reserved for those who had passed their third examination, patrimonial position for those who had passed only the second. The January 2 order made all judicial positions dependent on the third examination. At the same time, it greatly expanded the places available: the replacement of patrimonial with state judgeships opened up the possibility of 788 new positions.[11] Simultaneously, an entirely new institution, the state prosecutor's office (*Staatsanwalt*), was created, offering more than two hundred additional opportunities to those who had passed the third examination. Finally, the January 2 reorganization transformed the nature and qualifications of the Prussian bar by changing the lawyer's title from *Justizkommissarius* to *Rechtsanwalt* and making his academic qualifications the same as those of the members of the higher judiciary.

Taken as a whole, these reforms represented a major step toward the rationalization of the judicial system, a change that had been advocated by progressive circles for a number of years. Not only were the qualifications of the personnel equalized and the standards made universal throughout the country, but the judiciary underwent considerable professionalization at the same time. The superiority of a university-trained judiciary had long been recognized, but with the termination of patrimonial justice, entrance into the Prussian judiciary became for the first time dependent exclusively on a single standard of achievement. Thus the evolution that had begun more than a century before was completed, and the judiciary became fully professional in the modern sense of that term.

The new standards not only fulfilled the demands of those who had been calling for an increase in the quality of training for all those connected with the judiciary, they created new places for an estimated 300 Assessoren and thus allowed for the absorption of almost the entire surplus of underemployed. Whether this was the precise intention of the government is impossible to ascertain; certainly the abolition of patrimonial justice, which had been proposed by reformers for some forty years, was not motivated by expediency alone. But since judicial employment reforms had been a demand of both liberal and radical bureaucrats, the timing of these changes was almost certainly intentional, and many on the far right interpreted the expansion as one more instance of the appeasement of radicals at the expense of the taxpayer.[12] In the parliamentary debates that followed the reforms, a deputy named Fliegel, who was also a judge, defended the changes on the grounds that the increased cost of the system would pay the salaries of previously underpaid officials—to which Otto von Bismarck retorted that the reorganization of justice satisfied only one segment of the population, the bureaucrats themselves.[13]

Other aspects of the reform also appear to have been designed to eliminate long-standing grievances. The expansion of the number of judges and the general rationalization of the system promised to reduce the burdens on the junior members of the judiciary. By creating a new state prosecutor's office and assigning at least one Staatsanwalt to almost every court, the reform cut down on the tasks of the regular judiciary: relieved of the duties of prosecution, they could concentrate their energies entirely on adjudication.[14] In the higher courts, the collegiate principle, with its traditional authority pattern, was maintained; but the creation of one-man commissions and three-man deputations to operate on the local level gave lower-ranking judges an autonomy and degree of responsibility they had not previously possessed. And finally, the reform of the Prussian legal profession raised the status of the lawyer to the point where, for the first time, that profession could attract law graduates who might otherwise have entered the overcrowded judiciary or administration. Unfortunately, the numbers of Rechtsanwälte and Staatsanwälte were still controlled by the state. Neither rank could immediately become the safety valve the bureaucratic profession needed to relieve its own overcrowding, but nevertheless the first steps had been taken.[15]

This was only one side of the January reforms. If the modernization of the judiciary was aimed partially at pacifying the judiciary by eliminating certain causes of discontent, it also was intended to go hand in hand with tighter controls over the individual official. One effect of the universalizing and rationalizing tendency of the new law was to reduce the autonomy of the judicial process. Not only were all the former patrimonial judgeships brought under state control, but the number of positions directly appointed by the Ministry of Justice was substantially increased.[16] The naming of lower court judges remained in the hands of the members of the appeals courts. Unfortunately the creation of the one-man commissions and the three-man deputations increased the efficiency of the judiciary at the expense of its freedom.[17] The young, inexperienced judges who were assigned to the circuit courts were, because of their low pay and insecure position, less able to maintain their integrity against interference by superiors; moreover, recurrent overcrowding still made the process of promotion by seniority nearly impossible and encouraged favoritism and political interference. In this situation, the Minister of Justice, who was a political appointee, had an increasingly greater say in the naming and promotion of judges.[18]

The intrusion of the political factor into the personnel policies of the judiciary was a gradual development; but the creation of the state prosecutor's office had the immediate effect of reducing the autonomy of the judicial process. The Staatsanwalt did not share the formal independence of the judge; he was essentially an administrative official, subject to the same discipline as the other members of the executive branch.[19] One of the most significant aspects of the January reforms was the extent of the powers granted to this new agency. Only the prosecutor had the right to initiate proceedings, and thus cases brought before the courts were essentially dependent on the will of the administration. In addition to other advantages of a purely procedural nature, the prosecutor also had the power to appeal acquittals to higher courts.

The institution of jury trials, long a demand of the left, was supposed to offset the influence of the administrative branch. However, the new law stipulated that the list of prospective jurors should be chosen according to certain tax qualifications, and the only groups exempted from this exclusive practice were some types of professional men and some categories of bureaucrats.[20] Landräte and members of town councils, both traditionally conservative, were automatically eligible. For the purpose of individual trials, the district Regierungspräsident was to choose sixty persons from the original list, from which the presiding judges would select thirty-six. The prosecution and the defense would then dispute over the final twelve-man panel.[21]

The judicial reforms were only part of a series of laws and edicts that were issued in early 1849 for the purpose of pacifying the population while extending government control into areas of society not previously penetrated by the authority of the state. In quick succession the last vestiges of feudal manorialism were swept away, the guild system reformed, and factory improvement acts passed. A new local government ordinance was also brought under consideration, though it was not enacted until the following spring.[22] All the reforms embodied changes that had been demanded by progressive factions in the pre-March period: in most cases, the new measures appeared to be mere enactments of proposals made by the short-lived liberal ministries of the previous year, but in every case the changes went beyond the universaliz-

ing and equalizing tendencies of liberal legislation to include authoritarian measures. Liberals detected a revival of pre-March pater-
nalism; but by interpreting the changes simply as a revival of
feudalism, they ignored the modern elements embodied in the
new legislation.[23] Earlier governments had sought control through
the traditional corporations; the new conservatives were seeking
to control individuals more directly by isolating them from these
bodies and attaching them directly to the state by economic and
social means. Guild reforms, new factory laws, and agrarian improvements all involved the exchange of personal or group autonomy for the benefits of social welfare.

Prussia was rapidly becoming something very different from the
compromise of modern state and feudal society that had existed
under the General Code of 1794. The subjects of the Hohenzollerns now possessed equality of citizenship, not only with respect
to their obligations to the state but also in their relationships with
one another. Traditional regional and corporate bodies continued
to exist, and Prussian society was still riven with many of the
social distinctions of the pre-March period. But these institutions
were no longer part of public authority; now they were private
or semi-private organizations whose existence was dependent on
the individual member's right of free association. Before the revolution, the Prussian citizen had served the state through one or
more constituted bodies; he had owed his most basic rights to his
membership in them, and had been protected by them from the
arbitrary actions of the state. Now his rights and duties were derived solely from his status as citizen, and there stood between
him and the state no protection but the constitution.

This was the same constitution that the king liked to call "a mere
scrap of paper," dependent for its existence on the royal will alone.
His ministers were hardly more loyal to the principle of a constitution, but they were more aware of the power that this modern
system of law offered to a government willing to exploit its possibilities. Men like Brandenburg and Manteuffel were quick to

realize that there was no essential conflict between powerful executive authority and the existence of civil equality. Indeed, they believed that the times required the retention of the form if not the substance of the democratic concept of citizenship in order to sustain the power of the executive. "A good administration is the basic underpinning of the Prussian monarchy," remarked Graf Brandenburg. "It may be necessary to use it in certain instances to suppress the constitution, but it should never be employed to restore the corporate system."[24] This view, so clearly at odds with the ideas of the king and other influential proponents of restoration, as well as with the intentions of the liberal and democratic factions in parliament, was sure to arouse intense antagonism on all sides. Nevertheless, throughout the spring of 1849 the Brandenburg-Manteuffel government struggled to prove that constitutional government could be used for conservative purposes.

Although the country as a whole had experienced a shift toward the right during the final months of the revolution, the appearance of the new Lower House in January 1849 was strikingly similar to that of the Constitutional Assembly of 1848. Many familiar faces were present: Waldeck, Kirchmann, Jung, as well as other leading democrats, took up their old positions in the opposition. The social composition of the parliament was also much the same. Universal suffrage continued to benefit the intellectuals: the bureaucrats accounted for 42.2 percent of the total number of deputies. The judiciary had increased its percentage slightly, from 23.8 percent to 26.2 percent, while the administrative bureaucracy's proportion had risen sharply from 9.5 percent to 16 percent.[25]

The pattern of party affiliation among public servants, however, showed a marked change. The divergence between the judicial and administrative deputies had become greater, for while the majority of the judicial officials remained solidly on the left, the new administrators were primarily conservative.[26] Sixty-five percent of the judicial deputies belonged to the opposition parties; the proportion was only 21 percent in the administrative branch.[27] There was an equally sharp division between the older and younger ranks of the two bureaucracies, particularly in the judiciary, where fourteen of seventeen Assessoren stood with the Extreme Left or Left factions. This pattern was also true of the four administrative trainees represented, but to a lesser degree.[28] The low-ranking judges and administrators stood far to the left of those of their superiors who were elected to the Lower House. As in 1848, the younger members of the two services, especially the judiciary, formed the backbone of the democratic parties. Of the 140 deputies who composed the Extreme Left or Left factions of the January Parliament, fifty-three were members of the judiciary, including fourteen Assessoren and one Referendarius.[29]

These same elements formed the core of the democratic movement outside the parliament as well. The democrats' central committee consisted of Waldeck, Jung, von Unruh, and Rodbertus— all officials or former officials. Of the organization's provincial committees, almost a quarter were judicial officials; the entire Rhineland directory, for example, consisted of members of that branch of the civil service. Though the following of the democratic movement continued to be made up of shopkeepers and artisans, the leaders were members of the educated middle class.[30]

Evidence of continued radicalism within the bureaucracy itself could not help but attract the attention of Prussian conservatives, including the ministers themselves. The members of the Kreuz-zeitungspartei, who wished to restore the corporate system, were particularly persistent in attacking the continued presence of radical and liberal elements within the civil service. Otto von Bismarck, who at this time was closely associated with that faction, was moved by a belief that the collapse of the old order in 1848 had been caused less by the actions of the revolutionary than by the authorities' fear of him and by "the private sympathy of public officials for him."[31] According to tribunes of the far right, it was these very elements that by their indifference to or active participation in opposition movements might open the gates to a second revolution. In his initial speech to the new parliament Ludwig von Gerlach, a high ranking judge, demanded that the govern-

ment purge the members of the judiciary implicated in the tax
strike and other revolutionary activities.[32] The *Neue Preussische
Zeitung*'s charge that many of the higher officials sitting in parliament still played the dangerous game of compromise with revolution was seconded by Ernst Bülow-Cummerow, who declared
that the new constitution had expanded the bureaucracy's sphere
of activity by extending the officials' influence to the legislative
branch, thus concentrating tremendous power in the hands of a
subversive few.[33] The danger of a "representation by bureaucracy"
was twofold, argued Bülow-Cummerow: on the one hand it gave
an unscrupulous government a useful tool with which to manipu-
late the parliamentary body; on the other, it provided the civil
servants with the opportunity to satisfy their own selfish desires
and to further their "democratic tendencies."[34] Only a system of
representation based on a high property qualification would satisfy Bülow-Cummerow and the landed interests he represented,
and would fit the demands of the propertied bourgeoisie, who were
wary of any system of franchise that placed power in the hands
of the intellectuals.[35]

The Brandenburg-Manteuffel ministry was confronted with a
serious dilemma, for unless it did something to appease both its
conservative and its liberal critics it would be in a dangerously
weak position vis-à-vis the radicals. The king himself was particularly sensitive to dissent within the civil service and harped
constantly on the subject of discipline; moreover, his closest advisers, the members of the extremely right-wing Kamarilla, were
continually urging sterner action against radical officials, thus encouraging the monarch in his tendency to meddle in administrative matters.[36] From influential provincial notables such as Prince
Pückler-Muskau in Oppeln came complaints about the behavior
of the judiciary: "As excellent as the higher echelons of justice in
this district are, yet there are undignified obstructionists among
the judicial personnel. There is almost never an agitation in which
someone from this group does not play an important role."[37] Saxony's Oberpräsident von Bonin had also noted that the courts in-

variably complicated the work of the administrative authorities and made the task of restoring order extremely difficult. Bonin counseled Manteuffel to give the officials time to reform themselves; if they should refuse this grace, "then it is time to step in and dismiss them all wherever possible."[38] Advice of a more conciliatory nature came from Eichmann, the Rhineland Oberpräsident, who warned that precipitous persecution of all those involved in oppositional movements would be "politically unwise" and would only stir up further resistance.[39] Eichmann spoke for one of the provinces most deeply affected by dissent within bureaucratic ranks; the most uncompromising advice often came from those parts of Prussia where opposition was weak or scattered. Manteuffel and his colleagues seem to have taken this into account as they cautiously formulated their strategy in the spring of 1849.

A product of a relatively short but extremely successful career in public service, Otto von Manteuffel was representative of the senior ranks of the administration; honesty, devotion to duty, loyalty, and willingness for self-effacement were traits he shared with the most illustrious Prussian officials. While he was capable of understanding the implications of the changes that had taken place over the previous decade, he showed no sympathy for the behavior of the underprivileged members of his profession. As far as he was concerned, the younger generation was affected by the same intolerable disrespect for authority that infected the entire educated class. "Characteristic of this group is a combination of pride and cowardice, both of which are the products of godlessness," he wrote.[40]

From pride of profession as well as obligation to law and order, Manteuffel was determined to restore the virtue of obedience to both branches of the bureaucracy. Complete rehabilitation would have to wait upon the restoration of general social and political stability, however, for the Brandenburg-Manteuffel government would not be stampeded into hasty action, and certainly would not allow itself to be provoked into taking the step that the far right had been urging since December: a complete or partial restoration of the corporate system.[41] As Manteuffel was later to explain, the cooperation of the bureaucracy was absolutely indispensable during the critical years immediately after the revolution. The government had to steer a course between the twin dangers of foolhardy restoration and violent revolution. In rebuttal to those who argued that constitutional monarchy and representative institutions were the major sources of danger, he argued that any return to the old corporate system, including any action that would deprive the government of the support of its professional civil servants, would trigger further upheavals. "The Prussian state cannot be based on corporate institutions," he declared shortly after the Olmütz crisis of 1850. "It is essentially a bureaucratic and military system."[42]

In the late spring of 1849 the government was forced to adjust its policy of conciliation. The revival of revolutionary activity in southern and western Germany, together with renewed restlessness within Prussia itself, led to a harder line toward dissent. The crisis was provoked by the objections of the Lower House to the government's contention that it was parliament's role to revise and ratify rather than to legislate the Constitution. In particular, powerful opposition arose to the use of Constitutional Article 105, which allowed the government to enact major reforms even before the final ratification of the charter. The chamber's support for a motion by Lothar Bucher that the judicial reforms of January be declared illegal provoked the first serious confrontation between the executive and legislative branches.[43] Justice Minister von Rintelen voluntarily submitted his resignation and was replaced by a man of tougher temperament, Ludwig Simons.

But the issue of Prussia's relationship to a unified Germany brought about the final impasse. On April 21, the Lower House passed a motion to censure the king's rejection of the national crown offered by a delegation from the Frankfurt parliament. Using the pretext that the resolution was an unwarranted interference by the legislature in executive affairs, the government dissolved the legislature on April 27 and adjourned the upper chamber. The decision was not a sudden one: the government had, almost since the January elections, been biding its time, waiting for a favorable opportunity to rid itself of the rebellious parliament.[44]

Moving swiftly and using the authority of Article 105 of the yet-unratified constitution, the government issued a number of regulations and decrees that taken as a whole represented a turn away from the previous policy of conciliation. Of greatest significance was the revised franchise, issued on May 30, which established the three-class system of voting that was to remain the basic Prussian franchise until 1918.[45] The history of the evolution of this measure reveals that it was a compromise between the king's promise of "the broadest possible suffrage" and the demands of the powerful agrarian, business, and professional interests, which were pressing for a franchise based on high property qualifications. The solution reached was one that gave all males the vote but weighted the franchise according to the amount of taxes paid. In addition, the ballot was made public, thus depriving the voter of the privacy of his political decision.[46]

What amounted to a victory of the propertied classes over the radical intellectuals and their allies among the laboring poor could not fail to arouse opposition. The newly formed Union for the Preservation of Popular Suffrage met in Köthen in early June to issue a resolution calling on all democrats to abstain from the coming elections as a way of protesting against the new franchise system. Their act of passive resistance showed that the government had failed to stamp out all opposition within the ranks of its own bureaucracy. A number of officials and former officials, including Franz Hermann Schulze-Delitzsch, Hans Viktor von Unruh, and Johann Karl Rodbertus, were on the committee that drew up the Köthen declaration; and though most government agencies complied with the new electoral rules, there were reports of isolated incidents of opposition within the bureaucracy.[47]

The worst fears of the democratic opposition were justified when

TABLE I

Comparison of Distribution of Lower House Officials

Rank	January–April 1849 (universal suffrage)		July 1849–October 1852 (three class system)			
	Opposed to government	Loyal to government	Opposed to government	Neutral	Loyal to government	Unknown
Administration						
Ministers	0	2	0	0	4	
Regierungs- and Oberpräsidenten	0	4	1	1	4	
Regierungsräte	1	11	3	9	24	2
Landräte	4	13	7	9	40	6
Trainees (Auskultatoren, Referendarien, Assessoren)	3	2	2	1	0	
Judiciary						
Obertribunal Judges	1	2	0	0	0	
Presidents of Appeals Courts	1	1	2	0	0	
Appeals Judges and Directors of Lower Courts	14	19	10	17	17	4
Kreis Judges	3	2	8	2	7	1
Trainees	18	3	5	5	0	
Staatsanwälte	2	0	0	0	2	1
Rechtsanwälte	15	5	3	1	0	2
Total	62	64	41	45	98	16

the results of the July balloting were announced. Although the withdrawal of democratic candidates certainly had considerable effect on the outcome, there can be little doubt that the new system brought a decisive victory to the propertied classes.[48] The large landowners tripled their representation, and the industrial entrepreneurs also gained, though much less spectacularly. Equally significant were the results in regard to the bureaucracy: here, too, conservative elements made a startling breakthrough. The Landräte more than tripled the representation they had held in the previous parliament. Members of all ranks of the administrative branch flocked to parliament, for the first time since 1847, picking up 73 seats and raising their total from 40 to 113.[49] The number of judicial officials remained almost constant. Most striking, however, were the changes within the ranks of the two groups. These changes can be seen in Table 1, which shows the distribution of bureaucrats in the two parliaments.[50]

The new suffrage struck hardest at the lower ranks of the bureaucracy; the number of trainees was cut in half, while the superior echelons almost doubled their representation. Of equal interest is the shift in political affiliation—on all levels there was a movement to the right. In the January parliament 20 percent of the higher administrative officials (including all ranks) stood in opposition to the government; in July they were only 12 percent, if those who called themselves neutral but who, according to my findings, actually voted regularly with the government are counted as loyal. The corresponding percentage for the higher levels of the judiciary (excluding the Staatsanwälte and Rechtsanwälte) slipped from 58 percent in opposition to 34 percent. According to the same method of calculation, the proportion of opponents of the government among the trainees of both branches dropped from 81 percent in the earlier session to 54 percent in the later one.

The judiciary remained significantly to the left of the administration, the lower ranks far more radical than their superiors. Yet the composition of the July Lower House shows a clear victory for the propertied classes and their allies within the bureaucracy. This election marked the victory of the conservative coalition that had been in the process of formation since the March upheavals and that formed the basis of the solid majority won by the parties favorable to the government.[51] The lower, less affluent groups of Prussian society were virtually eliminated. Even more significant was the drastic reduction in the power of the radical intellectuals. Representation from the liberal professions—educators, clergymen, and doctors—was cut to about a third its previous strength. The subordinate ranks of the higher bureaucracy lost more than half their representation. The *Geistesproletariat* (intellectual proletariat), which had survived the November coup, had been dealt a severe blow by the discriminatory property qualification embodied in the three-class franchise system.[52]

The government's program to minimize internal opposition included more than franchise revision; before the July elections, new restrictions on the rights of assembly and association were issued, and the controls on the political press were tightened.[53] Of even graver consequence for the citizenship of state officials, however, were the ordinances of July 10 and 11 concerning the discipline procedures of the judicial and administrative branches. Their timing was not accidental, because since the suspension of the 1844 regulations the rights of officials had been under almost constant consideration. The July 1848 order had been meant to serve only as a guideline and was not specific enough to be definitive. The December constitution had promised more detailed legislation; and when, in January of 1849, the king asked the cabinet to move against dissident elements in the postal administration, the minister in charge had replied that the existing regulations were inadequate to deal with the situation.[54] In May, Manteuffel circulated a memorandum within the Ministry of the Interior dealing with the need for a stricter definition of the rights of officials: "The government cannot carry on successfully when its subordinate officials do not with all honesty guarantee their strongest support. All those who do not believe they can do this would do well to resign voluntarily; and where this is not done, it will be the duty of the ministry, in the interests of the country, to remove in a lawful manner those who fulfill their duties lackadaisically or grudgingly, as well as those who awaken distrust where, through education and understanding, trust should have been created."[55]

During the spring of 1849 pressure to do something about internal opposition mounted steadily. Events outside Prussia threatened to embroil Germany in a second revolution, and from the king came the command that those officials who had participated in the meetings of the national rump parliament at Stuttgart be investigated with an eye to possible punishment. In the provinces similar demands were voiced by those who feared that disorders in other states might spread to Prussia.[56] On June 8 the new Minister of Justice, Ludwig Simons, informed his subordinates: "It has come to the attention of the Minister of Justice from several sources that Referendarien and Auskultatoren have participated voluntarily in political demonstrations and rallies in which they have acted in such a way as to support convictions hostile to the king's government." Nontenured officials involved were to be warned, then dismissed if they persisted.[57] Ten days later, the Minister of Justice turned his attention to the entire judiciary: "Recent experiences have led to the conclusion that many, primarily younger, judicial officials have taken part in political demonstrations, have associated themselves with extreme movements, and have even become leaders of the same." Simons promised that persistent public protest would be dealt with in a severe manner. Responsibility for surveillance of the political activity of jurists was placed in the hands of the state prosecutors, who were to report all irregularities directly to the Minister of Justice.[58]

Pressure was building for more repressive measures. Representatives of almost a hundred conservative clubs, meeting in Potsdam in May 1849, submitted a petition to the Minister of Justice that put the rural and urban upper classes on record for tighter control: "It is with deep dismay that we observe that in many parts of the country the discipline within the bureaucracy has broken down, and that many civil servants, including judicial officials, have given support to the enemies of the monarchy and have even sided openly with them. . . . The honor of the bureaucracy, a quality for which Prussia is envied, has been undermined by the toleration of this sad state of affairs." The petition was signed by leading members of the landowning and business elites as well as representatives of the highest ranks of the bureaucracy itself.[59]

The outcome of these external and internal pressures was the formulation of a set of disciplinary regulations consistent with precedents set by the orders of the previous July and consonant with the new constitution, but aimed at an even tighter control of the politics of the civil service. As for the judiciary, it retained its formal independence in matters relating directly to its office. The judges—Staatsanwälte, Rechtsanwälte, and the personnel of the Ministry of Justice excluded—were to remain self-disciplining in matters concerning dereliction of duty. The courts of appeals were to constitute the authority for all but the highest judges, who were themselves under the jurisdiction of the Obertribunal. In no case could judges be dismissed or transferred without a formal proceeding before their professional peers. The provisions of the involuntary transfer clause of the 1844 regulations, which had caused so much stir, were thus slipped in under the guise of due process. In theory, the profession retained its treasured right of self-discipline; in practice, the new regulations meant that the government would work through the judicial bureaucracy rather than against it to obtain its political objectives.

The judiciary seemed to retain its old rights, but to the rights were attached duties that had not even been contemplated in the preconstitutional monarchy. It was clear that the government expected loyalty, or what they called "impartiality of adjudication," from its judiciary; but in this case impartiality in official business also meant neutrality in public behavior.[60] Appealing to the judiciary's sense of professional honor, the government warned that active participation by individual judges in organized opposition movements would destroy the nation's confidence in the entire judiciary.[61] The choice was clear: either the judiciary must abandon its political radicalism or face the possibility of the loss of independence.

The administrative bureaucracy was given no such choice, for it was subject directly to executive authority. The government explained that the introduction of constitutional government, with its separation of administrative and legislative authority, necessitated tighter control. The 1844 disciplinary code would be brought up to date; the ministries would control not only the personal conduct of subordinates but their political activities as well. Administrative officials would henceforth be liable to dismissal if they violated "the duty of loyalty" or did not practice "the courage" that their offices demanded, or showed themselves to be guilty of "hostile partisanship against the government." For most tenured officials there remained certain guarantees against arbitrary action by superiors. In most cases the accused was afforded a formal review by his peers in the form of a special discipline court or special review board of the provincial Regierung, and the right of appeal to the Staatsministerium and the king.[62] In this respect the new law provided all the guarantees that had characterized disciplinary procedures during the era of bureaucratic absolutism. However, there was one category of officials—later known as "political officials"— who were not secure against arbitrary discipline. Directors of the central ministries, Undersecretaries, Oberpräsidenten, Presidents and Vice-presidents of district governments, state prosecutors, state police chiefs, Landräte, and diplomats—all were liable to suspension with partial pension at the arbitrary discretion of their superiors. No regular procedure was established, no right of appeal guaranteed. In this regard, the July 11 order constituted a break with the past, a break with the tradition of corporate self-regulation characteristic of the preconstitutional period. Now the bureaucracy was divided into two groups: one reasonably free to exercise the rights of citizenship, the other virtually segregated from the rest of the political community.[63]

It must be noted that in most respects the July regulations did not depart from the consensus of liberal and conservative opinion that had been evolving since 1848. Except for the protests of the radicals who were the first victims, there was little open opposition on the part of the public or the bureaucracy itself.[64] When in April 1851 the appropriate committee of the Lower House reported on the disciplinary regulations, it recommended, with certain reservations, the passage of both measures. There were objections to the inclusion of vague language in the paragraph regarding the public responsibilities of administrative officials, but there was little antagonism to the principle that the government should be able to suspend certain categories of officials on political grounds without due process.[65] Ironically, these were precisely the powers that the members of the Left had demanded earlier: up to and during the revolution they had been unable to see that measures demanded in the name of progress might also serve the powers of preservation; now they were hardly in a position to reverse the trend toward centralization of authority they themselves had initiated.[66]

The conservatives, who by July dominated the parliament, welcomed the regulations; the *Kreuzzeitung*, which distrusted even the relative independence granted the judiciary, urged that the Ministry use its new powers vigorously.[67] In the debates on the bill only a few liberal voices were raised against the substance of the measure. Georg von Vincke, who had been the victim of disciplinary action in 1847, warned of the corrupting effects of the new laws, but most of his colleagues were too concerned with the restoration of order and stability to heed his admonitions about the future.[68] Although the Lower House had managed to tighten the language of certain sections of the code, the two disciplinary orders of July 10 and 11 were passed without substantial change and became law on May 7, 1851, and June 21, 1852, respectively.

Opposition factions would undoubtedly have been less willing to accept the disciplinary regulations if the government had made immediate and widespread use of them for political purposes. But during the July 1849 elections and for the rest of the period prior to the Olmütz crisis these powers were used sparingly, almost timidly. The government majorities in the Lower House had been achieved without the aid of undue interference in the electoral process; no attempt had been made to promote official candidates or to create a true governmental faction in parliament.[69] Brandenburg and Manteuffel were like doctors postponing radical surgery in hopes that the disease will cure itself. They believed both that the main body of the bureaucracy was healthy enough to effect a recuperation and that complications might arise if action were too hastily taken.

Some degree of political opposition was still permitted members of the civil service, as long as it was publicly discreet and did not intrude in any way on the operations of the government. This moderation was not at all popular with the influential right-wing faction, which was opposed as well to the government's liberal nationalist foreign policy. Clashes between the government and the Kreuzzeitungspartei were frequent, and the conservative majority in parliament was in an almost continuous state of disarray.[70] To men like Brandenburg and Manteuffel, who pictured themselves as defending the interests of the state against those of particular groups, the factionalism of the right was no less dangerous than the opposition of the left: they were of the old school of Prussian political theory that viewed any kind of partisan activity as dangerous to the stability of the state. According to this conception political parties, whatever their ideology, were too unstable to provide a firm basis of power. Above all, Brandenburg and Manteuffel were concerned with restoring order within the bureaucracy—the one body within the system that seemed capable of sustaining a stable government.[71]

In a circular of April 7, 1850, Manteuffel reiterated the government's position: "hostile partisanship" within the ranks would be suppressed. The constitution would be upheld, for "orderly and lawful conditions must be maintained at any price." With remarkable frankness, Manteuffel appealed for the bureaucracy's support in carrying through the government's current program of liberal reform of local government. Officials were assured that since "a considerable part of the difficult world-historical task of the Prussian state" fell to its civil service, the independence of the bureaucracy would be respected as long as the profession performed its duties in a loyal manner.[72] Most significant was the distinction made between different kinds of political partisanship—between a "hostile" or active opposition and a more passive difference of views. Manteuffel showed no desire to deprive the bureaucracy, even the so-called "political" officials, of their rights of citizenship. Like his liberal opponents, he viewed the participation of civil servants in public affairs as a necessary element of the Prussian constitutional system: they could serve as a stabilizing influence both in and out of parliament as long as the credibility and integrity of the profession was maintained. This required at least the appearance of independence from government control, and therefore Manteuffel was willing to settle for something less than total public obedience to government policy. Absolute loyalty in the fulfillment of official duties was demanded, but outside the obligations of his position the civil servant was still allowed considerable latitude as a private citizen. In most cases the individual official could vote for and even become a member of nongovernmental factions, so long as he remained passive or neutral and avoided public expression of dissent on those issues the government deemed crucial.

The tone of conciliation was still apparent. Manteuffel was still relying on persuasion rather than coercion—persuasion not only by the government itself but by those members of the civil service interested in restoring the honor of their profession. He had no illusions about restoration of the self-discipline of the Vormärz period. The constitutional system required a strong centralized government and tight control by the Berlin ministries; it did not, however, exclude the preservation of the traditional status of the bureaucracy as a privileged group, so long as the officials themselves were ready to unite in cooperation with their superiors.

Part Three

REACTION

Chapter Seven

A Break with Revolution

With the Olmütz crisis of November 1850 politics in Prussia entered a new phase. After two years of calculating compromise with the forces of liberalism, the government turned toward a policy much less tolerant of all forms of dissent. With the departure of Radowitz from the cabinet, the pretense of a liberal foreign policy was abandoned; and a reorganization of the government necessitated by the death of Graf Brandenburg in December further strengthened the power of the ultra-conservatives. Manteuffel succeeded as Prime Minister, assuming control of foreign affairs but relinquishing the post of Minister of the Interior to a man much closer to the Kreuzzeitungspartei, Ferdinand von Westphalen. At the same time Karl Friedrich von Raumer, an uncompromising conservative, was placed in charge of religious and educational affairs, replacing Adalbert von Ladenberg, a liberal who had resigned with Radowitz.[1] Earlier, changes in the cabinet had always been accompanied by assurances that the achievements of the revolution, in particular the constitution, were inviolable; but now the government made it abundantly clear that nothing would stand in the way of its program to eliminate all opposition. "Yes, this is a turning point in our political life," Manteuffel bluntly told the Lower House early in January 1851. "This must certainly be a break with revolution!"[2]

In the same speech, the new head of government spoke of the nature of the problem facing Prussia and expressed his determination to vanquish all the enemies of his regime: armed insurrection was no longer the foremost danger; now attention would have to be directed to the less obvious forms of subversion. Citing the recent involvement of public officials in the revolutionary activity in Hesse as an example of the kind of threat that still existed in his own country, Manteuffel warned: "I believe that revolution by bureaucrats (*Beamtenrevolution*) is an extreme danger, because while barricade fighters at least have the courage to expose themselves, officials play their part in dressing gown and slippers." To the cheers of the deputies on the right of the chamber, the Prime Minister pledged that every effort would be made to eliminate all subversive elements, no matter how highly placed, no matter how well protected by law or tradition.[3]

The initial impression left by Manteuffel's speech was one of implacable hostility to all manifestations of liberalism. The Kreuzzeitung greeted his statement as a sign that the Prime Minister had been converted to the ideological position of the ultra-right, and liberal elements, fearing the worst, assumed that the counter-revolution had finally begun. The next seven years were to show, however, that the "break with revolution" was not equivalent to the program of thoroughgoing restoration contemplated by some conservatives. Despite the efforts of the extreme right wing to resurrect the corporate order, Prussia retained its constitution and representative institutions were preserved. Despite the repressive atmosphere that prevailed after 1851, a feeble liberal opposition managed to survive. Elements of the progressive reforms of the previous period, including reorganization of the judiciary, were allowed to continue—though not for the purpose of creating conditions for greater freedom and equality, but to reinforce the authoritarian regime itself. The period of reaction that began with Olmütz by no means constituted a return to traditional political and social forms: old and new were now fused in ways scarcely conceivable in the pre-revolutionary period.

Despite his public statements, Otto von Manteuffel was not one of those who believed it possible to turn back the clock. He opposed any action that might threaten the legal and institutional continuity he had worked to establish during the previous three years. Yet even as Prime Minister he found it difficult to restrain those inside and outside the government whose commitment to gradualism was not as strong as his own. Particularly disturbing were those on the far right whose extralegal influence he criticized in a memorandum written in 1856. "There can be no doubt," he wrote, "but that the king of Prussia must have the right to choose his servants and to dismiss them. However, it violates the traditional organization of the Prussian system when he has, besides his official cabinet, still another; when he is advised not only by his ministers [but by others] and lets his orders be carried out by them. The counselors, adjuncts, and secretaries can only be the king's most intimate servants, never his counsel."[4] Manteuffel was directing his fire at two influences that complicated and sometimes disrupted the work of the responsible cabinet throughout the 1850's: the Kamarilla, the informal group of royal intimates who represented the views of the Kreuzzeitungspartei at court, and a man who often opposed the programs of both the ministers and the Kamarilla, Karl von Hinckeldey, the Police President of Berlin who, until his death in 1856, was one of Frederick William's most trusted advisers.[5]

Manteuffel was no more successful in curbing the intrigues of his own cabinet ministers than he was in controlling the Kamarilla and Hinkeldey. The Staatsministerium remained what it had been since the death of Hardenberg thirty years before, a loosely organized and badly coordinated body. Even the cabinet order of September 8, 1852, requiring all cabinet ministers with the exception of the Minister of War to inform the Prime Minister of their conversations with the king, did not provide Manteuffel with the authority he desired.[6] In his 1856 memorandum he complained bitterly of disunity and distrust among his closest associates. Only a man at once powerful and autocratic—and Manteuffel was no autocrat—could have achieved mastery over them.[7] Manteuffel was a firm administrator but not a dynamic political leader. Several times he subordinated his own views to those of Frederick William, even when he knew the king to be ill-advised on important matters.[8] Perhaps his bureaucratic background, which inclined him to tolerate what one observer described as a "federation of ministries," was at fault. A more plausible theory is that the unsettled conditions within the state itself made strong, unified control extremely difficult.

This helps explain how Manteuffel could preside over a government whose actions so often violated his principles of legality and gradualism. In relatively quick succession, several of the progressive reforms of the previous three years were rescinded. The judicial reforms survived unscathed, but the liberal local government ordinance of March 1850 was suspended, manorial police powers were reinstituted, and the authority to nominate the Landrat was returned to the privileged larger landowners. Symbolic of what seemed to be an almost total triumph of counterrevolution in the first months after Olmütz was the restoration of the pre-March provincial estates by executive edict in May 1851—an act that struck many supporters as well as opponents of the regime as a violation of the constitution and the first step in the restoration of the entire corporate order.[9]

The actions of the government provoked opposition not only among the general public but also within the very group Manteuffel had previously tried so hard to pacify, namely the bureaucracy. During May and June of 1851 it seemed that all the unifying labors of the previous administration had come to naught. This time there was dissent among the higher as well as lower ranks of the civil and foreign service. The internal rebellion was led by a number of respected officials, some of whom had previously been close to the ultra-conservatives. The split came when Moritz von Bethmann-Hollweg broke with the Kreuzzeitungspartei over the reactivation of the provincial estates. His new *Wochenblattpartei* (named for the party newspaper) immediately attracted the support of a number of officials who were concerned over the breach of the constitution, including Robert Graf von der Goltz, Albert Pourtalès, Karl von Usedom, and Justus Gruner, younger members of the diplomatic corps, as well as Oberregierungsrat Ludwig Mathis and other officials of the internal administration. Bethmann-Hollweg and his intimate collaborator Klemens Perthes were professors at Bonn University; and when the faction was represented in the Lower House after the election of 1852, its fourteen deputies included six administrators and one member of the judiciary.[10]

The program of the new party was by no means radical, and its flexible conservatism—so strongly reminiscent of the traditions of the Reform Era—won the support of the Prince of Prussia, the future William I, whose Koblenz residence soon became the rallying point for what was largely a western-based party.[11] Yet despite the essentially loyal character of the new faction it was soon embroiled in a bitter fight with the Kreuzzeitungspartei and its ultraconservative allies within the government—a conflict so sharp that it threatened to tear open the wounds that had been healing since the revolution. The ultras felt sufficiently confident of their own strength to insist that the dissenters, regardless of rank and reputation, either support their policies or give up office. Resistance by members of the Wochenblattpartei and their supporters among the general public only seemed to stiffen this demand for absolute obedience, and as time went on the most uncompromising among them began to take the position that their opponents not only submit but also actively support the government's reactionary policies.

This almost fratricidal conflict within conservative ranks gave those who were already advocates of total obedience a chance to press their demands. Even before the split had occurred there were indications that there were those in high places, including the king himself, who were tired of depending merely on the "neutrality" of the bureaucracy and wanted to demand more of the civil service than passive assent. As one of his first acts as Minister of the Interior, the ultra-conservative Ferdinand von Westphalen had issued an unusually frank circular outlining a new policy toward the rights and duties of state officials. In it he vowed to pursue the "strengthening of the constitutional monarchical order" with vigor and zeal, and he called on all officials to do the same. "The means to this end lie in the true fulfillment of duty by the unanimous active cooperation of the governmental agencies and in the trust and obedience of every official toward his superiors. I place my confidence in the qualities of the Prussian spirit, especially in an honest, loyal attitude toward his Royal Majesty—unshaken by the political confusion of the times." Active support of the government would be rewarded and opposition punished: "One spirit and one will must permeate and animate the entire administration."[12] Gone were the old appeals to the corporate honor of the bureaucracy. The demand for obedience overwhelmed the plea for cooperation; submissiveness was openly encouraged, and for the first time the bureaucracy was called upon to abandon all pretense of neutrality in civic affairs and to join actively in the defense of government policy.

Ironically, it was the emergence of a conservative opposition that provided the first opportunity to implement the new policy. In the spring of 1851 two Oberpräsidenten and at least two Landräte who opposed the reactivation of the provincial estates were suspended from office. The popular Oberpräsident of the Rhineland, Rudolf Auerswald, was replaced by a well-known member of the Kreuzzeitungspartei, Hans von Kleist-Retzow; and his Posen counterpart, Bonin, also a liberal-conservative, was replaced by the authoritarian Puttkamer. The Oberpräsident of Saxony, Witzleben, seems to have resigned voluntarily; his replacement was Ernst von Senfft-Pilsach, another ultra-conservative.[13]

The number dismissed undoubtedly represents only a small part of those who opposed the government. It is known that the king favored a sweeping purge; he seems, however, to have been overruled by his more cautious ministers.[14] Despite the small numbers involved, the changes that did take place signified a departure from the government's previous policies, for those who were dismissed from key positions were now being replaced by men who would not only support the government's position in a passive manner but would actively pursue its policies in the way a political ap-

pointee might be expected to do. The offices involved, though designated as "political" by the 1852 disciplinary code, had not been
used previously for purposes of control. Now, however, the appointments assumed a different character, with manipulation of
public opinion and influence over representative institutions taking precedence over purely administrative considerations.

Neutrality was clearly no longer enough; the government felt it
was time to eliminate all opposition inside and outside the bureaucracy. A ruthless battle against the well-known members of the
Wochenblattpartei who were still in government was initiated.
Members in the diplomatic service were better protected than those
in the internal bureaucracy, and were able to retain their positions
as long as they supported the government's foreign policy. Fortunately for them their views were still close to Manteuffel's, and
until the spring of 1854, when the issue of Prussia's involvement in
the Crimean struggle was still undecided, there existed a kind of
precarious alliance between them and government. But in the crisis
over the Vienna Convention in March 1854 this coalition was shat-
tered. The realistic Manteuffel refused to commit himself to the
western alliance to which the Wochenblatt diplomats were ideologically sympathetic. Bunsen, Goltz, Gruner, and Pourtalés were
forced out of office. The party lost favor at the Berlin court, and
after 1854 what little influence it had was limited to the no-man's
land of the press and the impotent parliament.[15]

A combination of considerations, both pragmatic and ideological, had prompted what would prove to be a very important change
in the government's attitude toward the bureaucracy. The demand
for almost total obedience to public and political as well as internal and administrative programs of the cabinet could not but affect
the civic attitudes of the individual official. Now that he was
viewed as an instrument of political manipulation his freedom of
action was narrowed; even more important, the distinction between his obligations as a citizen and his duties as a servant of the
state was practically eliminated. The change in the collective atti-

tudes and behavior of what was still one of Prussian society's most influential social groups was bound to have an enormous impact on both the general tone of civic affairs and the character of party politics.

The feeling that the time was right to demand something more than neutrality was encouraged by those close to the king, who had been appalled at the independence of certain officials.[16] When the right of officials to join political organizations had been discussed in 1849 the ministers had been wary of making too hasty a decision. At that time, they had waited almost a year before banning membership in an organization known to be hostile to the government.[17] Now, feeling more secure, and urged on by the king and the Kamarilla, they began an intensive housecleaning in both branches of the civil service. The unrepentant who occupied positions that came under the discipline code's "political" category were transferred or suspended. Such was the fate of Westphalian Landrat Florenz von Bochum-Dolffs, a target of government hostility since before the revolution.[18] Several other Landräte apparently met the same fate during the post Olmütz period, and even some judges lost their positions for political reasons.[19]

As might have been expected, it was the lower-ranking members who bore the brunt of the pressure. Although there is little information concerning the fate of trainees, there is some indication that a number were dismissed.[20] From the records of the highest disciplinary organ for subaltern officials, the *Dizciplinhof*, it is possible to piece together a partial picture of the kind of actions that were directed against the lowest officials. In 1852, twelve subaltern officials (including some teachers and clergy) were prosecuted for political opposition; in 1853, there were two cases; in 1854, one. Of this total, seven are known to have been relieved of their offices; the rest of the cases were either dismissed or referred back to lower levels of jurisdiction.[21]

The fact that there were few such cases would seem to indicate a certain leniency; on the other hand, it may only serve to indicate the effectiveness of the less formal pressures in use at that time. Usually it was not necessary to bring opponents of the regime before the disciplinary tribunal: they were either intimidated by subtle means or were forced out through denials of salary raises or promotions. In 1853 the king had ordered that all decisions concerning officials who were in any way suspected of radical activity during the years 1848–49 be brought to him for review.[22] The lists submitted to him by the Ministry of Justice show that it was primarily the younger officials who came under this type of surveillance.[23] As long as the immediate superior would vouch for the loyalty of the junior official, the king was almost always willing to endorse a pay raise or promotion; but this procedure placed the younger members at the mercy of those above them and thus struck one more blow at the principle of the political independence of the individual official.[24]

The same tendency was manifested in the restoration of the secret Konduitenlisten, the hated symbol of outside interference that had been suspended by popular demand in July 1848. The objection at that time had been largely to the kind of information included in these reports, and when in 1849 a system of reports was established that did not include information of a moral or political nature, there was no widespread dissent. However, the senior members of the bureaucracy soon found this system inadequate: information on the political tendencies of the official insofar as he was "hostile to the government" was deemed necessary, and in 1854 the old Konduitenlisten were reactivated.[25]

Not only the ministers but all the senior officials who cooperated in this screening process were accomplices to the gradual subordination of the bureaucracy to external political control. Reports of judicial authorities show to what extent the members of the bureaucracy were being made to conform in their daily lives to the will of the government in power. Only those judges whose political attitude was "thoroughly conservative" were to be considered for promotion, noted one directive; and only those former radicals who had "abandoned all political activity" were to be granted a raise in salary.[26] Politics was rapidly becoming a prime consideration in the personnel policies of the once-independent judicial branch.

The government found the administrative bureaucracy somewhat easier to control than the judiciary, both because its institutions permitted tighter rein and because more administrative officials were initially sympathetic to the conservative cause. Even before 1848 the judiciary had been associated closely with the political opposition. The radical movements of the pre-March period waved the banner of judicial independence when they found that they could expect from that branch the strongest support for programs of reform; and during the Revolution of 1848 the younger members of the judiciary had caused more concern than the administration, though it should be remembered that the loyalty of the administrative bureaucracy had also been called into question at that time.[27]

Some historians have suggested that the reasons behind these political differences were essentially social: that ever since the late eighteenth century the judiciary had become increasingly bourgeois in composition while the administration had followed just the opposite path.[28] But although it was true that by mid-century the majority of the judiciary were of somewhat lower social origin than their administrative counterparts, the backgrounds of the higher echelons of the two branches were not yet markedly different. In the highest courts and in the Ministry of Justice itself, the nobility continued to dominate, so that in effect the same group that controlled the administration decided the personnel policy of the judiciary as well.[29] Once again the significant difference was not between the two branches, but within the ranks of each. For example, when the issue of administrative versus judicial authority became the focus of the struggle in the 1850's, the higher echelons of the judiciary sided with the conservatives who wished to strip the courts of their right to prosecute members of the executive who, in the exercise of their official duties, had broken the civil law. As they had done so often in the past, the lower ranks stood in opposition.[30]

The question of judicial review of the administrative process was not new; the debate can be traced back to the eighteenth century. In 1797 regulations for the newly organized province of East Prussia had established the jurisdiction of regular courts over administrative officials who had violated the civil law. Although this principle was extended to all parts of Prussia in 1808, it soon became apparent that in practice the administration was still independent of judicial review. In 1842 a new law strengthened the executive's hand by leaving it to the accused's superiors to decide whether or not the contested action had been a dereliction of duty and was therefore punishable by the regular courts. This in effect reestablished the formal immunity of the administration in civil cases.[31]

The liberal upsurge of the 1840's included new pressures for judicial review: one of the major goals of the Left in 1848 was the abolition of the immunity of administrative officials; and the constitution of 1850 appeared to uphold the liberal concept that no superior should have the right to exonerate his own subordinates.[32] The law did not, however, exclude the possibility of an independent nonjudicial power deciding on the matter of jurisdiction in cases of conflict between judicial and administrative authority, and this was the loophole the government used when it proposed that the administration should have the right of appeal to the special Court of Competency. Such a body had existed since 1847 and was recognized by Article 96 of the Prussian constitution. Now the conservative government argued that it should be granted the power to decide on the right of the courts to try individual administrators. The government's bill easily passed the Upper House, slipped through the Lower by a slim 156–131 margin, and on February 13, 1854, became the law of the land.[33]

The worst fears of the opposition were not realized, however, for the new Court of Competency, a quasi-judicial board composed of both judges and executives, proved impartial in its decisions. Yet it was in principle rather than practice that the new law had its greatest impact. "Few laws of this period," wrote constitutional historian Edgar Loening, "had such a damaging effect on the morale of the people as did the law of February 13, 1854. In it they saw the completion of the police state."[34]

Although more administrative than judicial officials had voted for the bill when it passed the Lower House, there had once again been significant division between the ranks.[35] Where the principle of government under the rule of law was at stake, the upper and lower ranks of the judiciary were sharply divided; but the issues involving social antagonisms cut across rather than between the two branches of government and transcended the question of administrative versus judicial authority. The core issue was one of power, and the upper echelons of both branches rallied in support of laws that reinforced discipline, even when the laws curtailed the rights of the general public and the individual official.

The internal histories of both the administration and the judiciary during the post-revolutionary decade are full of illustrations of the self-serving attitude of the higher echelons. In December 1848 the Obertribunal at Berlin had felt it necessary to issue a public letter rebuking one of its own members, Benedikt Waldeck, for his active support of democratic radicalism during the previous nine months. In their message they made it quite clear that their greatest concern as members of Prussia's highest court was not the rights of the individual but the respectability of their profession: "We owe it to God and to man to make certain, with all the strength at our disposal, that this court retains the trust and respect of the country." Waldeck was told the most honorable thing he could do was to resign voluntarily from the judiciary.[36]

Benedikt Waldeck was not ready to give up his rights as judge and citizen quite so easily; he interpreted his duty in a different manner. Waldeck told his colleagues in a public reply that "in the interest of the whole judiciary, in the interest of the Obertribunal itself, in the interest of the public, and in the interest of the parliament, I have a holy obligation to retain my office."[37] His personal struggle against the attempt to subordinate the individual to the interests of an authoritarian state was ultimately rewarded, but it did not deter other courts from attempting to squeeze out other radicals, for example, Jodocus Temme, Julius von Kirch-mann, and Julius Gierke. Many refused to submit silently to the pressure of the authorities, but not all were successful in retaining their positions.[38]

Contemporary critics were not slow to perceive that the political conservatism of the upper echelons of the judiciary was due in large part to a desire to preserve the profession's social respecta-bility. On the issue of the admission of Jews to the civil service, members of the higher courts had shown themselves to be as exclu-sive as their administrative counterparts.[39] In their desire to main-tain their social status, they desperately tried to dissociate them-selves not only from political radicals and religious pariahs but from all those who, because of their social background, reflected unfavorably on the profession. The members of the judiciary were so transparently snobbish that Theodor von Schön described them as "guild-like" in their attitude; and Rudolf Gneist observed: "No respectable artisan guild has ever felt so completely the master class as do the jurists when it comes to their ostracized and neglected colleagues."[40]

Nothing demonstrates this trend so clearly as the political trials of the post-revolutionary decade. The government's prosecution of the deputies involved in the tax strike resolution was only the first of a series of actions instituted against the opposition.[41] The new jury system set up under the January 1849 reforms proved initially to be no great obstacle to the government's objectives. The first jury trial, the May 1849 prosecution of the playwright Robert Springer, who was accused of insulting the king, was a triumph for the conservative cause: the jury, carefully chosen to provide a favorable decision, sentenced Springer to two and a half years in prison. It seemed for the moment that the government would be free to use the jury system as a tool with which to offset the radi-cal tendencies of the professional judiciary.[42]

During the period of martial law, which lasted for most of 1849, military tribunals handled political cases. Yet the most famous trial of the period was a civil one: the prosecution of Benedikt Waldeck for treason in November and December of that year. Waldeck had been arrested and imprisoned in May, but was not formally charged until November, partly because the government had some difficulty in building a case against him. The state's most important evidence, a letter from the well-known radical Carl D'Ester, implicating Waldeck in a revolutionary plot, was disqualified in a preliminary hearing as a forgery. The state's case had to be revised, and it was not until November 28 that the accused was brought before a Berlin jury and charged with having knowledge of a highly treasonable enterprise but failing to report it to the authorities. The state's chief witness and Waldeck's codefendant, Joseph Ohm, then showed himself to be a perjurer. At this point the proceedings became so embarrassing that the chief state prosecutor, Sethe, was forced to ask for Waldeck's acquittal. On December 3 the proceedings ended, the jury acquitted Waldeck and recommended action against Ohm. In one of the most impressive mass demonstrations since the March Days of 1848, a large crowd of Berliners greeted Waldeck as a conquering hero.[43]

Soon after Waldeck's acquittal, another Berlin jury found innocent all but one of those accused in connection with the tax strike resolution.[44] In April 1850, the government began prosecution of those Prussian deputies to the Frankfurt National Assembly who had participated in the Stuttgart rump parliament. Jodocus Temme and Johann Jacoby, among others, were tried for treason against the German Confederation and the Prussian state. Temme, then Vice President of the Münster Court of Appeals, was acquitted by the jury. The government, determined to remove him from that post, then moved to charge him under the provisions of the 1849 discipline regulations with neglect of office. Early in 1851 the Obertribunal found him guilty of this charge, and he was dropped from office without pension. The king later offered Temme the dependent position of Staatsanwalt, but he refused it and made a career for himself as a journalist and parliamentarian.[45]

The trial in 1850 of Gottfried Kinkel and those who participated

with him in the abortive Rhineland insurrection of May 1849, and
the famous proceeding against eleven members of the Communist
League, held in October 1852, concluded the series of prosecutions
that had begun in December 1848.[46] The government's enthusiasm
for the jury system had gradually and understandably diminished,
and it was turning increasingly to the professional judiciary as an
instrument more suitable to its purposes. In April 1853 a law was
passed transferring the jurisdiction of all political crimes—treason,
insurrection, assault on the king—to the Berlin Kammergericht.[47]
But even with this weapon at its disposal the government still
found it necessary to use extralegal means. In the October 1854
Kammergericht trial of the democratic journalist Dr. August Ladendorf and nine others charged with high treason, the government was again exposed to ridicule when it was revealed that the
police had planted an *agent provocateur* in the Ladendorf circle.
During the early stages of the investigation one judge, Schlötke,
and a state prosecutor, Nörner, refused to prosecute the case. They
were replaced by two more amenable officials, Judge Holzapfel
and Oberstaatsanwalt Schwarck. All but one of the Ladendorf
group received prison terms.[48]

Except for a few jurists like Schlötke and Nörner, the Prussian
judiciary seems to have been willing to cooperate with the executive branch by overlooking cases of illegal action on the part of
the police. By the mid-50's the police were able to evade even the
constitutional right of all prisoners to be charged and brought before a judge within a reasonable time, an evasion that would not
have been possible without the consent of the judicial officials.
According to Wilhelm Stieber, secret meetings during the 1850's
between representatives of the Ministry of Justice, the state prosecutor's office, and Hinkeldey's police paved the way for an accommodation permitting such practices: the judiciary agreed to look
the other way while the police arrested, searched, and confiscated
without legal sanction.[49]

Contemporary observers could not help but note the degree to
which the judiciary subordinated its obligation to the law to the

requirements of government policy. The administration, particularly the police, were not only allowed to violate the constitutional guarantees of individual rights, but were permitted to encroach on the independence of the courts.[50] The state prosecutor's office was serving the authoritarian purposes for which it was designed, transforming the Prussian court system into an instrument of political oppression. Even the lower ranks of the judiciary, persuaded and coerced by every instrument available to the authorities, were gradually coming to view themselves as instruments for the protection of the state against its enemies.[51]

The changing attitude of officials toward their professional duties was part of a more general transformation that also encompassed the individual bureaucrat's conception of his responsibilities as a citizen. The post-Olmütz policy of imposing ever-tighter controls over administrative and judicial personnel was bound to extend to that area as well, and in the 1850's there was a definite tendency toward greater conformity in the private as well as the public life of the profession. Westphalen's demand for complete obedience on the part of each and every official admitted no distinction between the individual's roles as citizen and functionary. Although the goal of total conformity was never achieved during the 1850's, a point was reached in the history of the bureaucracy when the traditional concept of the double role of the official had a diminishing influence on the behavior of both branches of service.

Before 1851 little attempt had been made to use officials in electoral politics. The government had been content to warn its employees against open opposition and to rely on their neutrality on issues that presented a conflict between their obligations as servants of the state and their interests as private citizens or elected representatives. The government had not attempted to organize its own parties within the parliament, partly because men like Manteuffel distrusted modern representative institutions, partly because they entertained some vague hope for the eventual restoration of an estate system. But when this proved totally impracticable even the most stubborn conservatives began to look upon parliament as a stabilizing force that might not only curb radical tendencies among the general population but could also serve as a check on opposition elements within the apparatus of the state itself. At first suspecting the parliament to be an instrument of bureaucratic radicalism, conservatives had come to see it as a tool to be used against their domestic enemies.[52]

They began cautiously, testing new ways of controlling parliament until they found the ones most useful to their purposes. It did not take long to determine the utility of the bureaucracy itself in electoral matters; and beginning with the by-elections in late 1850, the conservative faction began to bring the weight of the civil and military services into play.[53] By virtue of their numbers alone, state employees represented a formidable political weapon in Prussia. Those directly or indirectly employed by the state— railway men, certain kinds of construction and mining workers, some local officials, as well as lower and higher administrators, judges, Protestant clergy, and all levels of the teaching profession— numbered an estimated 98,000. The addition of some 132,000 military personnel brings the total of men within the real or potential scope of government control close to 230,000.[54]

Such a figure seems insignificant in a country with an eligible voting population of almost three million, but when the low voter-participation rate of the 1850's is considered, the number begins to take on its true importance. In 1855, when participation reached its lowest point, only 471,170 of the 2,908,156 eligible to vote chose to do so. What this could mean in a garrison town or an important administrative center is shown by the July 1849 election in Trier: of 2,663 qualified voters, only 707 exercised their right; of this group, 370 were state employees, a fact that aided the conservatives enormously in their successful attempts to win and hold the Trier electoral district during the 1850's.[55]

The government was now encouraged to begin to bring pressure on those officials already in parliament whose position might be influenced by subtle forms of persuasion or coercion. Prime targets were the moderate liberals, a group that could be counted on to follow the government lead only so long as the official policies were compatible with their principles.[56] During and after the Olmütz crisis, members of this group were confronted with a serious moral-political decision, the choice between the demands of their consciences and those of their profession. Under pressure from the government to support its policies, some chose to go into active opposition, while others decided to abandon their principles. A few, on the other hand, volunteered during the Olmütz crisis to lay down their mandates, thus solving the conflict between conscience and office by renouncing politics altogether. At least one official was ordered explicitly to relinquish his political rights; and if the government's own reports are correct, there were several more who volunteered to remove themselves from public affairs for the sake of their careers.[57]

The government moved swiftly to reinforce its position by supporting reliable deputies. On October 16, 1850, Manteuffel ordered the district presidents to direct their attention to the encouragement of conservative candidates in by-elections. Despite efforts to win seats made vacant by resignations, the results were indifferent: four conservatives were elected, but so were two liberals.[58] Nevertheless a new tactic was revealed, the full implementation of which awaited the general election of October 1852. On October 7, two weeks before the balloting, Minister of the Interior Westphalen issued a series of instructions assigning the heads of the administration in each province responsibility for marshaling their subordinates. They were told that passive support of the government program was no longer sufficient: vigorous, active participation by all officials in the "conservative" crusade was required. Westphalen warned that the political activities of all officials would be under surveillance—a threat that did not need elaboration.[59]

The 1852 election also represented a turning point in another important respect. Previously the government had been willing to depend for support on those traditional conservative groups, primarily the landed aristocracy, who were already well represented in parliament. Together with the more conservative elements of the industrial bourgeoisie, they had been the ones who had provided the major support for government programs and were the major point of contact between the state and society outside the formal channels of the bureaucracy. Now, for reasons that were tactical as well as strategic, the government began looking for new ways of controlling parliament that would make the cabinet less dependent on the old elites. Because he had been engaged in a bitter dispute with the Kreuzzeitungspartei over tariff policies throughout the summer of 1852, Manteuffel was extremely eager to dispense with the support of that particular group.[60] He ordered officials to support only those candidates who had shown themselves to be absolutely loyal to government policy, and "above all else to guard against division and self-interested objectives within the conservative party itself."[61] Thus the Manteuffel regime turned its back on a major segment of its former allies and began building new bases of strength in and outside parliament.

The strategy was to use the bureaucracy in a way it had not been used before: immediately, as an instrument with which to elect hand-picked candidates; ultimately, as a reservoir of such candidates. Beginning in 1852 members of the civil service were to play a leading role in the formation of a new governmental party, a party as distinct from the old right as from the old left. The burden of the task fell to the administration, particularly the state officials in the towns and the Landräte in the countryside. In 1852 they were ordered to avoid all appearance of direct intervention, but to find suitable candidates and support them with whatever legal means were at their disposal.[62]

The shift in bases of support could not be accomplished overnight, and the elections of October 1852 were a disappointment to the more optimistic in the Manteuffel cabinet. The old moderate liberal factions lost about a quarter of their former strength, but a new opposition party, the Catholics, emerged to fill this gap.

Reacting against recently imposed restrictions on the freedom of the priesthood, the Catholics demonstrated their great political power.[63] In all, the liberals and Catholics combined could count on more than two hundred votes, a majority of the Lower House. The government could be assured of the absolute loyalty of only 121 members. The Kreuzzeitungspartei, numbering twenty-six, continued to play the role of right-wing opposition.[64]

The government was more careful in preparing for the next general election, to be held in October 1855, which would involve the crucial issue of Prussia's role in the Crimean conflict. Once again the conservative right was in disarray; both the Wochenblattpartei and the Kreuzzeitungspartei opposed the neutrality policy of the ministry, thus making it even more necessary that the government create its own loyal faction.[65] On May 18, 1855, Westphalen issued an unprecedented circular to the Oberpräsidenten setting forth the tactics to be used in the coming electoral contest.[66] It established a precedent for later government interference by sanctioning every device short of ballot-stuffing. Officials were ordered to propagandize the government's program in the local press. Conservative clubs and associations were to be mobilized in the interest of the state; local officials were to use their influence in the election committees to eliminate opponents from the voter lists. Beyond this, they were to consider the possibilities of the "appropriate structuring of electoral districts."[67] Before the 1855 election gerrymandering became general practice, with the normally liberal urban and conservative rural areas effectively segregated, safe districts combined, and areas of opposition isolated.[68] In addition, the administration was encouraged to select polling places that would by the nature of their location favor the loyalist cause.[69]

Of equal significance was the pressure brought to bear on the bureaucrats themselves. Reliable officials were urged to present themselves as candidates; known dissenters were warned to stay out of politics. The Landräte were informed that where reliable conservative candidates were not available, it would be "advisable" for the Landräte to present themselves for election.[70] In at least one case the government, distrusting the loyalty of the local Regierungspräsident, sent in its own agent to supervise the organization of the election.[71] In a circular to all district presidents on September 15, Westphalen warned that in earlier sessions of parliament a number of officials had been conspicuous in the ranks of the opposition, but that now this condition would be tolerated no longer. Local officials were told that they could expect the active cooperation of all the other branches of government, including the clergy and the teachers.[72] Even the supposedly "impartial" judiciary had been instructed to support the governmental candidates.[73] On September 19 Raumer pledged the full support of his subordinates to Westphalen's policies, and three days later Heydt promised the allegiance of the postal, telegraph, railroad, construction, and banking officials as well.[74]

The total strength of the bureaucracy had been mobilized in an attempt to create what amounted to a single-party parliament. The government had learned its lessons well. In contrast to 1852, religious differences were to be minimized and ideology subordinated to the interests of electoral victory. Westphalen, who was normally sympathetic to the Protestant cause, reprimanded the Rhineland's pietist Oberpräsident Hans von Kleist-Retzow for displacing a Catholic Landrat from one of the Düsseldorf district election committees. The man in question had had a long record of political loyalty; his removal would only be detrimental to the government cause.[75]

The primary target of the government's campaign was partisanship, whether of the left or the right. This was a theme that had been heard before—though now the definition of hostile partisanship was expanded to include neutrality toward, as well as opposition to, the official position. The success of this strategy was recorded in an overwhelming victory by governmental candidates. The left opposition (including Catholics) was reduced from over

200 deputies to 125; the loyalist faction now numbered 190, a gain of some seventy seats, while the independent conservatives managed to elect only 42 deputies. Most striking was the increase in the number of administrative officials, particularly Landräte, whose numbers increased from 52 to 76. Because of their victory the next session of the Lower House was called by critics the Landratskammer.[76]

Westphalen was understandably pleased with the results of the elections of 1855. He could report that despite the attempts by the Catholics and the partisans of Bethmann-Hollweg to elect "socalled independent men," the bureaucrats had proved useful in building a governmental majority. Only in Berlin, Frankfurt an der Oder, and Königsberg had there been any serious opposition among civil servants—and steps were being taken to prevent a recurrence of that unfortunate situation. A few notables like Freiherr von Bunsen, Robert von Patow, and Count Schwerin had resisted government pressure, but their number was too small to cause concern. The bureaucracy as a whole had proved obligingly loyal in matters political; the government could be assured, said Westphalen, of a solid working majority in the next session of parliament.[77]

On the basis of the election returns of 1855, few would have been willing to contest Westphalen's optimism. It seemed that the government had successfully transferred its base of power from the coalition of traditional conservative groups that it had relied on immediately after the revolution to an almost totally obedient bureaucracy. Ironically, though the shift had an immediate effect on Prussian political development, it was of little use to the Manteuffel regime in 1858, when a combination of events surrounding the incapacitating illness of Frederick William IV brought about a major cabinet reorganization in which both Westphalen and Manteuffel were forced out of office. Nevertheless, the effect of their manipulative tactics on the bureaucracy itself was undoubtedly profound and lasting.

As far as politics was concerned, the period of transition that had begun in the 1840's was now coming to a close. Prussia had found a new and definite direction during the decade of reaction; the policies regarding the bureaucracy initiated at that time had set her on a course that would be adjusted but not basically altered in the decades to come. As the decade turned, the changes in the political character of the bureaucracy were still more potential than actual; nevertheless, a transformation of great significance had begun that was to set the precedent for the future.

Chapter Eight

The Bureaucracy and the Politics of Reaction

From the very beginning the government's policy of using members of the civil service for political purposes led to intense controversy. Spokesmen for both the extreme left and the extreme right denounced it, the former as a threat to the principle of liberty and equality for all citizens, and the latter as an example of the dangerous centralization of power that had taken place in the 1850's. These were the groups most adversely affected by the intrusion of the civil service into political affairs; they were, in addition, the groups that recognized the irreparable harm that was being done by the corruption of individual officials and destruction of public confidence in the integrity and impartiality of the profession. Johann Gustav Droysen seems to have summarized the feelings of a broad spectrum of opinion when he wrote of the Landratskammer that "its deeper meaning lies in the confirmation of the complete dependence of the once proud and independent Prussian bureaucracy."[1]

Not all Prussian officials surrendered their political independence, nor did public respect for the profession disappear suddenly during the period under consideration. Nevertheless, it is possible to detect the growth of a political timidity and conformity that manifested itself in the parliamentary politics of the post-revolutionary decade. During the 1852–1855 session of the Lower House, 65 percent of the administrative personnel (including Landräte) and 23 percent of the judicial officials (including prosecutors, but excluding lawyers) who sat as deputies were members of factions that can best be described as pro-government. An analysis of the deputies elected in 1855 reveals that the percentage had risen since 1852 to 78 percent for administrators and 53 percent for judiciary—changes in line with trends that began as early as 1849.

These figures would hardly be an indication of changes within the bureaucracy as a whole if they represented external pressure rather than internal evolution. Therefore it is important to compare the allegiance of the "political" officials, who were particularly vulnerable to government influence, with that of the regular officials, whose tenure was relatively secure, to determine whether the shift toward conservatism was real or only apparent. The results show that the regular officials had a similar if not greater tendency to align themselves with the pro-government factions during the 1850's. Even the most independent branch, the judiciary, demonstrated a trend that must be interpreted as more than just a temporary phenomenon.

The offices that were designated as "political" in 1849 had traditionally been strongholds of conservatism. In the 1852–1855 session of the Lower House, 74 percent of the cabinet ministers, Ober- and Regierungspräsidenten, and Landräte were already closely aligned with the pro-government factions; 80 percent of the Staatsanwälte, the only "political" offices within the judicial ranks, were also loyal. These percentages increased slightly during the next session of parliament, but on the whole the pattern of conservatism among the office-holders followed a predictable pattern.

Of the regular officials, whose tenure was relatively secure and who were less subject to government pressure, there was a convincing shift toward conformity during the same period. In the 1852–1855 session of the Lower House 38 percent of the regular administrators in parliament who belonged to a recognized faction were members of the pro-government coalition; in the next session, the percentage remained about the same. But among the judges who were members of parliamentary parties during the same two sessions, the percentage of loyalists rose from 12 to 33 percent.

When these figures are broken down by rank it is found that the same drift toward conformity occurred on every level of the judiciary. In the 1852–1855 parliamentary session all the lower-ranking judges had been members of opposition factions; after the 1855 elections, only two-thirds were in opposition. The middle ranks of the judicial branch show a similar though less radical shift of allegiance.[2]

These figures do not tell us all we would like to know about the attitudes of the bureaucracy, but they serve to indicate a turning point in the political history of the profession. While it is true that the officials who won seats in parliament were not entirely representative, and that some officials who opposed the government had been forced out of public politics, while many more had simply withdrawn in order to protect themselves against harassment, there can be little doubt that the attitudes of those who were still active reflected a general shift away from the patterns of the previous decade. As far as the members of the higher echelons were concerned, loyalty to the government had been a habit; they were the men closest to power, and it was their ideas that were embodied in many of the government programs. The gradual submission of the lower ranks constituted a far more significant change, however, for it signaled the easing of some of the earlier divisions and the emergence of a new breed of officials, drawn both from the senior ranks and from among the disillusioned younger men but practicing a form of politics different by virtue of its pragmatism from that of either the traditional corporate conservatives or the democratic radicals.

One other related trend is worth noting. Throughout the 1850's the proportion of officials who avoided confrontation between their consciences and the orders of their superiors by staying aloof from political action grew steadily. In the 1852–1855 session 13 percent of the administrators and 2 percent of the judiciary personnel were designated as independent. In the next session the proportions of unattached officials were 19 percent and 13 percent, respectively.[3] The officials who gave their loyalty to the government factions and those who opted for neutrality might seem to represent two opposing tendencies, but in reality they represented the same general pattern of behavior: disengagement from independent participation in political affairs.

The effects of a decade of political reaction were nowhere more clearly revealed than in the events that immediately followed the termination of the Manteuffel-Westphalen administration. In 1858, when the future William I became regent in place of the ailing Frederick William, one of his first acts after forming a moderate liberal government was to forbid all direct influence in the electoral process. The new cabinet, which included several members of the Bethmann-Hollweg party who had themselves been victims of such interference during the 1850's, were scrupulous in their behavior during the elections held in the fall of 1858. Pressure on officials to support selected candidates ceased and the government made no attempt to form its own party. The 1858 elections resulted in an overwhelming liberal victory that swept into office many officials who had not sat in parliament for almost ten years. The composition of the Lower House reverted to a pattern much like that of early 1849: the number of Landräte was cut to a third, and the judiciary doubled its representation. A number of the radicals of the 1840's, including Kirchmann, Unruh, Schulze-Delitzsch, and Waldeck, took up their old places either in 1858 or in elections held during the early 1860's.[4] Everything gave the impression of a complete return to the pattern of the pre-Olmütz period, as if nothing had happened during the intervening period of reaction.

On closer observation, however, it becomes clear that much had been altered. The whole spectrum of opinion had shifted so far to the right that those who sat on the left of the House elected in 1858 were moderate liberals or members of the Catholic faction rather than the radical democrats who previously dominated that position. Even former radicals who had returned to take up their places in parliamentary life were no longer inclined to the same position they had taken a decade before. The majority had long since dissociated themselves from all revolutionary action and were ready to work within the existing system in support of gradual reform. They were older now, better established in the professions, and generally more willing to compromise with the very forces they opposed with such fervor a decade before. Noticeably missing among the oppositional officials in the parliaments of the 1860's was the type of younger man so prominent earlier. Of twenty bureaucrats who were disciplined for their parliamentary opposition by the Bismarck government during the 1860's, the average age was forty-seven in 1862—considerably older than the radical officials in 1848. The fact that the leaders in the 1860's were the survivors of previous decades was a clear sign that no new generation of radicals was stepping forward. When they were gone, a unique epoch in the history of the bureaucracy would be over.[5]

During the constitutional conflict of the period between 1862 and 1867 some of the old oppositional tendencies of the bureaucracy, particularly among members of the judiciary, appeared to revive, and for a short time it seemed that the radicalism of the 1840's had not disappeared entirely. A fifth of the membership of the Progressive Party, the leading opposition faction, was composed of judicial officials; and most of the bureaucrats elected to the Lower House during those years were members of the anti-government coalition.[6] The resurgence of what Otto von Bismarck scornfully called "Geheimrat liberalism" did not fail to arouse the concern of conservatives who remembered 1848. No one was more determined to reimpose discipline than Bismarck and his ruthless Minister of the Interior, Graf von Eulenberg. With the weapons that the Manteuffel-Westphalen administration had placed at their disposal, they proceeded to issue a series of orders reminding officials of their duty to provide "unreserved support to the crown." Offenders were subjected to considerable harassment, and eventually two Oberpräsidenten and four Regierungsräte were transferred, while two Staatsanwälte and one Landrat were removed by suspension.[7] The judicial offenders proved more difficult to discipline, but again the government found the higher courts willing to act against dissenting junior officials. Using the conservative Obertribunal as its primary disciplinary agent, the Bismarck ministry managed by one means or another to remove sixteen judges from office.[8]

Yet despite these attempts to repress dissent, the Bismarck-Eulenberg government did not resort to the mobilization of officials for electoral purposes on anything like the scale of the 1850's. With a few exceptions, they were content with passive obedience rather than active support—a highly significant change of tactics that illustrated a shift in the politics of the bureaucracy itself.[9] Apparently Bismarck did not feel it necessary or advisable to use officials as instruments for establishing a governmental party; indeed, he tried to have officials excluded from the new Reichstag. He may have been influenced by the fact that a part of the bureaucracy, notably the judiciary, was already in opposition to the government over the constitutional issue, but it is unlikely that this was his only reason. The Manteuffel government had used its bureaucracy despite this type of internal opposition, and Bismarck could undoubtedly have done the same—but now there was another, more compelling reason, why the bureaucracy could not be relied on as a basis for political support inside and outside parliament, namely, the tendency among Prussian officials since the late 1850's to withdraw from active participation in politics. The constitutional crisis of the 1860's, in which many bureaucrats participated, would seem to prove the opposite; but it was a temporary phenomenon, and by the 1870's the percentage of officials in parliament began a steady decline. Bismarck must have realized that Manteuffel's experiments in the 1850's had to a certain extent misfired, insofar as the pressure on officials had made this group generally less accessible to both the government and the opposition. This may have influenced his decision to rely on a brilliant foreign policy rather than internal coercion to build support for his government.[10]

The withdrawal of officials from politics was a gradual one whose true proportions were not entirely evident until after the 1860's. The constitutional conflict and the crisis of German unification were the last occasions for the involvement of large numbers of state officials in parliamentary politics. In the decades between unification and World War I, the percentage of civil servants in the Lower House declined considerably. During the period 1848–1867 the proportion of state officials in the Prussian Lower House averaged 38 percent—the highest point being reached at 50 percent in 1855 and the lowest at 29 percent in 1848. In the years 1873–1912, the average declined to 24 percent, with a low of 17 percent in 1904.[11] Even the efforts of Puttkamer in the 1880's to ensure the conservatism of the provincial bureaucracy produced very mixed results and did not reverse the trend away from politics.

This notable decline in the participation of state officials in parliamentary politics is attributable to a number of factors, only some of which are related to the changes in the bureaucracy itself. In part, it was simply a reflection of the transformation of Prussian political life—particularly the displacement of the educated elites, of which the bureaucracy was the most prominent. With the emergence of organized political parties, local notables were no longer able to dominate electoral politics: voters made their choices less on the basis of local loyalties or social deference and more on ideological positions or interest-group calculations. As the broader political and constitutional concerns of the revolutionary period were replaced by specific economic, social, and religious issues, the qualities that the members of the bureaucracy could offer, namely, training in jurisprudence and practical experience with legal problems, were no longer at a premium. New groups such as the Catholic clergy, landowners, businessmen, lawyers, and journalists were overcoming their former inhibitions about participation in public affairs and emerging as representatives of the interest groups that soon were to dominate Prussian political life. Only in those cases where the state official was closely associated with some special interest group, as were the Catholic judges or the Landräte of the eastern provinces, was he willing or able to draw on the kind of support necessary for election. For most bureaucrats there was little opportunity or incentive to participate in an activity so for-

eign to their training and to the day-to-day tasks of their profession.[12]

Some of these factors were already at work in the 1850's. The
organization of political parties was still in a primitive state, but
the shift from general to specific issues and the tendency toward
interest-group politics were already apparent. The constitutional
crisis of the 1860's injected political and legal issues once again,
but once it was solved, the trend away from the older forms of
politics resumed at an accelerated pace. The reactionary 1850's had
made their own unique contribution to these trends, however.
To all those factors in society at large that were working to exclude
state officials from politics, there must be added the effect of the
government's manipulation of the civil service at a time when
political consciousness of the bureaucracy was in a formative stage.
Something that is not revealed by the election results of the decade
of reaction is the fact that government pressure on officials had
actually proven unproductive: instead of resulting in the desired
involvement of officials in public affairs, it had influenced many
of them to retreat to the safety of apolitical attitudes and to disen-
gage from all forms of civil responsibility. By 1860 much of this
change was more potential than actual; nevertheless, it is possible
with a small amount of hindsight to detect those trends that became manifest in the 1870's and 1880's.

Prussian civil servants had discovered that there was little to be
gained and much to be lost by drawing attention to themselves
through political activity. In other European political systems a
man might enhance his career by partisan affiliations, but such
rewards were limited in the already highly professional Prussian
bureaucratic system. In France and England a parliamentary career often led to high office, but in Prussia the positions officially
designated as "political" were used only sparingly for patronage
purposes; and when a man was so rewarded, care was taken that
he become reasonably well qualified for the position either through
practical experience or academic training. Furthermore, the num-

ber of positions set aside for political patronage were few in comparison to the large number of offices that were available for that purpose in France, England, and other European countries. Ministerial rank and the office of Oberpräsident were the plums most often awarded for political loyalty, and there were only about twenty of these positions available. Of course there were the nonbureaucratic offices and honorary positions, but these would not have been attractive to members of the civil service. The tradition of seniority also discouraged the practice of advancement through patronage, so that relatively few officials entered politics with any hope of bettering their careers.[13]

On the other hand, activity in public affairs, even when free of all taint of opposition, was potentially damaging to a man's professional chances. A distrust of democratic politics lingered among the higher ranks of the government. The king had never completely reconciled himself to the public activities of state officials; and those bureaucrats who held most strongly to the corporate tradition felt that party politics was a demeaning endeavor incompatible with the professional standards of the Beamtenstand.[14]

Traditional inhibitions against political participation were reinforced by the social and economic difficulties that continued to plague the bureaucracy throughout the 1850's. As long as overcrowding and underemployment persisted, many found it desirable to lay low. Ironically, some of the same forces that had first produced political activism now—under the shadow cast by the failure of the revolution—encouraged withdrawal from public affairs. To the dedicated minority for whom the exercise of the rights of citizenship was a matter of democratic principle, this did not really matter; but for the vast majority of officials who had to make the choice between political rights to which they were only partially committed and the security of an office on which they were wholly dependent, discretion proved the better part of valor. On the whole they preferred to relinquish their rights of citizenship rather than risk the possibility of incurring the disfavor of their superiors, whose notations in the secret personnel files might damage their careers irreparably.

Some, like Rudolf von Delbrück, rationalized this behavior by convincing themselves that active citizenship would decrease rather than increase their influence on public policy.[15] They learned to argue that they could accomplish more behind a desk than on the floor of parliament, and from this narrowly professional point of view evolved a concept of citizenship that was strongly elitist in character. The government encouraged this subordination of public to private values by following a policy of rewarding those of its opponents who were willing to give up their political opposition in return for employment. On the assumption that a man could be controlled inside more easily than outside the bureaucracy, Manteuffel and Westphalen made ever effort to lure former enemies into the civil service. Jodocus Temme, who had been dismissed as a judge, was offered a state prosecutor's position, while Hans Viktor von Unruh was encouraged to return to his job in the state railway system by the same men who had persistently harassed him.[16] Two other noted democrats of the 1848 period, Wilhelm Stieber and Friedrich Held, were placed in official positions, and others, both democrats and liberals, were absorbed by the establishment during the course of the 1850's.[17]

Perhaps the most notable application of this subtle tactic was the government's handling of Benedikt Waldeck, the Supreme Court judge who had become the symbol of the resistance within the bureaucracy. All attempts by his colleagues on the higher court to persuade Waldeck to resign failed; his trial for treason in late 1850 ended in acquittal. That such a man should be allowed to continue in public service seemed improbable, yet he was permitted to remain at his post. Documents of the Ministry of Justice reveal, however, that Waldeck's tenure on the high court was contingent on one all-important stipulation—his withdrawal from all political activity. In a reply to a query from Frederick William concerning the wisdom of Waldeck's retention, Minister of Justice Ludwig Simons assured the king: "Since those years [1848–49] Waldeck had held back completely from political activity and has not taken up his mandate as a deputy again...." Since Waldeck's immediate superiors found him quite competent in the fulfillment of his professional duties, there were no grounds for further action.[18]

After his trial Waldeck had refrained from opposition politics, reemerging only in the early 1860's as a member of the liberal opposition to Bismarck. While he seems to have mellowed somewhat toward the Manteuffel regime, his motives for staying in office seem also to have been based on a realistic appraisal of the slim chances for radical activity in the hostile environment of the 1850's.[19] There were others who remained in office for similar tactical reasons, but many more gave up their political rights because they had no alternative but state employment. As Hans Viktor von Unruh wrote of his fellow countrymen: "There are times when immediate material interests predominate so much that they not only submerge ideal goals and the love of civic freedom, but they even force the most obvious disadvantages of reactionary government into the background."[20] Most officials seem to have accepted the de facto limitation of their constitutional rights passively, for after the excitement and confusion of the revolutionary period they had become totally absorbed in their particular functions and were no longer interested in viewing Prussia's problems from a broad political perspective. As Johann Gustav Droysen observed, the Prussian government became no more than "a federation of ministries, and every ministry a federation of officials, each with his own specialty."[21] The Prussian bureaucracy was now frequently compared to an impersonal machine, its members to well-drilled automatons. Karl Varnhagen von Ense, a liberal, described the contemporary civil service as being made up of spiritless little men, capable of no higher idealism, "indifferent to right and wrong, choking on truth, insolently cherishing lies."[22] The conservative Kreuzzeitung was equally vociferous in its attacks, equating "neutrality" with an absence of moral principle.[23]

The pattern of bureaucratic behavior was not much different from that of Prussian society as a whole. The civil service, particularly its upper ranks, had abandoned its claims to political leadership and become one among a number of competing interest groups. By the 1850's its members had established an unenviable reputation for crass opportunism, for putting their own social and material needs ahead of the common good. Wilhelm Lette, a liberal with extensive bureaucratic experience, wrote of the careerism within the civil service; and Rudolf Gneist, speaking contemptuously of the quality of liberalism among a large part of the judiciary, wrote: "With fixed salaries, with a set promotion to higher positions, with the irremovability and untransferability of judicial personnel, they think they have everything necessary to maintain the independence of the judiciary."[24]

This is not to say that the private integrity of the average official had been corrupted. On the contrary, the Prussian bureaucracy remained remarkably free of petty scandal; its reputation for honest, efficient government was hardly challenged throughout the period of transition. What suffered was not the personal morality of the civil service, but the civic spirit of the members. As early as 1849 Rudolf Gneist noted that the higher bureaucracy was afflicted by a peculiar form of schizophrenia. "I have often been shocked by the theoretical radicalism of the higher officialdom and the way it often appears honest in private, while in official life, for reasons understood only by itself, it accommodates itself to the system. Among these important and formerly important men there develop two different natures, the official and the private, the latter often amiable and liberal, but the former ready to sell out to the system as long as it facilitates admittance to the circle of the initiated.... To learn how one can serve a system against one's conscience and conviction for an entire lifetime, one must be a Prussian official; to know how one covers the disgrace of abandoned conviction with a title or a decoration, one must know the secrets of the higher bureaucracy."[25]

For those Prussians who believed that the public responsibilities of the members of the bureaucracy should transcend the narrow limits of self-interest, these trends were deeply disturbing. Members of right and left found themselves united in condemning a system that deprived the public life of the country of the talents of

one of its most respected groups. Many conservatives, remembering
the role that the bureaucracy had once played under the preconstitutional system, yearned for a return to the guidance of a public-
spirited elite. The liberals and democrats defended the right of the
individual official to the full exercise of citizenship, not out of a
desire for the return of the bureaucratic absolutism, but as a matter
of constitutional principle. One liberal Geheimrat is reported to
have forbidden his four sons to follow in his professional footsteps
and to have apprenticed them to businesses where, as he put it,
"they can still have their honor with their bread and some freedom
besides."[26] Josias Freiherr von Bunsen, the Prussian ambassador to
London whose conflict with Manteuffel during the Crimean War
had led to his own ouster, wrote to his son: "I will not educate one
more son for that miserable diet (*Hungerbrot*) of servitude, the
bureaucracy. Believe me, the country demands from our class during this next thirty years men who will promote the good of the
community, men who have neither bureaucratic training nor juri-
dical expertise, but independence. It is Germanic foolishness to
believe that one can create a free people through officials and
professors."[27]

Bunsen was a distinguished representative of the educated notables who during the previous thirty years had served as Prussia's
political elite. Now men with the broad sense of public service that
Bunsen possessed were becoming increasingly rare in high office.
Some had left office rather than submit to the authoritarianism
that had become part of the routine of government; most stayed
on, attempting to maintain their private moral integrity by making compromises with the existing system. For the most part the
civil servants of the 1850's were simply prisoners of their careers,
one-dimensional men attempting to buy personal security by sur-
rendering their civil rights.

The more the government succeeded in deactivating the bureaucracy politically, the more it reinforced the very aspects of bureaucratic absolutism that its leaders sought to avoid. In effect, the

Manteuffel-Westphalen regime had deprived Prussia of a vigorous independent parliament, thereby forfeiting its own opportunity to free itself from the kind of excessive dependence on bureaucracy that had plagued its predecessors in the preconstitutional period. After the November coup a parliamentary democracy was out of the question, but the possibility of an effective working relationship between the executive and the legislature that would allow the cabinet to use the Lower House as a sounding board for its policies was not out of the question. There were those in the conservative government, including Manteuffel himself, who foresaw a role for parliament consistent with the Prussian tradition of strong executive authority; and if they had felt that they could rely on parliament for responsible advice and consent, they might have invested it with greater power.[28] But in the 1850's the Prussian Lower House was already showing the signs of faulty leadership and internal disunity that were to plague it for the duration of the century. A parliament that was too malleable, too sensitive to government influence, was no more useful than one that was too rigid in its opposition; and the relatively abrupt shift from one extreme to another during the decade following the revolution did little to convince doubters of the usefulness of a relatively strong, well-organized legislature.

It was in large part the government's own fault that it was forced to rely on officialdom in much the same way that it had done in the preconstitutional era. The history of the pre-March parliaments in other parts of Germany had shown that the executive could permit its officials the right of public dissent without unduly endangering its own power. In Baden a moderate degree of tension had existed between the government and a parliamentary opposition without disruptive effects, and the parliament had been sufficiently representative of public opinion to provide the government with an accurate indicator of the effectiveness and popularity of its programs. State officials acting in their capacity as elected representatives had shown themselves capable of assuming the role of responsible citizens while at the same time continuing to function efficiently as employees of the state.[29] In Prussia such a relationship was nearly impossible, because the bureaucrats who sat as deputies could not be expected to perform both as puppets of the government and reliable witnesses to public opinion. When they did occasionally break ranks, it was too often for purely selfish reasons, as in the case of the opposition to the budget during the 1855-1858 session, when officials demanded higher salaries as the price of their support.[30] On most issues in which the public interest was involved they were simply unresponsive, and no government could rely on their attitude to measure the popularity of its programs.

Other social groups were not yet ready to assume the role of public leadership that had previously been the bureaucracy's. In depriving the parliament of the most important single source of intelligent leadership, the government had forfeited the opportunity to emancipate itself from dependence on its own functionaries. Much of the difficulty that Manteuffel experienced in maintaining the unity of his cabinet was directly attributable to the absence of representative institutions strong enough to require the effective leadership of a prime minister. The various departments went their own ways, often more under the control of their permanent staff than the minister in charge. As Bismarck found when he took command in 1862, the ministerial bureaucracy was capable of exercising enormous influence by virtue of its expertise.[31] The absence of a strong, independent legislative branch also made it more difficult for the prime minister to control the influence of both the king and such extraconstitutional bodies as the Kamarilla, whose power would have been far more limited had the cabinet been able to use the argument of ministerial responsibility against its intrigues.[32]

If the forced withdrawal of the bureaucracy from active citizenship crippled the legislative institutions of the new constitution, it was also a blow to constitutionality itself. The new legal system needed strong advocates to gain the respect of the general population, and in Prussia such men were notably lacking. The legal profession was too weak and dependent to fulfill the function that members of the bar performed in the Anglo-American countries, so that it fell to the bureaucracy to sustain the public legal order.[33] The Prussian bureaucracy had shown a strong feeling for law in the pre-March period, and its loyalty to institutional forms of legality was generally undiminished in the 1850's; but where the new constitutional rights of the citizen were concerned, the bureaucracy was less than courageous. Its public advocacy of civil rights was often so obviously self-interested as to be of little real influence. As we have seen, the government had ordered its subordinates to honor the constitution, but had done so only in the service of law and order. Both Brandenburg and Manteuffel viewed the new constitution from a utilitarian point of view—for them, the continuity of law was a basic requirement of stable government. Beyond this pragmatic consideration, most bureaucrats had no strong attachment to this particular form of public law.[34]

The lack of personal commitment to constitutionality among the members of the bureaucracy made it difficult for Manteuffel to check those tendencies toward arbitrariness among his subordinates that sometimes threatened his own authority. Not only did he have difficulty limiting the illegal activities of the king and the Kamarilla, but he found it almost impossible to stop the illegal and extralegal activities of the more powerful members of the bureaucracy. His frequent clashes with the chief of the Berlin police, Karl Ludwig Friedrich von Hinckeldey, provide some of the most illuminating examples of the way in which members of the bureaucracy threatened the rule of law during the 1850's. In the eyes of the general public as well as his own subordinates, Hinckeldey became a symbol of the bureaucracy's disregard of the constitution. He was "a man who in the interests of counterrevolution frequently set himself above the existing laws," wrote one of his closest collaborators, Wilhelm Stieber.[35] He shared with Manteuffel the traditional bureaucratic sense of *Staatsräson* (the interests of the State), but lacked the prime minister's sense of the necessity of legal continuity in times of social and political upheaval.[36]

Even his most determined opponents could not deny that in his role as police president of Berlin (1848–1856) and in his broader capacity as director of police in the ministry of the interior (1854–1856), Hinckeldey achieved much in the way of material progress. He moved where Berlin's municipal government feared to tread, forcing through improvements in fire protection and sanitary conditions over the protests of the economy-minded city councillors.[37] The city's social problems were of great concern to the energetic Police President: he was convinced that to allow them to fester was to strengthen the hand of the opposition parties. As he wrote to a Hanoverian colleague: "The worst thing that the police can do in such matters is to remain immobilized. The people want to see that someone worries about their hunger."[38] To alleviate the chronic problem of fluctuating food prices, Hinckeldey began to interest himself in the mechanics of the grain exchange, intervening with state funds and personal influence to regulate bread prices.[39]

Because he placed great hopes on the ability of police activity to undercut the popularity of the opposition movements, Frederick William IV had a great interest in Hinckeldey's experiments. Both the king and his police president regarded the orderly procedures that had for so long governed the work of both the administration and the judiciary as too confining, and they were quick to use any means that seemed suitable to their ends. Hinckeldey was particularly frank about his actions: "I have learned much from these democrats. We must see to it that their influence is exhausted by the police bringing about improvements."[40] That his methods were autocratic, that he undercut not only institutions of self-government but also established bureaucratic practices mattered little; all was in the interest of the state.

When Hinckeldey took over the post of police president, one of his first acts was the professionalization of the municipal police. No attempt was made to restore the pre-March *Gendarmen,* a body dissolved during the revolution, but the same old faces and methods reappeared soon after the November coup.[41] The size of the police organization grew, and so did the scope of its functions. The police had a hand in regulating the rights of press and assembly; it checked identification cards at the railway terminals, censored theaters, and even invaded classrooms to check the contents of students' notebooks. " 'Police permission' is now a cliché and catchword in all aspects of daily life!" noted Karl Varnhagen von Ense. "To rent a furnished room, to sell a couple of straw covers, to dance, to sing, to listen to music, to meet friends, to travel—all require 'police permission.' "[42]

Hinckeldey acquired additional powers in 1854 when he was appointed to the newly created position of *Generalpolizeidirektor* in the Ministry of the Interior. Now his activities outside the Berlin city limits, which before had been only semi-official, were given full sanction. He became what amounted to a Prussian minister of police and had powers rivaling not only those of his nominal superior, von Westphalen, but even those of Manteuffel himself. Using his special relationship to the king to bypass the cabinet, Hinckeldey disrupted both legal institutions and long-established bureaucratic traditions. His advice to Frederick William ranged far beyond the jurisdiction of his office; foreign as well as domestic policy came within the scope of his intrigues. Spying on members as well as enemies of the government, he ingratiated himself with the monarch and earned the enmity of all the responsible ministers. Yet because of this man's remarkable influence, even his most determined enemies, including the Kamarilla, could not succeed in discrediting him.[43]

In March 1856 Hinckeldey's career was ended in a duel with Hans von Rochow, a member of an aristocratic club that had been the subject of police harassment. The crowd of some 100,000 that paid homage to him at his funeral remembered only what he had done for their economic and social welfare; they ignored the means he had used, and forgave the fact that the duel in which he died had been an illegal one.[44] He had aroused the opposition of the Kreuzzeitungspartei through his arbitrary use of authority, but he had won a great many other conservatives to his Machiavellian stand. At a time when even the once-proud Berliners were willing to exchange the abstract principles of liberty for the concrete rewards of an authoritarian system, the bureaucracy could no longer be expected to let legal or moral scruples stand in their way.

Among those most influenced by Hinckeldey's example were the men who had served under him. Wilhelm Stieber, a relatively recent recruit to government service, who during the Revolution of 1848 had been involved in left-wing politics, was typical of the members of the younger generation who adopted the values that Hinckeldey represented. Stieber's enthusiasm for activism had been quick to wane with the failure of the revolution, but he had remained close to the left opposition, working as a defense lawyer for accused democrats during the political trials just after the revolution. When the 1849 judicial reforms threatened to exclude all those who had not yet passed the Third Examination from the public defender capacity, Stieber, who had never become an Assessor, was forced to seek other employment. The judiciary denied his application for entry into that branch of government, and for a time his future seemed dim. Then in November 1850, apparently on the recommendation of the king himself, Stieber was made a *Polizeiassessor* in charge of the security section of the Berlin police department. As Hinckeldey's righthand man he rose rapidly, becoming in 1854 the *Polizeidirektor* in charge of political affairs. In this position he actively participated in the persecution of the political opposition that only months before he had publicly defended. At the same time, he was also active in or privy to almost all police activity.[45]

What was it like to be a key police official during the 1850's? During a series of prosecutions instituted against him in the early 1860's for his conduct during those years, Stieber spoke candidly of this role. "Under Herr von Hinckeldey," he told the court, "we police officials lived in a state of innocence concerning constitutional matters. If the king himself had ordered us to arrest the *Minister-präsident*, we would have arrested the entire cabinet."[46] Under these conditions the subordinate official was not expected to judge the rightness or wrongness of his own actions, but only to obey his superiors. "According to the arrangement of the royal department of police, which was not organized collegially, so that all decisions were completely in the hands of the police president, I was not permitted to remonstrate against the orders of Herr von Hinckeldey or to presume to criticize them in any way."[47] Stieber argued that the duty of the official to obey his superiors was absolute and that it transcended all moral obligations, including the citizen's responsibility to the constitution. Thus he hid behind the authority of his superiors, protecting himself against prosecution by refusing to acknowledge in any respect the double obligation of the official to the state and society.[48]

More revealing than Stieber's testimony itself was the way it was received by the courts. They accepted the argument that the individual official owed no responsibility to anyone except his superiors; and it was only after three prosecutions that Stieber's opponents were finally able to obtain his dismissal from public office. The evidence presented during the trial was sufficiently damaging to both the administrative and judicial branches that it brought about the resignation of Ludwig Simons, Minister of Justice in the Manteuffel era, who was still in office under the Auerswald-Hohenlohe administration; but it effected no great changes within the bureaucracy itself.[49]

There were probably few Prussian officials as ruthless and unprincipled as Hinckeldey and Stieber. A certain respect for the conventions of the profession was characteristic of most bureaucrats, no matter how powerful; and there were still many officials on all levels who incorporated a respect for law in their personal moral code. But for the vast majority of officials, there was too much to be lost and too little to be gained for them to endanger themselves by standing up for a strict interpretation of the law. It was convenient to be "innocent" of the constitution, particularly when one's superiors were encouraging indifference toward the protection of the individual citizen's civil rights. In an atmosphere of doubt and fear, few could afford to adhere to the letter of the constitution.

The result was the multiplication of opportunities for arbitrary action on the part of the state. Without the check that an active parliament would have provided, nothing but the bureaucracy stood between the citizen and the power of the state. Economic and demographic growth during the 1850's was forcing an expansion of both the size and the scope of government; and under these conditions it was more important than ever that law or custom or both moderate and limit this enormous power. Conservatives had condemned revolution for tearing the delicate web of traditional constraints that had formerly surrounded the operations of the monarchy; now they themselves had furthered absolutism by encouraging members of the civil service to disregard, in the name of the authority of the state, not only their own civil rights but the rights of others. They should not have expected the bureaucracy's traditional sense of honor and integrity to survive such a process, for the disregard of one set of standards necessarily led to a violation of limits in other important areas.

It would be inaccurate to say that the Manteuffel administration was responsible for all these changes; some of the trends can be detected even before 1848. First the revolution, then the reaction had helped bring them to the surface, and other events, including the industrial boom of the 1850's, were also influential. Furthermore, it is clear that the changes were far from complete by 1860. Future events, including the constitutional conflict of the next decade, unification, and the period of the great depression of the 1880's and 1890's would leave their imprint on the bureaucracy. But important precedents were being set, and the political trends of the post-revolutionary decade, affected by the social, economic, and cultural transformations of the same period, were already evident. It now remains to be seen how the bureaucracy's interaction with other social groups and institutions contributed to the replacement of older traditions with a new complex of values and behavior.

Chapter Nine

The Bureaucracy and Society

Industrialization, urbanization, and rationalization are terms that can be used to describe the broad dimensions of the profound transformation that touched virtually every group in Prussian society during the early 1850's. As for the bureaucracy, the pace of modernization was reflected in its further professionalization—in the substitution of increasingly specialized standards for the rather general criteria of competence sufficient at an earlier period. The trend toward higher academic norms had begun early in the 1800's, but the effects of this change only became evident around the middle of the century. As a new breed of bureaucrats more attuned to the specialized needs of an industrialized society arose, professionalization ceased to be a cause of division within the bureaucracy and became a source of a new kind of consensus based less on traditional corporate concepts such as honor than on pride in expertness and efficiency. Members of the bureaucracy found themselves identifying with those groups in the population, namely the industrial bourgeoisie, the military, and the entrepreneurial landowners, who placed the greatest emphasis on functional utility and achievement. A new upper class was emerging, made up of men proud of their property and power and bound together less by a reverence for tradition than by respect for success.[1]

It is important to note that the types of social relationships these changes ultimately produced were in an embryonic state in the 1850's: evolution was gradual and even by the end of the century had not reached its ultimate point. Nevertheless, we must attempt to understand the direction of change as well as its dynamics, since the significance of the events of the 1850's for this study lies in their effect on the bureaucratic politics of the second half of the century.

In the 1840's the senior members of the bureaucracy still thought in traditional terms. Their sense of superiority was based on their belief in the historic mission of the Beamtenstand rather than on the consciousness of special technical competence, a factor more important to the younger men. Both generations were moved by the ethic of service, but while the tendency of the older men was to subordinate individual achievement to the honor of the group, the junior members were concerned with recognition of individual merit. The growth of individualism at the expense of traditional collective goals derived from the transformation of the values of members of the bureaucracy and the peculiar condition of the profession during the mid-century period. The conflict between the two generations involved ideals and economic interests in a way that required that any resolution result in the improvement of the material conditions of the civil service as well as the creation of a new consensus on goals among its members.

The problem of underemployment, which had so plagued the profession during the 1840's, was not so much eliminated as modified. The judicial reforms of 1849 had provided only temporary relief, and by 1858 there were 470 unpaid Assessoren awaiting promotion to the tenured ranks. The number continued to rise in the early 1860's, and in 1862 there were 868 Assessoren, of whom only 86 were paid allowances.[2] The situation was considered so serious that in May 1857 the government issued a circular to the secondary schools outlining the prevailing conditions and urging prospective candidates to reconsider their career expectations. Early the next year the Minister of Justice issued his own warning to prospective jurists.[3] He repeated the arguments used in earlier warnings and added that increased overcrowding required that the government discourage all but those who could afford the long wait for appointment to tenured position.[4]

To all outward appearances it seemed that little had changed. But although the conditions that had caused so much conflict a decade before did not disappear immediately, the response of both the junior and senior ranks was now very different. No longer were the frustrations of the younger officials or the sensitivities of the senior men so easily generalized into social and political struggle. The tensions that earlier had involved a confrontation between two different value systems were now accepted by both sides as a necessary part of the day-to-day life of their profession. The younger men no longer looked upon their grievances as social or political issues, for they had come to view underemployment as an unavoidable aspect of the economics of their profession, involving problems soluble only by the bureaucracy itself and unrelated to broader issues. By the end of the postrevolutionary decade they were accustomed to appealing to their superiors on the grounds of common interest and the well-being of their profession. In 1860, when Assessoren petitioned for higher salaries and more secure working conditions, they refrained from calling the authority of their superiors into question. Instead, they tactfully reminded them that times had changed and in the changing had altered the goals and aspirations of their profession: "Every period has its own special code, which subjects every *Stand* to its necessities. More than ever before, the measure of a profession will be its ability to provide for the material well-being of its members. Those that cannot guarantee [their members] a living will forfeit their prestige."[5]

The senior members of the bureaucracy did not always satisfy the demands of the petitioners, but their responses showed how much their attitude toward intraprofessional problems had changed since the Vormärz period. They no longer reacted as if their status had been challenged; they met the rational-utilitarian arguments of the junior ranks not with references to the sacred tradition of the Beamtenstand or to the infallibility of age and experience, but by explaining the necessity of open competition, with its favorable and unfavorable consequences. They defended the system of unpaid apprenticeship on the grounds that any other system would foster favoritism and corruption, and their arguments against greater security for the Assessoren were based on the notion that such a system would deprive the aspirants of incentive.[6]

The point worth noting is that both sides were now talking the same language, arguing from similar assumptions, and displaying essentially the same social value system. They continued to talk of the necessity of upholding the honor of the Beamtenstand, but they meant by this the achievement of higher standards of professional competence rather than the maintenance of traditional social standing. And although they could not resolve the problems that divided them, each now tended to place responsibility on the contradictions within the system itself rather than blaming the other side for the predicament of overcrowding and underemployment. In a sense, the area of conflict between the ranks had been legitimized by the isolation of what had come to be regarded essentially as economic concerns from the social relationships within the profession.

The lessening of tensions was also a result of the decline in the number of candidates that occurred in the late 1860's. Yet this alone is not enough to explain the changing attitudes within the bureaucracy. Overcrowding would recur in later decades, and university graduates would continue to find the adjustment from student life to professional status full of frustrations, but their response would not be that of the mid-century period.[7] A new sense of professionalism had the effect of isolating this kind of conflict from the larger social and political questions; it was no longer considered proper to bring intra-occupational affairs to public attention.

A more important factor in depoliticizing this type of intra-professional tension was the fact that the older generation was being replaced by the younger. University graduates of the 1830's and 1840's were taking over the higher positions, and although their values were not always identical to the values of their subordinates, the gap was not nearly so wide as it had been between them and their own superiors in years gone by. The new leaders of the profession were men whose modern education had prepared them to accept the trend toward individualism at the expense of the traditional collective goals; they valued efficiency above custom and were much more willing to reward merit than the previous generation had been. This did not make it any easier for them to resolve the problems of their profession. Although many had personally experienced conditions of underemployment and social deprivation, they found that once they were in control of the highest ranks of the profession, they were in no position to do much about the inequities resulting from open competition. Partly out of apathy, but mainly as a result of the realism that had become so fashionable in the 1850's, they accepted the situation without much questioning.

The mood of pessimism and apathy that pervaded all aspects of life in the postrevolutionary decade may have accounted for the passivity of the junior ranks. The new men were accustomed to the abrupt transitions that mark the socialization process of any modern profession. Their academic training was increasingly oriented toward specialization, and they were encouraged to look upon themselves less as intellectuals concerned with general problems than as experts equipped for specific functions.[8] As academic training became more task-oriented, the adjustment from the role of student to that of apprentice, then from apprentice to tenured member, became easier. The hurdles of secondary and university education accustomed those who passed them to the habit of deferring gratification and taught them to accept the fact that any system of open competition produces both winners and losers. This did not happen suddenly, but as the concept of the broadly educated individual gradually lost its appeal in the second half of the century, young men learned to blame their failures on themselves rather than the system. With a few exceptions, they would demand only a fair administration of the existing rules and procedures, taking for granted the less desirable consequences of open competition.

Even the seniority system, which had been a focus of controversy in the pre-March period, now appeared in a different light. In 1857, when the Oberpräsident of the Rhineland, Hans von Kleist-Retzow, questioned the utility of seniority, he was told that to abandon the system would lead to a demoralization of the Beamtenstand.[9] Discussion among the members of the cabinet revealed that there were strong reservations about too strict an application of the seniority concept, but that none of the ministers saw any alternative to the existing system. This time however they did not defend the seniority system with the argument of tradition, which had been used so frequently a decade before—the position of the cabinet ministers was significantly more pragmatic and utilitarian now. Age itself was no longer given as a justification; instead, it was pointed out that the Prussian examination system provided no objective means of ranking individual candidates, and that reliance on the recommendation of superiors would open up the possibility of favoritism and corruption. Seniority was the only equitable alternative.[10]

By the 1850's the seniority system was no longer really at issue, even among the younger members of the profession. The growing monopoly by university graduates of offices in both branches had restored a reasonable balance between the qualifications of the junior and senior ranks. There would continue to be young officials who would regard their recent education as superior to that of their elders, but the cultural gap was not so great as to contribute to deep social divisions. Another source of discontent, the unequal work load, had been alleviated by the various reorganizations that had taken place since 1848. The higher bureaucracy had been gradually expanded since the revolution, which eased the burden that had fallen on the younger men: in the years 1850 to 1900 it was to grow by 75 percent.[11] In addition, rationalization was helping to remove some of the load from the previously overworked junior ranks by distributing tasks more evenly among an increasingly hierarchical system of authority. The gradual abandonment of the collegiate system in both branches meant that the younger official was provided with a measure of real authority commensurate with his share of the day-to-day work of the profession. Furthermore, in the more monocratically organized bureaucracy, the lines of responsibility were more sharply drawn, providing the individual official with a clearer picture of the limits of duties than had been possible under the collegiate arrangement.[12]

The aspect of modernization that seems to have contributed most to the restoration of unity within the profession was the increasing specialization of function. Although by virtue of their legal education many higher officials continued to think of themselves as generalists capable of holding any civil office, the institutions within which they operated were placing more and more emphasis on specialization of duties. By 1858 officials were no longer transferring from one branch of service to the other with the same ease they had a decade before. In the 1840's there had been an average of 28 transfers per year from the lower ranks of the judiciary to the administration; in the next decade the average had dropped to 23 per year.[13] In addition to the growing specialization of function, a number of other factors, including progressive overcrowding in the administration, may have contributed to this result—but whatever the cause, the effect was the same. The official was coming to think of himself primarily as an expert in a particular field, suited only for one type of employment in one particular profession.[14]

In this sense careerism had a healing effect socially, because it helped relieve the individual official of the burden of conforming to the demands set by the traditional corporate system—demands that were often out of line with his actual resources. Specialization tied him closer to one particular group within the profession, but it freed him from the tyranny of collective standards, which in the bureaucracy's case tended to be set by those whose wealth and status was out of reach of the majority. Prussia's civil servants did not cease to be aware of their membership in the broader unity of the Beamtenstand; indeed, the traditional sense of common identity remained remarkably strong despite the growing size and complexity of the bureaucratic organization. Yet the increasing specialization of function had the effect of redefining social aspirations in such a way that the old corporate pressures to conform to the standards of those officials who had the highest salaries were no longer as strong as before. The judiciary, whose pay was not as high as that of the administrative ranks, began to set its own social standards, thus relieving its members of some social pressure to conformity. By the end of the century judicial office was no longer assumed to require the equivalent of the wealth and status of the administrative branch.[15] Raises in the salary levels of the lower ranks of the bureaucracy, which began in the late 1850's, also contributed to the easing of financial burdens.[16] Although the social requirements of both branches of service remained relatively high compared to the rest of Prussian society, its members were apparently finding better ways to cope with this than had been available in the pre-March period.

The growth in the number of technical officials, men not trained in law or concerned with general matters of administration, accelerated this trend. These were people less sensitive to historical traditions, who brought with them a definition of success at odds with the standards of the old social order. They too tended to be more concerned with the recognition of their individual achievements than with the honor ascribed to members of the Beamtenstand.[17] Their values echoed the demands of an industrializing society, and it was in that direction that the bureaucracy as a whole was moving, slowly but surely, in the second half of the century. To fully understand the nature and cause of this change we must go beyond the forces working within the bureaucracy and examine the changing nature of Prussian society itself.

The sudden termination of the legal dimensions of the corporate monarchy in 1848 was not paralleled by an equally abrupt transformation of the social consciousness of the bureaucracy. Many officials, particularly those of the older generation, refusing to define themselves in anything but traditional terms, continued to consider their association with one of Prussia's historical Stände sufficient reason to think themselves a step above even the wealthiest members of the industrial bourgeoisie. As has so often been noted, corporate identities were retained in Prussia longer than in most European countries.[18] But here symbol must be separated from substance, for while certain forms of corporate imagery survived well into the second half of the century, new behavioral patterns were emerging that were very different from those of pre-March society.

Officials could pretend to reject the values of the businessman's acquisitive society, but they were as deeply affected as any other group by the general transformation in behavior and values occasioned by economic development. The 1850's brought an enormous expansion of the industrial system accompanied by renewed inflaation. Once again the government was flooded by appeals from the lower ranks of the bureaucracy. Reports recalled the hungry 1840's and warned, "If present conditions continue as they are, and salaries are not adjusted to grain prices ... there will be sad consequences for the whole Prussian bureaucracy."[19]

The Lower House was also the recipient of such complaints, and from 1855 on it placed increasing pressure on the government to do something to raise the salaries of the civil services. At first the cabinet was reluctant to act. Minister of Finance Bodelschwingh argued that funds were inadequate to cover a general increase.[20] Other ministers tried various measures, including selective raises and bonuses, but could not stem the protests. After three years of steady pressure, from inside and outside the profession, from the left and also from the right, the government finally granted salary increases to most of the lower and middle levels of the bureaucracy, including the subaltern.[21]

The raises were not large but because the salaries of the highest ranking officials were not increased at that time, the existing gap between their salaries and those of their subordinates was diminished to some degree. In view of the general increase in consumption standards throughout the entire bureaucracy, this was an important step toward easing the economic frustrations inherited from the previous decade. It acted as an important precedent for future salary reform and also demonstrated the government's concern for the well-being of its employees. Perhaps most important of all, it showed that the higher ranks had freed themselves from some of their inhibitions about economic matters and were moving toward an accommodation between traditional concerns with honor and status and the economic realities of an industrial age. The movement for higher wages, both inside and outside parliament, had involved every rank—a sign that material concerns were no longer considered unbecoming to members of the profession.[22]

This did not mean that the bureaucracy had been converted to the businessman's ethic. The change was not, as some contemporaries and later Marxist historians would have it, a corruption of professional ethics.[23] On the contrary, the expressions of concern for things economic were perfectly consistent with the transition to a modern profession. As far as the bureaucracy was concerned, the abandonment of corporate values stopped well short of the acceptance of the profit motive. For the modern official as well as the capitalist entrepreneur, individual achievement was becoming much more important than the ascribed qualities of birth, age, religion, and geographical origin. This did not mean that the type of achievement that bestowed prestige was the same in both groups: for the business classes, achievement was measured largely by accumulated wealth, while in the bureaucratic profession, rank and title were the symbols most sought after. Although the individual official was not concerned with profit, he was no more altruistic than the businessman. His particular institutional setting simply authorized a different set of goals and rewards—and it was these rather than the achievement ethic itself that distinguished his group from the rest of society.[24]

The difference between the rewards of the professions and those of business or landowning were never absolute, however, and as time went on the two tended to converge. As industry became increasingly more complex and business practice ever more specialized, the kinds of goals sought by businessmen more and more resembled those of the professionals. As the entrepreneurs were transformed into a managerial class, rank and title became as important to them as to the members of the state bureaucracy. In Prussia, where the capitalist class had traditionally occupied a socially inferior position, this tendency began earlier and remained more pronounced than in other countries. Even in the 1850's Prussian entrepreneurs were reaching for the titles and positions associated with state service.[25] Their sons were entering the professions in ever larger numbers, just as members of the bureaucracy were moving in the opposite direction—an indication of acceptance by the profession of certain values previously despised as earmarks of the acquisitive society. The government was well aware that by offering higher salaries, industry was drawing many recruits from the ranks of the civil service.[26] It was also well known that those who stayed in the profession were using their spare funds to speculate on the stock market and to invest in land—activities that the bureaucracy tried to control rather than eliminate.[27]

Some alteration in the bureaucracy's system of values was to be expected in a period when businessmen's sons were beginning to enter civil service: to some extent the accommodation with the stock market that took place during the 1850's was the result of one generation replacing another. Yet it was not only that younger officials were more open in their recognition of economic realities. If the change in the attitude of the bureaucracy is to be fully understood, the economic difficulties during the previous decade must be taken into account. As we have seen, few officials were actually corrupted by this situation. Most managed to arrive at some kind of balance between their desire for economic well-being and their responsibilities to public service. It was a credit to the older generation that as early as the 1840's it recognized and acted on the threat of corruption that the new profit opportunities posed. While the conflict-of-interest laws that they initiated seemed unnecessarily strict at first to those whose salaries were inadequate, in the long run the new codes proved to be an effective compromise between the traditional ethic of service and

the modern necessities of social consumption. Fortunately for the
profession, this balance was sustained by the other reforms of the
postrevolutionary period. The expansion of opportunity within
the profession and the increase in salary levels were as important
as the codes themselves in preventing the kind of corruption that
might have occurred in the difficult times of transition.

The first instinct of the bureaucracy when faced with the social
and economic crisis of the mid-century period was to protect its
own. The concern for the well-being of the general community
was often given only secondary consideration, and nowhere was
this more evident than in the recruitment practices of the 1850's.
In theory the profession remained open to all who were academically qualified, but no attempt was made to aid those for whom
higher education was financially difficult or impossible. The idea
of universal free education, which had been part of the democratic
platform in 1848, found no favor among the conservative government or its allies in the upper classes. As the primary beneficiaries
of a free labor market that favored the well-to-do, they were opposed to any form of subsidy.[28]
    It is not surprising that as higher education became more time-
consuming and expensive the Prussian universities became less
and less representative of society as a whole, gradually restricting
the opportunities for upward mobility they had offered earlier in
the century. For example, the proportion of sons of lower-middle
class families in the student body at Halle declined in the second
half of the century. After the brief surge in attendance at the Law
Faculty in the early 1850's caused by the expansion of the bureaucracy, the proportion of peasant and artisan sons among those
studying law sank from 10.6 percent to 8 percent in the late 1870's.
On the surface this decline did not seem to represent an abrupt
change in the recruitment patterns of the bureaucracy. There were
still a substantial number of lower-middle class sons entering the
higher bureaucracy, and the proportion of those from the subaltern ranks and other nonacademic professions studying in the

same faculty actually rose during the same period.[29] But the social pyramid had broadened enormously at its base, and groups like the peasants and artisans, which had previously represented a large part of the lower orders of the traditional social hierarchy, were now rapidly becoming an isolated minority within the lower classes of the new industrial society. Beneath them had grown the great urban and rural proletariat, a group whose members had little or no representation in either the Law Faculty or the student body in general.[30]

Prussian universities remained open to their traditional clientele but were virtually inaccessible to the new working class; schools in the new industrial centers were inadequate; no attempt was made to recruit talented workers; and little encouragement was given to those few sons of the proletariat who were motivated to seek the benefits of higher learning.[31] Even when the laboring poor wanted to send their sons to the universities, the absence of adequate scholarships prevented them from doing so. We do not know how many workers' families managed to reach the bureaucracy by first attaining a lesser degree of education and occupying white collar jobs for a generation, but however large this number may have been, the socialization process required to reach the higher civil service usually severed any ties between the upwardly mobile individual and his class origins.[32]

Faced with their own economic difficulties, the bureaucrats of the 1850's were in no mood to sponsor the mobility of outsiders. No attempt was made to ease the conditions of professional apprenticeship. The argument that economic disadvantages were barring from the civil service many talented but poor individuals fell on deaf ears. By 1860 it was already clear that those who controlled the personnel policies of both branches were determined to make no concessions to men who for lack of funds were unable to meet their standards. The already stiff financial requirements for entry into the profession were applied even more strictly during the 1850's,[33] and greater attention was paid to the candidate's sources of income, because the superior ranks were now determined to exclude all those whose financial condition might prove embarrassing to the profession.

This tightening of procedures was the direct result of the new wave of overcrowding that began in the early 1850's, but it also seems to have represented a premonition of permanent change in the profession's own criteria of social acceptability. Enforcement of high financial requirements might be a guarantee against the kind of internal crisis that had plagued the bureaucracy in the previous decade, but it was also a sign of a new social consciousness that placed a higher value on wealth than the members of the old Gebildeten had. The belief that wealth was a sign of capacity had penetrated even the educated professions, and the government had no problem justifying its policy of exclusion to those who believed the rich deserved their privileges. As a result of their own economic difficulties, members of the bureaucracy were less likely to look at the wealthy with the contempt they had occasionally displayed earlier. While it is clear that wealth alone was never enough to obtain the respect of the Prussian educated elite, it is true that they were much more aware of what wealth could provide in terms of education and other symbols of status than they had ever been before.

The members of Prussia's old cultured elite were better able than most to adapt to modern institutions of higher education, but even they encountered difficulties in meeting the financial requirements for education. They had believed their position was assured because they belonged to a natural aristocracy of talent; now they were forced to accept the fact that the nouveaux riches were in many cases better able than they to gain access to the certifying institutions. Ascriptive characteristics that had always facilitated admittance to the select professions no longer carried the same weight, and the number of sons of bureaucrats who were entering the Law Faculty was not enough in the third quarter of the nineteenth century to match the growth of the student body as a whole. By the 1870's there appears to have been an actual decline in the absolute numbers of sons who were competing for places within their fathers' professions.[34] This trend seems to have been the result of a desire on the part of some bureaucrats, particularly those in a weak economic position, to conserve their financial and social resources by marrying late and limiting the size of their families. As the century progressed the number of available males seems to have declined, due to the smaller number of children per family and the increase in the proportion of unmarried officials.[35] Data concerning the administrative bureaucracy of the late nineteenth century indicate that the less fortunate the individual official's financial situation, the less likely he was to marry early and raise a large family.[36]

In the second half of the century the proportion of the bureaucracy drawn from the ranks of the professional classes declined. Even the bureaucracy itself was no longer contributing as great a proportion as it had in the previous half-century. Sons of professional men were shifting increasingly to faculties like philosophy, where financial requirements and social demands were less than those of law. It can be estimated from the Halle records that the percentage of officials' sons in each class preparing for civil service careers fell from 51 percent in the 1850's to 36 percent at the end of the 1870's; and the percentage of sons of the higher bureaucracy alone declined from 28 to 16 percent in the same period.[37]

The willingness of some sons of the educated elite to enter occupations that their fathers had considered beneath the dignity of a cultivated man accounts in part for this change. There seems to have been a trend not only toward entry into business and industry but also toward military careers, and during the 1850's junior officials regularly complained that peers who had entered the army were better off both economically and socially than they were.[38] This trend indicated a relatively sharp break with tradition, for prior to 1848 those who went to the university were, to all intents and purposes, exempt from military service; and many academic youths avoided the army for social as well as political reasons. Civil officials had championed the popular *Landwehr* against the regular army, and during the Revolution of 1848 radical bureaucrats had been among those who had advocated the abolition of the traditional military establishment. It seems, however, that a decade later Prussian officials followed the lead of the industrial middle class in accepting the institutions of the regular army;[39] and subsequently they looked to the army as an institution capable of providing them with access to status and power. By the 1860's the bureaucratic families were second only to the officer corps itself in the number of sons they presented for candidacy in the officer ranks of the military, and half a century later they had surpassed even the professional soldiers in that respect.[40] By then it was clear that both the army and the bureaucracy had come to cherish an arrangement that provided the former with a source of acceptable and talented candidates and the latter with a prestigious occupational alternative for their sons.[41]

The ties formed with the military and big business helped shape the bureaucracy's social and economic position in the new industrializing society. Together with membership in the right student fraternity, affiliation with an aristocratic regiment in the reserve officer corps became an important means of getting ahead, particularly in the administrative branch. The record of an individual's military service helped his superiors identify him socially; this kind of information became after 1888 a regular part of the annual personnel reports. By the end of the century almost 70 percent of the Rhineland's higher bureaucracy were associated in some way or another with an army unit.[42] Many young men were to discover that the absence of military associations was a serious liability in bureaucratic circles.[43]

These changes meant that institutions like the army were taking over some of the selection and socialization functions that the bureaucracy had once reserved to itself. In the future Prussia's civil service would no longer exercise such exclusive control over the composition and character of its own membership, but would rely on a complex of organizations whose class and political interests complemented its own. Some of the functions were taken over by the schools and universities, and particularly by the highly conservative student corps, which became increasingly powerful after 1848. They were influential in imposing uniformity of political views on the candidates, because they acted as a sort of informal screening board that rejected those students whose attitudes were unacceptable.[44] The military carried the same burden of responsibility: it too acted to separate the desirables from the undesirables and to implant the qualities of absolute loyalty and obedience. It is impossible to determine precisely the extent of change that this alteration in the nature of socialization produced, but it seems clear that it encouraged conformity and authoritarianism in political behavior.

Borrowing prestige from aristocratic institutions was only one method used by the bureaucracy to secure its social position; new patterns of recruitment served the same purpose. As noted earlier, the number of landed aristocrats and industrial-commercial bourgeoisie entering the profession increased substantially after 1848. For the first time in almost a century, the *Landadel* emerged as a powerful source of recruits, who together with the sons of the upper middle class gradually began to dominate the universities, transforming them from channels of upward mobility into preserves of wealth and title. At Halle the percentage of landowners' sons in each law class rose from 10 percent to 14.5 percent during the period 1850–1870; during the same period, the proportion of businessmen's sons increased from 9 percent to 17 percent.[45] Both groups adapted rapidly to professional requirements, and by the end of the century their sons formed the largest part of the regular bureaucracy.[46] Of the fathers of higher administrators (excluding Landräte) serving in the Rhine Province in 1905, 21 percent were administrative and 16 percent judicial officials; 17 percent were larger landowners; 30 percent were in business or industry; 6 percent were military officers; and 10 percent were in other occupations.

A more complete survey of the changes over the second half-century indicates that the wealth of the bureaucracy had increased.

TABLE 2

Composition of the Rhineland Bureaucracy, 1850–1905

Position	Provincial origins		Religion		Estate		Independent source of income	
	Eastern	Western	Protestant	Catholic	Noble	Commoner	Yes	No
1850								
Regierungsrat or higher	50%	50%	57%	43%	24%	76%	43%	57%
Regierungsassessor	59	41	69	31	35	65	50	50
Landräte	33	67	41	59	40	60	58	42
All positions	46	54	52	48	34	66	52	48
1875								
Regierungsrat or higher	48	52	79	21	49	51	47	53
Regierungsassessor	60	40	63	37	66	34	40	60
Landräte	24	76	44	56	41	59	73	27
All positions	39	61	61	39	43	57	60	40
1905								
Regierungsrat or higher	46	54	69	31	13	87	64	36
Regierungsassessor	63	37	91	9	29	71	55	45
Landräte	20	80	48	52	44	56	84	16
All positions	30	70	66	34	23	77	63	37

SOURCE: Koblenz Staatsarchiv, personnel reports for 1850–58, 1875, and 1905.

From incomplete records of the sources of income it is possible to document a considerable increase in the proportion of independently wealthy men on almost every level of the profession (see Table 2).[47]

Of those who reported some independent wealth in 1905, many had inherited money, most of it apparently in liquid assets. Only 11 percent of the Rhineland officials owned substantial amounts of land.[48] The rest who had wealth seem to have invested it in savings or stock; a few among the highest ranks were board members of large business concerns.[49] No less than half the administrators of the Rhineland bureaucracy at the turn of the century were from landowning or business families that presumably could be expected to provide support for their son's career; and more than half were married to women who came from families of the same background.[50] Of the fathers of women married to administrators in the Rhine Province in 1905, 15 percent were administrative and 19 percent judicial officials; 7 percent were larger landowners; 48 percent were in business or industry; 9 percent were military officers; and 2 percent were in other occupations.

The figures drawn from the personnel records of Rhineland administrators do not tell us all we would like to know about the social origins of the bureaucracy as a whole, but they do seem to substantiate the conclusion that the bureaucracy had been aligning itself ever more closely with other elements of the Prussian upper class ever since the middle of the century. A new ruling class was emerging, which combined the formerly separate elements of industrial and agrarian wealth with the professional elites and cut across all provincial boundaries.

It is difficult to say whether the figures on geographical origins indicate any significant change, though it may be that the slight rise in the percentage of westerners in the highest echelons may indicate a further decline of the old Prussian custom of assigning officials to districts outside their native provinces.[51] On the other hand, the reduction of old tensions between the eastern and western territories may have been offset somewhat by a recurrence of anti-Catholic discrimination, which in the second half of the century took the form of hostility not so much to the religious as to the political manifestations of Catholicism. The statistics on religious affiliation indicate that religion was again becoming important as a factor of selection after 1848. As indicated in Table 2 the most severe effects were felt in the regular bureaucracy (excluding Landräte) after 1870, though the organization of Catholic opposition factions in 1852 had already introduced the possibility of political complications in the recruitment of Catholics long before the *Kulturkampf*. The situation of Catholics in the civil service seems to have improved toward the end of the century, at least as far as the upper echelons were concerned. It is important to note that during the entire nineteenth century the Rhine Province had no Catholic Oberpräsident, and although a number of Regierungspräsidenten were members of that faith, the upper ranks as a whole were dominated by Protestants.[52] Those Catholics who had made successful careers in administration were presumably either strongly conservative or at least politically neutral—usually men of title or members of the upper levels of the Catholic bourgeoisie. Apparently religion per se was not always a factor, but it appears that some Catholics who were perfectly loyal in every respect were passed over because of the association of Catholicism with political opposition.[53]

The same patterns seem to have held for the judiciary. This branch had a reputation for being less socially exclusive than the administration, and Catholics appear to have made greater headway, though they were woefully underrepresented in all but those provinces where their religion was in the majority, and largely excluded from the higher ranks, including the Ministry of Justice itself.[54] Of equal significance was the fact that only 23 percent of the state prosecutors were Catholics while the proportion among lawyers was 41 percent. Clearly the Protestants remained firmly in control of those offices that carried the greatest power and left the less influential offices to the outsiders.[55] Next to the judiciary itself, the legal profession remained the least prestigious of the occupations open to men trained in law, and its membership was a composite of Prussia's undesirables: Catholics, Jews, and radicals.[56]

For many of Prussia's landed aristocrats a university degree and a place in civil or military service had become an alternative to the difficulties of agriculture. Even before the revolution the Landadel had been seeking new bases of economic and social support and reaching out to make alliances with groups and institutions with which it had enjoyed little contact previously. Although agriculture prospered during most of the nineteenth century, the landed aristocracy found that it could maintain its economic position only by closing ranks with the nonnobles who now owned a large share of the eastern agricultural properties. By the end of the century there had been formed what Hans Rosenberg has called an "aristocracy of the land," composed of noble and nonnoble landowners whose common economic interests were solidified by social and political ties.[57]

The evolution of the bureaucracy's relationship with the landed aristocracy followed much the same pattern, though its basis was less economic and political than social. The Landadel did bring some wealth to the profession, but most of those who made it their career stayed free of personal concern for the landed interest. Only among the Landräte did the politics of the agrarian interest groups find strong allies, and that was because many who served in that position were drawn directly from the ranks of the larger landowners. Most of the regular officials, including those with recent associations with the land, appear to have been involved politically only so far as government policy directed them to be. Their contacts with the landed aristocracy were more social than political; the nobility enjoyed the security that civil office offered, and the bureaucracy welcomed the prestige that sons of the Landadel brought to their profession.[58]

From the ministerial level down, the number of nobles from landed families seems to have increased by the end of the century.

In the Rhineland administration, sons of Landadel outnumbered sons of Dienstadel—a sign that the long separation of these two important groups was coming to an end. With respect to marriage, too, the old social barriers were going down before social and economic necessity. Sons of landed aristocrats with an eye to furthering their careers were marrying into established bureaucratic families, while young officials were marrying the daughters of the landed classes in an effort to gain economic and social security.[59]

Because the higher bureaucracy had expanded at a more rapid rate during the second half of the century, even the fresh blood provided by the landed nobility was not enough to preserve the noble caste's proportional strength. In 1839 nobles had made up 46 percent of the higher bureaucracy, but by 1914 they accounted for only 25 percent. With respect to the entire bureaucracy, including the technical officials and the subaltern ranks, they were now but a tiny minority.[60] Yet men of title and members of the industrial bourgeoisie had managed to maintain control of the profession by dominating the commanding positions in the heirarchy of authority. Just as the expansion of the officer corps in the 1860's had caused the nobility in the army to regroup in select social enclaves, so the growth of the bureaucracy resulted in the retrenchment of that profession's old elites within a few select ranks.[61]

The first positions to be abandoned were those of the subaltern bureaucracy; even by the mid-nineteenth century it was rare for either the rich or the titled to seek employment there. For a time the upper classes seemed also to be deserting the judiciary, which for most of the second half of the century was filled largely by men of lower social standing. The judiciary, once the exclusive domain of the nobility, became like the artillery in the army, a branch of service whose lower levels were filled almost entirely by the less socially desirable. Not until the very end of the century did the upper classes begin to turn to the judicial branch in larger numbers, though even in the 1840's and 1850's men of title and wealth dominated the highest courts and the Ministry of Justice itself.[62]

The upper levels of the administration, particularly the Ober- and Regierungspräsident positions, as well as the strategic Landrat office, also remained the preserve of the upper class. In 1818 nobles had made up 70 percent of the Oberpräsidenten rank; in 1828 their number had fallen to 44 percent; for the rest of the century, however, it hovered between a half and three-quarters, with only occasional variations.[63] The ratio of nobles to commoners among the Regierungspräsidenten declined from three to one in the 1820's to an almost even count in 1914. The percentage of nobles among the Landräte fell from 73 percent to 56 percent in the same period. As far as both positions were concerned, the change was not one involving the triumph of one class over another, but simply evidence of further professionalization that was bound to bring the percentages more into line with the ratio of three nonnobles to every one noble that was characteristic of the bureaucracy as a whole at the end of the century.[64]

The disproportion of members of the aristocracy in higher positions did not indicate the dominance of the landed interests as such. What it did show, however, was the tendency of those in power to ascribe to members of the nobility a set of values and aptitudes that supposedly qualified them especially for certain sensitive positions within the bureaucratic hierarchy. By virtue of their connections and heritage, sons of the nobility were thought to command a greater degree of authority in the general community and to have superior discrimination in using the power at the bureaucracy's command. In the 1850's, when the talent for authoritarian leadership was so much in demand, nobles were favored for strategic positions—not because of family connections or ties with the land, but because it was supposed that they would be more willing and useful tools of government policy. During that period the pre-March trend of replacement of noble Landräte with nonnoble was temporarily checked, and though future regimes could not stem the flow of bourgeois bureaucrats into these sensitive positions, they continued to favor men of title for offices that required the exercise of considerable personal authority.[65]

It was in this way that politics entered into the selection and promotion process. The positions most affected were those that had never been much subject to the rules of seniority, namely those designated as political. No office illustrates the social effects of this peculiarity of the Prussian system better than the Landrat post. Before 1848, candidates for that office had been nominees of the owners of the larger estates, but beginning in 1848 and continuing under the Manteuffel regime, the position became increasingly subject to appointment by the central government. By the end of the 1850's it was already a part of the regular bureaucratic ladder— a stepping-stone for young administrative officials on the move to higher positions.[66] But despite the fact that it had been virtually removed from the patronage of local landowners, the proportion of nobles in the Landrat position remained relatively high. These men were no longer simply local landed aristocrats, but nobles with full professional training; yet they owed their appointments to the assumption that the qualities traditionally ascribed to nobles made them particularly well suited to that post. Whether or not the noble official was actually the best equipped for the position hardly mattered to successive governments concerned with maintaining their political authority in the countryside. In this indirect manner the intrusion of the political factor, which was not consciously designed to favor any one party or interest group, necessarily worked to the advantage of the landed aristocracy and their allies among the upper-middle class.[67]

It is one of the features of the Prussian bureaucracy that its professionalization went hand in hand with a trend toward social exclusiveness and political authoritarianism. In other countries the introduction of high academic standards for admission was accompanied by the diminution of the intrusion of social and political factors into the everyday workings of the civil service. But in Prussia the conditions of the bureaucracy's transition to modernity encouraged a different course of development—one that aligned the bureaucracy ever more closely with the other powerful elites.

In some countries the termination of political patronage appointments and the introduction of a system of open competition for civil service positions had the effect of opening the eyes of the bureaucracy to a broader spectrum of interests, or at least detaching it from its previous close association with the traditional estates. As far as England was concerned, the reduction of royal influence and the creation of a professional civil service had just such an effect on the social and political position of its bureaucracy, thus helping to guarantee the neutrality of its bureaucrats in parliamentary democracy.[68] In Prussia's case, however, the authoritarianism of the state, combined with the exclusiveness of the powerful landed aristocracy and industrial bourgeoisie, worked in the opposite direction.

Members of both branches of the Prussian service were able to accept discrimination against Catholics, Jews, and members of the working classes on the grounds that the interests of the community were best served by limiting the entrance of members of groups alleged to be hostile to the state. This policy, which represented an intrusion of political considerations unknown before the revolution, was certainly due in large part to the nature of the mid-century upheaval. The coincidence of an important turning point in the institutional development of the bureaucracy with the massive social, economic, and political crises in which members of that group were so deeply involved could not but have an enormous impact on the future. In the 1850's, when the policy of political exclusion was initiated, Prussia had just emerged from a period of revolution during which the old elites' fears of all those groups that did not possess what it considered to be the appropriate rank, status, or property were heightened considerably. The conservative government of that period had played on these anxieties, using them as an excuse to exclude its own enemies from the civil service. The bureaucracy itself, which at that time was attempting to cope with internal difficulties, was not as scrupulous as it might have been about the kinds of restrictions that were imposed. The government began by excluding known radicals from government employment, but ended by discriminating against whole groups whose reputation for loyalty had been brought into question during the revolution or in the period of reaction. When men began to be excluded from the bureaucracy on the basis of their backgrounds and associations rather than for what they had actually done or believed, a new nondemocratic factor began to intrude into what was supposed to be an open process of selection. Although it must be acknowledged that in the early postrevolutionary period some attempt was made to deal with each case individually and to determine which candidates actually held subversive views, the beginnings of this process of discrimination can be traced to the 1850's.

The events of the mid-century did not necessarily make the conservative alliance of landed aristocracy and Protestant upper-middle class inevitable. The constitutional crisis of the 1860's, the events of national unification, the Kulturkampf, and the eventual emergence of a powerful socialist opposition all had their own impact on the composition and character of the Prussian bureaucracy. But it is undeniable that it was the politics of revolution and reaction, together with the economic and social changes of the 1840's and 1850's, that laid the foundation for these later developments. This was the bureaucracy's metamorphosis from a privileged body, proud of its cultural and social leadership in a corporate society, into a dependent element of a new upper class.

Chapter Ten

Conclusion

Consciousness of social change is often slow to develop: it was not until 1915 that a German social scientist, Otto Most, published the first systematic investigation of changes in the composition of the bureaucratic elite, which demonstrated that economically weaker elements, including many of the oldest bureaucratic families, were abandoning the service and being replaced by representatives of the more prosperous industrial and agrarian entrepreneurial classes. His conclusion that the new heterogeneity of social background was helping to erode the bureaucracy's sense of tradition was hardly original, however, for those who had witnessed the changes of the mid-century period were already aware of the consequences not only for the existing social order but also for the future of Prussian politics.[1] The effects of transition from a corporate to a class society were already visible in the emergence of patterns of political power that were to remain dominant until the end of the monarchy in 1918 and even beyond, into the uncertainties of the Weimar Republic.

In one sense at least, the civil service had become more inclusive in the second half of the century. Whereas it excluded Jews, Catholics, members of the working class, and the politically unreliable, it had opened itself to groups not previously associated with the educated professions, namely the urban and rural entrepreneurial classes. The entry of larger numbers of sons of landowners and businessmen into the profession diluted its homogeneity by replacing the old familial and cultural bonds with a more complex

combination of ties based on wealth, military service, student fraternity membership, and political affiliation. As men from diverse
backgrounds entered the profession, the life-style of the bureaucracy was gradually altered, becoming less distinct from that of
the other upper classes and embodying a combination of various
tastes and forms borrowed from new elements. Though Prussian
officials might continue to refer to themselves as a Stand, the loyalties that held them together were based less on the feeling of being
part of a group whose role was legitimized by tradition than on
a common association with the interests of certain contemporary
institutions: the university, the army, and the increasingly specialized bureaucratic institutions themselves. Thus one of the bureaucracy's sources of solidarity, its sense of being part of a sacred
chain of continuous generations, lost its efficacy at mid-century.

New blood helped the civil service maintain its prestige and
economic position, but this was of little comfort to those members
whose resources were inadequate to the steadily rising cost of living, a trend that was interrupted only by the great depression of
the 1880's and early 1890's.[2] The newcomers increased the pressure of competition within the profession, weakening rather than
strengthening the solidarity of the group. Growth in size also contributed to this result, further diminishing the corporate sense of
community by making close personal relationships within the profession increasingly difficult to sustain. This was bound to change
the elite's image of itself and affect its relationship to other groups
in Prussian society. The belief in the bureaucracy's historical role
as the guarantor of the well-being of the state and society, shaken
at mid-century, never regained its hold on the popular imagination.
Both the profession and the public were coming to view the civil
service as only one elite among many, a competitor for a voice in
policy-making but no longer a claimant to omniscience in public
affairs. In this respect the bureaucracy had gone through a kind
of desanctification process. The Revolution of 1848 had disclosed
divisions within its ranks, and the politics of the era of reaction
had removed the aura of aloof detachment that had previously en-

veloped its activities. Hegelian metaphysics provided no suitable definition of the bureaucracy's new role; an alternative self-image was needed if it was to regain the sense of collective purpose that had motivated its individual members prior to the 1840's.

The task of formulating a new set of goals in a rapidly changing society was made more difficult by the increasing heterogeneity of membership. Newcomers brought with them new concepts of the ideal role of the civil service. Before 1840 the continuity of generations had insured a remarkably strong, stable sense of purpose; but now that the composition of the bureaucracy was broader and less cohesive, a clear and coherent notion of the role of the elite was much more difficult to come by. Instead of emphasizing the position of leadership as it had in the early nineteenth century, the civil service came to see itself as a conciliator between conflicting interests. Members of the bureaucracy liked to imagine themselves as mediators in the conflict between the various class elements of industrial society, but in reality their role was confined to conflicts within upper-class circles rather than between these elites and the emerging industrial proletariat. The advanced state of the bureaucracy's professionalism and its traditional commitment to Prussian Staatsräson precluded complete identification with the interests of any one element of the Prussian upper classes; but it also made it virtually impossible for the bureaucracy to assume the position of neutrality called for by its own code of conduct. This disparity between ideal and reality, which was evident as early as the 1840's and 1850's, was to trouble the profession for the remainder of the century.

The fact that the civil service of the second half of the nineteenth century had attachments to diverse groups whose interests were often at odds did not make it any easier for it to regain the public's confidence. The role conflicts that the bureaucracy as a group encountered tended to be reflected in the lives of individual officials, producing the feeling of lack of direction and purpose about which contemporaries were already concerned in the 1850's. The evaporation of the original sense of a historically sanctioned mission made it difficult for individual officials to define their place in the state and in society and left them with a sense of insecurity. Lacking the strong sense of purpose that had moved the more homogeneous Beamtenstand of the early nineteenth century, the rising generation had a much more functional attitude toward their occupation. Their conception of their own responsibilities tended to be narrower; they avoided situations in which their actions were not covered by explicit instructions; and in their private lives they withdrew from public affairs as much as possible. Highly professional but politically inert, avoiding issues leading to conflict, each official so affected mirrored the uncertainty of purpose that was overcoming the bureaucracy as a whole. The rationalization of this condition was the expedient doctrine of neutrality, the attitude of *ohne mich* ("Not me!") that had become so prevalent by 1914.[3]

Ralf Dahrendorf has explained the tendency of German elites to avoid conflict as part of their society's general pattern of aversion to all forms of competition. He tells how during the second half of the nineteenth century elites formed defensive "cartels" to protect themselves against the pressures to which they were subjected.[4] Certainly the bureaucracy could never have regained the position of leadership it held before 1848—but its unwillingness to face squarely the social and political problems of the new age affected the performance of legitimate administrative and judicial functions, and its members' lack of respect for constitutional forms of government helped undermine the belief in legal procedures that its own institutions required. Lacking faith in their own ability to confront and master major social and political problems, Prussia's higher civil servants ultimately lost the respect of a large segment of society.

The history of bureaucracy in the period of revolution and reaction provides an insight into the origins of this process. The events of the 1840's shook the self-confidence of the Beamtenstand, and the structural changes resulting from revolution and reaction made it impossible for the elite to regain its old position of respect and power. Faced with the emergence of parliamentary democracy, the English civil servants of the mid-nineteenth century had gracefully accepted a position of principled neutrality, eschewing political decision-making and restricting themselves to advising ministers. In Prussia this kind of neutrality was virtually impossible: the country's political tradition demanded the inclusion of officials in political affairs, and the bureaucracy's self-image, shaped during the crucial period of revolution and reaction, made it difficult for the profession to accept a position of principled neutrality. The solution arrived at in the formative period of the 1840's and 1850's was therefore one that took into account the necessity of constitutional government, but in no way made allowance for the evolution of that system toward parliamentary democracy. From the beginning, the relationship between the government and its officials was authoritarian: when crises arose, the Prussian state always demanded active support rather than passive neutrality from its higher civil servants. Although in quieter times governments were content to allow this increasingly conservative elite considerable latitude as far as the civil and political rights of its individual members were concerned, it became standard practice during periods when parliamentary and extraparliamentary movements challenged government policy to suspend the neutrality of the civil service.

The manner in which the Prussian civil service adjusted itself to social changes laid the groundwork for a sham constitutionalism. Its members adopted a pose of neutrality, yet their noninterference was prompted not by respect for the principle of separation of powers but, in most cases, by a calculated self-interest. Above all else, it was the desire to avoid a recurrence of serious internal and external conflicts that caused many Prussian officials to turn their backs on the constitution and ultimately on their own right to political participation, except, of course, when their superiors ordered them to enter the lists in the line of duty. In the 1850's many of these men rationalized their withdrawal of support of the constitution by adopting the notion that more could be done behind closed doors than in the bright light of parliamentary debate. This contributed to the weakening of the rule of law generally and led ultimately to the undermining of the representative institutions that might have been used to counteract arbitrary rule by the monarch and his chancellors.

In England the neutrality of the civil service was a precondition of the evolution of strong and independent representative institutions, but there the abstention from political interference involved a prior commitment to the separation of powers—something that was missing in the Prussian case. This tendency toward neutrality was strengthened by the fact that during the crucial phase of the evolution of English parliamentary democracy there occurred changes in the social composition and professional disposition of the English bureaucracy that favored constitutional government. Although the English higher civil service began in time to recruit primarily from among members of the upper middle class, whose qualifications included a broad literary university education, the possible harmful effects of increased social homogeneity were offset by the growth of a new service ethic that guaranteed a greater degree of social as well as political neutrality to the new elite. Thus the English civil service was capable of contributing to the successful political democratization of the country.[5] The passive withdrawal of the Prussian bureaucracy fostered authoritarianism by encouraging successive governments to treat the civil service as a tool of their policies and to use individual officials for partisan purposes when the occasion required. The political conditions under which the Prussian bureaucracy had lost its earlier corporate consciousness had been unfavorable to the formation of the kind of principled neutrality that is necessary to a democratic political system. Likewise the difficult social transition from aristocratic exclusiveness to integration in the modern class structure worked against the kind of conscientious detachment typical of the English profession.

Of course, it is impossible to say what the fate of the Prussian bureaucracy would have been if its political and social development not been interrupted by the revolution of 1848 and the decade of reaction that followed. Nor can we presume to know how the position of the bureaucracy might have changed if the revolution had succeeded in creating a democratic constitution. What can be stated with certainty, however, is that the origins of the similarities and differences between the Prussian experience and that of other Western European countries are to be found in crisis periods, including the Reform Era, the period we have just examined, and the revolution of 1918. Because of its manifold official duties, the bureaucracy was a critical agent in these events. Equally significant, however, was the way in which the group was affected by the internal changes that resulted from the efforts of its own members either to alter or to conserve its social and political character. What this study reveals is not only that officials were often in conflict with one another over the future of their profession, but that as individuals they were often torn between duties imposed by the state and personal commitments prompted by conscience. The conflicts and contradictions have been emphasized here in an effort to counteract the oversimplified, organic image of the Prussian civil service presented in much of the historical literature. The advantages of viewing the bureaucracy as a complex social and political organization should be abundantly evident: only from this perspective can its role in Prussian history be fully understood.

REFERENCE MATTER

Notes

Complete authors' names, titles, and publication data are given in the Bibliography, pp. 257–63. The following abbreviations are used in the notes:

AHR	*American Historical Review*
BA Koblenz	Bundesarchiv Koblenz
FBPG	*Forschungen zur Brandenburgischen und Preussischen Geschichte*
GS	*Gesetzsammlung für die Königlich Preussischen Staaten*
HA Berlin	Hauptarchiv Berlin-Dahlem
HHS	*Handbuch über den Königlich Preussischen Hof und Staat*
HZ	*Historische Zeitschrift*
KPS	*Königlich Preussischer Staatskalender*
JMB	*Justizministerialblatt*
MB	*Ministerialblatt für die Innere Verwaltung*
SA Düsseldorf	Staatsarchiv Düsseldorf
SA Koblenz	Staatsarchiv Koblenz
SBV	*Stenographische Berichte über die Verhandlungen des Hauses der Abgeordneten* (Lower House) 1849–
VCV	*Verhandlungen der constituierenden Versammlung für Preussen 1848*, 7 vols. (Berlin, 1848)
VSWG	*Vierteljahrsschrift für Sozial- und Wirtschaftsgeschichte*

Introduction

1. George Iggers, *The German Conception of History* (Middletown, Conn.: 1968), pp. 232–38.

2. Otto Hintze, "Behördenorganisation und allgemeine Verwaltung in Preussen beim Regierungsantritt Friedrichs II," in *Acta Borussica. Behördenorganisation*, Vol. 6, Part 1 (Berlin: 1901), pp. 3–614; also his numerous essays in *Staat und Verfassung* (Leipzig: 1941) and *Geist und Epochen der*

preussischen Geschichte: Gesammelte Abhandlungen (Leipzig: 1943). Schmoller's work on the eighteenth-century bureaucracy is exemplified by *Acta Borussica. Behördenorganisation,* Vol. 1 (Berlin: 1894); and by his essays in *Umrisse und Untersuchungen zur Verfassungs- Verwaltungs- und Wirtschaftsgeschichte* (Leipzig: 1898). See Rosenberg, *Bureaucracy.*

3. Joachim Lampe, *Aristokratie, Hofadel und Staatspatriziat in Kurhannover: Die Lebenskreise der höheren Beamten an den kurhannoverschen Zentral- und Hofbehörden 1714–1760,* 2 vols. (Göttingen: 1963); Helen Liebel, *Enlightened Bureaucracy versus Enlightened Despotism in Baden, 1750–1792* (Philadelphia: 1965); Koselleck, *Preussen;* Runge.

4. Kehr, "Zur Genesis der Bürokratie," and "Soziale System," pp. 31–52, 64–86. Much less useful is Hartung, "Studien," pp. 223–74.

5. For a general discussion of the concept of political modernization as it relates to bureaucracy, see Joseph La Palombara, ed., *Bureaucracy and Political Development* (Princeton, N.J.: 1963), pp. 9–14; and Bendix, pp. 105–41.

6. Conditions in the Rhineland before and during the Revolution of 1848 are described in Faber, *Rheinlande,* pp. 384ff; and Repgen, pp. 47–49, 305–7.

Chapter One

1. The essays in Conze, *Staat und Gesellschaft im deutschen Vormärz 1815–1848* (Stuttgart: 1962) are some of the first attempts to treat the pre-March decades on their own merits.

2. Riehl, *Die bürgerliche Gesellschaft,* pp. 3–4.

3. *Ibid.,* pp. 4–6.

4. Tocqueville, p. 228.

5. The most useful analysis of the *Allgemeine Landrecht* is Koselleck, *Preussen,* pp. 23–149. Also see Uwe-Jens Heuer, *Allgemeines Landrecht und Klassenkampf* (Berlin: 1960); Epstein, pp. 372–87.

6. "Von den Rechten und Pflichten der Diener des Staats," *Allgemeines Landrecht für die Preussischen Staaten,* Title X, para. 68–145.

7. Tocqueville, p. 229.

8. Epstein, pp. 386–87.

9. Koselleck, *Preussen,* pp. 153–62; Walter M. Simon, *The Failure of the Prussian Reform Movement, 1807–1819* (Ithaca, N.Y.: 1955), pp. 3–40.

10. Koselleck, *Preussen,* pp. 331–32.

11. See Henderson; Hamerow, pp. 1–94; and John H. Clapham, *The Economic Development of France and Germany, 1815–1914,* 4th ed. (Cambridge, Eng.: 1936), pp. 29–52, 83–103.

12. Hans Wolfram Graf Finck von Finckenstein, *Die Entwicklung der Landwirtschaft in Preussen und Deutschland 1800–1930* (Würzburg: 1960), pp. 79–201; Koselleck, *Preussen,* pp. 487–89; Conze, "Die Wirkungen der liberalen Agrarreform auf die Volksordnung in Mitteleuropa im 19. Jahrhundert," *VSWG,* Vol. 38 (1945), pp. 2–43.

13. Gunther Ipsen, "Die preussische Bauernbefreiung," *Zeitschrift für*

Agrargeschichte und Agrarsoziologie, Vol. 1 (1953), pp. 29–53; Wolfram Fischer, "Soziale Unterschichten im Zeitalter der Frühindustrialisierung," *International Review of Social History*, Vol. 8 (1963), pp. 415–35.

14. Brunschwig, pp. 47–72; Wilhelm Treue, *Wirtschaftszustände und Wirtschaftspolitik in Preussen 1815 bis 1825* (Stuttgart and Berlin: 1937), pp. 6–31, 160–81; Rosenberg, "Demokratisierung," pp. 459–86.

15. Conze, "Vom 'Pöbel' zum 'Proletariat,'" pp. 333–64; Conze, "Staat und Gesellschaft in der frührevolutionären Epoche Deutschlands," *HZ*, Vol. 186 (1958), pp. 1–34; Koselleck, *Preussen*, pp. 606–9; Wolfgang Köllmann, *Sozialgeschichte der Stadt Barmen in 19. Jahrhundert* (Tübingen: 1960).

16. Peter Reichensperger, quoted in Noyes, p. 23.

17. Hamerow, pp. 3–93; Noyes, pp. 15–33.

18. Koselleck, *Preussen*, pp. 607–9; Wolfgang Köllmann, "Anfänge," pp. 28–44; Carl Jantke and Dietrich Hilger, eds., *Die Eigentumslosen* (Freiburg and Munich: 1965), pp. 7–48.

19. Koselleck, *Preussen*, pp. 599–601; Zunkel, *Rheinisch-Westfälische Unternehmer*, pp. 34–46.

20. "Über die Zahl der Urwähler im Preussischen Staate und deren Vertheilung nach Geschäften und Erwerbszweigen," *Mittheilungen des statistischen Bureaus in Berlin*, Vol. 2 (1849), pp. 17–32.

21. Holborn, pp. 359–84; W. H. Bruford, *Culture and Society in Classical Weimar* (Cambridge, Eng.: 1962), pp. 1–11, 389–425.

22. Gerth, pp. 16–96, 109–17. For a brief overview of the professions in the 1840's, see O'Boyle, pp. 374–83.

23. "Statistische Übersicht," pp. 33–51.

24. On the clergy, see "Pfarrer," *Die Religion in Geschichte und Gegenwart*, 3d ed., Vol. 5 (Tübingen: 1961), pp. 286–87; and Paul Drews, *Der evangelische Geistliche in der deutschen Vergangenheit* (Jena: 1924), pp. 126–28. On the medical profession, see Paul Diepgen, *Geschichte der Medizin*, Vol. 2, Part 1 (Berlin: 1951), pp. 69–82, 220–25; Alfons Fischer, *Geschichte des deutschen Gesundheitswesens*, Vol. 2 (Hildesheim: 1965), pp. 52–70, 369–87; Erwin H. Ackerknecht, "Beiträge zur Geschichte der Medizinalreform von 1848," *Südhoffs Archiv für die Geschichte der Medizin*, Vol. 52 (1932), pp. 87–89.

25. Between 1800 and 1850 the total Prussian bureaucracy increased from 23,000 to 25,000. The higher bureaucracy remained almost constant during the same period. Figures on the entire bureaucracy from Finer, p. 710. For additional information, see Eckart Sturm, "Die Entwicklung des öffentlichen Dienstes in Deutschland," C. H. Ule, ed., *Die Entwicklung des öffentlichen Dienstes* (Cologne: 1961), pp. 33–35.

26. Weissler, pp. 421–48, 528–30.

27. "Statistische Übersicht," pp. 35–36.

28. *Ibid.*, pp. 38–45. On university enrollment, see Conrad, pp. 12–16.

29. Conrad, pp. 48–60.

30. Riehl, pp. 292–308; O'Boyle, pp. 375–80.

31. Prussian budgets are compared in Gerstfeldt, pp. 1–61. See also Koselleck, *Preussen*, pp. 438–47.

32. Rosenberg, *Bureaucracy*, pp. 192–201, 221–28; Hintze, "Österreichische und Beamtenstaat," pp. 401–44; Fann.

33. Stein to Hans von Gagern, 1821, quoted in Thiede, pp. 41–42.

34. Fann, pp. 120–22.

35. Hartung, "Studien," pp. 238–40.

36. Hans Schneider, *Der preussische Staatsrat 1817–1918* (Munich and Berlin: 1952), pp. 110–12; Koselleck, *Preussen*, pp. 79–83.

37. Georg Wilhelm Friedrich Hegel, *Philosophy of Right* (Oxford: 1958), para. 297, p. 193.

38. See Wilhelm; and Koselleck, "Staat und Gesellschaft," pp. 87–93; Huber, Vol. 2, pp. 374–80.

39. Henderson, *State and Industrial Revolution*; Wilhelm Treue, "Adam Smith in Deutschland, Zum Problem des 'politischen Professors' zwischen 1776 und 1810," *Deutschland und Europa* (Düsseldorf: 1951).

40. Richard Tilly, *Financial Institutions and Industrialization in the Rhineland, 1815–1870* (Madison, Wis.: 1966), pp. 13–15, 137.

41. See Köllmann; and Hans Joachim Henning, "Preussische Sozialpolitik im Vormärz," *VSWG*, Vol. 52 (1965), pp. 485–539.

42. Hermann von Petersdorff, *König Friedrich Wilhelm der Vierte* (Stuttgart: 1900), p. 28.

43. Hartung, "Regierung," pp. 1–9; Huber, Vol. 2, pp. 477–84.

44. For the effect of size on social organization, see Peter Rassow, "Social and Cultural Consequences of the Surge of Population in the Nineteenth Century," in Herbert Moller, ed., *Population Movements in the Modern European History* (New York: 1964), pp. 62–65.

45. Hans Rothfels, "Theodor von Schön, Friedrich Wilhelm IV und die Revolution von 1848," *Schriften der Königsberger Gelehrten Gesellschaft* (Halle: 1937), pp. 106–8; Huber, Vol. 2, pp. 484–87.

46. Schön, pp. 3–4.

47. Koselleck, *Preussen*, pp. 337–97; Hamerow, pp. 56–93; Krieger, pp. 273–340.

48. Koselleck, *Preussen*, pp. 392–94; Karl Griewank, "Vulgärer Radikalismus und demokratische Bewegung in Berlin 1842–1848," *FBPG*, Vol. 36 (1924), pp. 14–37; Faber, *Rheinlande*, pp. 175–77, 312–14; Jacques Droz, *Les révolutions allemandes de 1848* (Paris: 1957), pp. 25–146; Valentin, Vol. 1, pp. 24–101.

Chapter Two

1. Otto Camphausen to Ludolf Camphausen, Nov. 10, 1843, in Hansen, Vol. 1, p. 609; Varnhagen von Ense, Vol. 2, p. 127; Heinzen, pp. 12–13.

2. *Allgemeines Landrecht*, Title X; Perthes, pp. 68–70; Koselleck, *Preussen*, pp. 78–115.

3. For percentages of officials in various provincial diets during the 1830's and 1840's, see Koselleck, *Preussen*, pp. 692–93.

4. Freiherr vom Stein to Ernst Moritz Arndt, 1817, quoted in Thiede, p. 41.

5. Gerhard Ritter, *Stein* (Stuttgart: 1958), pp. 282-83; Heffter, pp. 69-77.

6. Koselleck, *Preussen*, p. 386.

7. *Ibid.*, Chapter 2, Part 3; Fann, pp. 202-27.

8. Hartung, "Studien," pp. 231-32.

9. Wehnert, *Über den Geist der preussischen Staatsorganisation und Staatsdienerschaft* (Potsdam: 1833), pp. 60-61.

10. Fann, pp. 201-18.

11. On the administration's requirements, see Clemens von Delbrück, pp. 2-9; and Friedrich, pp. 129-48. On the judiciary's standards, see Wilhelm Hedemann, "Justizverwaltung und Wissenschaft," in *200 Jahre Dienst am Recht* (Berlin: 1938), pp. 249-71.

12. Information on the family origins of officials does not appear in the personnel records of the Rhineland bureaucracy until the 1880's. Therefore the best sources of data on the social backgrounds of officials are the student records of the Halle and Berlin universities, which list the occupations of the fathers of law students. Not all those studying law were destined to enter the bureaucracy, but enough did enter to make these records an adequate index of the changing composition of the civil service. In 1820, 43 percent of the law students at Halle University were sons of state officials. If the sons of other professional men are included, the proportion of students from the cultivated elites rises to more than 60 percent. The Berlin University figures, which are less precise, show that over half of those studying law in 1820 were from the cultivated elites. For the Halle figures, see Conrad, pp. 51-52; for the Berlin figures, see Lenz, p. 522. A list of the academic preferences of secondary school graduates during the period 1789-1806 shows that 47 percent of those who elected to go on to the study of law at the university level were sons of civil servants, two-thirds of whom were of the upper ranks. Another 22 percent were sons of other professional men and only 31 percent were from families engaged in trade or agriculture. This information was compiled from tables of students in Paul Schwartz, *Das Gelehrtenschulen Preussens unter Oberschulkollegium und das Arbiturientenexamin*, 2 vols. (Berlin: 1910-11). Further evidence of the self-perpetuating character of the higher bureaucracy in the early nineteenth century is provided by Fritz Maas, "Über die Herkunftsbedingungen der geistigen Führer," *Archiv für Sozialwissenschaft und Sozialpolitik*, Vol. 41 (1916), pp. 144-86; and by Lotz, p. 402.

13. Hartung, "Studien," pp. 242-44, 252-56; Loening; Otto Hintze, "Preussens Entwicklung zum Rechtsstaat," *Geist und Epochen der preussischen Geschichte* (Leipzig: 1943), pp. 105-73.

14. Documents relating to the evolution of the *Konduitenlisten* are to be found in HA Berlin Rep. 90 Nr. 2318. For contemporary comment, see Heinzen, p. 171.

15. Lotz, pp. 364-76.

16. *Ibid.*, pp. 423-24; Most.

17. Lotz, p. 376; Naudé, pp. 1–22.

18. Most, pp. 183–88. For comparison with benefits of other bureaucracies, see Anderson and Anderson, pp. 217–22.

19. Rosenberg, *Bureaucracy*, Chapter 7; and Walter L. Dorn, "Prussian Bureaucracy in the Eighteenth Century," *Political Science Quarterly*, Vol. 46 (1931), pp. 403–23; Vol. 47 (1932), pp. 75–94, 259–73.

20. Perthes, p. 45.

21. Figures compiled from *HHS*, 1820.

22. Henning von Bonin, "Adel und Bürgertum in der höheren Beamtenschaft der preussischen Monarchie 1794–1806," *Jahrbuch für die Geschichte Mittel- und Ostdeutschlands*, Vol. 15 (1966), pp. 139–74.

23. Rosenberg, *Bureaucracy*, Chapter 8.

24. These figures include only those elevated to ordinary titles of nobility. Compiled from *Chronologische Matrikel der Brandenburgisch-Preussischen Standeserhöhungen und Gnadensacte*, ed. Maximilian Gritzner (Berlin, 1874).

25. Preradovich, pp. 115–23.

26. Conrad, pp. 51–52.

27. *Heidelberg Universität Matrikel*, 2 vols. (Heidelberg: 1905).

28. Mühler memorandum to Staatsministerium, Jan. 22, 1841, HA Berlin Rep. 90 Nr. 2007.

29. Kamptz memorandum to Staatsministerium, Dec. 29, 1840, *ibid.*

30. Holtze, pp. 56–57.

31. Stein, "Beurteilung des Rehdiger'schen Entwurfs über Reichsstände," *Freiherr vom Stein*, ed. W. Hubatsch, Vol. 2, Part 2 (Stuttgart: 1960), p. 853. For background, see Johanna Schultze, *Die Auseinandersetzung zwischen Adel und Bürgertum in den deutschen Zeitschriften der letzten Jahrzehnte des 18. Jahrhunderts* (Berlin: 1925); and Fritz R. Martiny, *Die Adelsfrage in Preussen vor 1806* (Stuttgart: 1938), pp. 80–86.

32. W. H. Bruford, *Germany in the Eighteenth Century* (Cambridge, Eng.: 1953), pp. 236–69; Holborn; Ludwig Beutin, "Das Bürgertum als Gesellschaftstand im 19. Jahrhundert," *Blätter für deutscher Landesgeschichte*, 90. Jahrgang (1953), pp. 132–65; Horst Beau, *Das Leistungswissen des frühindustriellen Unternehmertums in Rheinland-Westphalen* (Cologne: 1959); Zunkel, *Rheinisch-Westfälische Unternehmer*, pp. 23–67; Zunkel, "Beamtenschaft," pp. 262–74.

33. The distance between these groups is illustrated by Wolfram Fischer, *Die Bildungswelt des deutschen Handwerkers um 1800* (Berlin: 1955), pp. 43–51, 180–232.

34. Rudolf von Delbrück, Vol. 1, p. 194.

35. Lotz, pp. 401–2, 423–24; Most, pp. 181–87; Koselleck, *Preussen*, pp. 103–4, 114–15, 245–46.

36. Boehn, *Biedermeier*, pp. 150–51; Fann, pp. 246–50.

37. Rosenberg, *Bureaucracy*, pp. 183–86; Fann, pp. 11–19; Ringer, pp. 15–25.

38. Conrad, pp. 51–52.

39. Naudé, pp. 1–22.

40. The continuity between the Napoleonic and Prussian administrations in the Rhineland has been described by Faber, "Verwaltungs- und Justizbeamte," pp. 350–88. In 1858 the population of the Rhine province was 76 percent Catholic, as compared with 38 percent of the Prussian population as a whole. The personnel records of the administrative district of Trier for the year 1840 show that 45 percent of the higher administrative officials (including *Landräte*) were Catholics. That confession's proportion of the trainees in the Trier Regierung was even higher—60 percent (figures compiled from personnel reports of Trier district for the year 1840 in SA Koblenz Abt. 442 Nr. 3401). Of those who became Assessoren in the judiciary during the period 1824–35, almost 30 percent were Catholic. Many of the Catholic candidates were assigned to areas in which that faith was predominant, but the records of the Ministry of Justice show that even in the predominantly Protestant provinces the proportion of Catholic judges was at least 10 percent, and apparently rising. Figures from lists of Judicial Assessoren to be found in BA Koblenz P135 2791/2792.

41. The tabulation below shows the religious affiliation of all higher administrative personnel serving in the Rhine province during the years 1850–58. The figures are compiled from personnel reports, which only began to supply complete information on religion, geographical origin, date of birth, and history of career in 1850. The reports of the Koblenz, Köln, and Trier Regierungen are found in SA Koblenz Abt. 430 Nrs. 15043/5318/14556; reports of the Aachen and Düsseldorf districts are in SA Düsseldorf (Schloss Kalkum) Abt. 1 Nr. 68 and Fach 19 Nr. 1448/8481. Henceforth this source will be referred to as *Personnel Reports 1850–58*.

Rank	Protestant	Catholic
Oberpräsident	3	—
Regierungspräsident	5	1
Oberregierungsrat	5	8
Regierungsrat	27	19
Landrat	33	48
Total	73	76

42. Faber, "Verwaltungs- und Justizbeamte," pp. 381–88; Max Bär, *Die Behördenverfassung der Rheinprovinz seit 1815* (Bonn: 1919), p. 180.

43. The tabulation on p. 232 shows the geographical origins of administrators serving in the Rhine Province 1850–58 (from *Personnel Reports 1850–58*).

44. Stoelzel, pp. xxxvi–xlviii; Gustav Croon, *Der Rheinische Provinziallandtag bis zum Jahre 1874* (Düsseldorf: 1918), pp. 101–2.

45. Fann, p. 246. See also Perthes, p. 54.

46. Quotation from Ernest Kohn Bramsted, *Aristocracy and the Middle Classes in Germany* (London: 1937), p. 42. See also Koselleck, *Preussen*, pp. 433–43.

TABULATION FOR NOTE 43

Rank	Western (Rhineland and Westphalia)	Eastern
Oberpräsident	—	3
Regierungspräsident	3	3
Oberregierungsrat	8	4
Regierungsrat	20	14
Landrat	28	14
Total	59	38

47. Zunkel, *Rheinisch-Westfälische Unternehmer*, pp. 82–98; Koselleck, *Preussen*, pp. 440–47.

48. The proportion of businessmen's sons among those studying law at Halle rose from 9 percent in 1820 to 18 percent in the 1870's. Conrad, pp. 51–52.

49. Zunkel, *Rheinisch-Westfälische Unternehmer*, Chapter 4.

50. *Ibid.*, p. 118.

51. Naudé, pp. 9–16.

52. Figures for Halle taken from Conrad, pp. 51–52. For a similar trend at Berlin beginning in the 1840's, see Lenz, p. 522.

53. Leopold von Wiese, *Das höhere Schulwesen in Preussen* (Berlin: 1864), p. 520.

54. The number studying law at all Prussian universities was 938 in 1820, 1,533 in 1830, 964 in 1840, and 1,470 in 1850. Conrad, p. 108.

55. Weissler, p. 530.

56. Gerstfeldt, "Beiträge" (cited in note 31 to Chapter 1), pp. 27–28.

57. Most, pp. 181–86.

58. Michael Mulhall, *The Dictionary of Statistics*, 4th ed. (London: 1898), p. 258.

59. Most, pp. 185–87. For contemporary criticism, see Heinzen, pp. 188–210; Loos, pp. 51–56; and Weidemann. Additional material concerning complaints and protest is found in records of Ministry of Justice, BA Koblenz P135 7165.

60. *JMB*, 1839, p. 416.

61. *Ibid.*, p. 415.

62. Prior to the 1830's, the number of candidates had usually matched the needs of the judiciary. During the period 1756–1800 the average number taking the third judicial examination was 13 per year; during the period 1801–1936 it was 36 per year. Figures from Gneist, *Freie Advocatur*, p. 31. The figures on examinees in the years 1841–62 are listed in the table on the opposite page.

63. Conrad, pp. 105–19.

TABLE FOR NOTE 62
Results of Judicial Examination, 1841–62

Year	Number of examinations given	Number passed (No. becoming Assessoren)	Number failed	Percentage failed
1841	227	179	48	21%
1842	230	188	42	18
1843	180	157	23	12.5
1844	230	201	29	12.5
1845	221	193	28	12.5
1846	226	185	41	18
1847	246	182	64	26
1848	282	196	86	30.5
1849	180	118	62	34.5
1850	195	132	63	21
1853	293	209	84	29
1854	309	180	129	42
1855	360	198	162	45
1856	358	220	138	30
1857	483	315	168	35
1858	470	314	156	33
1859	457	309	148	32
1860	447	323	124	28
1861	351	270	81	23
1862	408	292	116	28

SOURCE: Compiled from *JMB* (1855), pp. 68–69; (1858), pp. 95–96; (1863), pp. 39–40.

64. See table on p. 234.

65. The administration faced a period of overcrowding in the late eighteenth century, but this seems to have been temporary and without results similar to those of the later period. See Brunschwig, Appendixes 3 and 4.

66. See table for note 64, p. 234.

67. *JMB*, 1858, pp. 300–304.

68. Wagner, pp. 41–44.

69. Judicial officials made unfavorable comparisons between their conditions and those of the administration in the 1850's. Petition of subaltern officials at court at Culm, 1855, BA Koblenz, P135 7165.

70. *JMB*, 1858, pp. 19–20.

71. Figures compiled from seniority lists of Presidents and Directors of Oberlandesgerichten, *Jahrbuch der preussischen Gerichtsverfassung*, 1856.

TABLE FOR NOTE 64

Number of Assessoren in Judicial Service, 1836–48

Year	No. as of Jan. 1	New Asses- soren	Retiring Asses- soren	Deaths	Appointment to:		Transfer to admin- istrative branch or retire- ment	Other causes for re- moval
					Rat	*Justiz- kommis- sarien*		
1836	676	152	39	4	14	10	8	3
1837	787	181	60	8	15	17	16	4
1838	908	193	57	7	18	14	16	2
1839	1142	205	52	6	13	21	11	
1840	1292	222	92	18	13	37	24	
1841	1420	184	100	3	21	42	34	
1842	1504	183	78	3	20	42	18	
1843	1609	162	108	16	26	39	26	1
1844	1663	190	104	16	16	32	39	1
1845	1749	199	146	14	47	47	37	1
1846	1802	178	129	22	19	46	38	4
1847	1851	192	124	19	19	58	26	2
1848	1919	197	86	15	14	43	13	

SOURCE: Compiled from BA Koblenz P 135 2792.

NOTE: Figures for 1836–38 do not include Rhine Province.

72. Gneist, *Freie Advocatur*, pp. 22–24.

73. Friedrich von Ammon (p. 101) remembered much speedier advancement early in the century.

74. Figures compiled for career records of administrative officials who served in Rhine Province 1850–58. From *Personnel Reports* 1850–58.

75. Bülow-Cummerow, *Preussen*, pp. 218–22; also Eberty, p. 365.

76. Hartung, "Studien," p. 234; Loos, p. 88.

77. In the Rhine Province in the 1850's, the average age of the Regierungspräsidenten and Oberregierungsräte was 55; among the Regierungsräte, the average age was 49.

78. The stagnation within the upper ranks is described by Heinzen, pp. 188–202.

79. Circular from Minister of Justice, May 6, 1840, *JMB*, 1840, p. 217. For the examination results, see table for note 62, p. 233.

80. HA Berlin Rep. 90 Nr. 2318.

81. Heinzen, p. 171; Loos, pp. 48–51.

82. *GS*, 1844.

83. Loening; Plathner.

84. BA Koblenz P135 2528 and P135 3140; also SA Koblenz Abt. 403 Nr. 2522, and Koselleck, *Preussen*, Chapter 3, part 3.

85. Memorandum from Minister of Justice, Nov. 23, 1837, BA Koblenz P135 2529.

86. Fann, p. 272.

87. Frederick William IV to all government departments, May 12, 1841, BA Koblenz P135 2486.

88. Memorandum from Minister of Interior, Dec. 12, 1842, BA Koblenz P135 2486.

89. Regulation of Jan. 24, 1843, *JMB*, 1843, p. 21.

90. *Trier Zeitung*, Feb. 20, 1843. This and other articles plus pamphlets critical of the bureaucracy can be found in BA Koblenz P135 2486.

91. Report of Oberlandesgerichtspräsident Lange, Feb. 6, 1844, BA Koblenz P135 2486.

92. Minister of Justice Mühler to Lange, March 1, 1844, *ibid.*; also *JMB*, 1843, p. 106.

93. *Preussische Staats Zeitung*, Nr. 341, 1841, Beilage; also BA Koblenz P135 6034.

94. *GS*, 1839, p. 235.

95. Ruling by Minister of Justice Mühler, Aug. 25, 1840, *GS*, 1840, p. 287; also BA Koblenz P135 3383.

96. On the development of conflict-of-interest regulations, see Zunkel, "Beamtenschaft," pp. 270–72; and Eichholtz, pp. 150–81.

Chapter Three

1. Brunschwig, pp. 147–58.

2. Schorn, Vol. 1, p. 237.

3. Clemens von Delbrück, pp. 6–9; Finer, pp. 794–95.

4. On Stein's attitude toward incompetent, pedantic officials, see Thiede, Chapter 2.

5. Friedrich, pp. 139–43.

6. On the effect of reforms, consult Paulsen, *Geschichte des gelehrten Unterrichts*, pp. 278–362.

7. Schulze and Ssymank, pp. 274–78; Ringer, pp. 14–42. For a comparative approach to the role of students in the formative periods of the histories of modernizing states, see Edward Shils, "Intellectuals in the Political Development of New States," *World Politics*, Vol. 12 (1960), pp. 329–68.

8. William Howitt, *The Student-Life in Germany* (London: 1849), pp. 427–40; Boehn, *Biedermeier*, pp. 243–52; Schulze and Ssymank, pp. 278–99.

9. Eberty, pp. 422–25; Ernsthausen, Vol. 1, p. 80.

10. A vivid description of the examination system is provided by Richter, pp. 43–44, 88, 103–13; also Eberty, p. 405, and Finer, p. 798.

11. See table for note 62, Chapter 2. See also Boehn, *Biedermeier*, p. 245; Eberty, pp. 422–25.

12. Paulsen, *Geschichte des gelehrten Unterrichts*, pp. 286–300.

13. Clemens von Delbrück, pp. 6–8.

14. Griewank, pp. 9–21. Tensions within the university faculty are discussed by Busch, pp. 41–57; and Obermann, pp. 165–202.

15. Griewank, pp. 7–12; Paul Wentzcke, *Geschichte der deutschen Bur-schenschaften, Quellen und Darstellungen zur Geschichte der Burschen-schaft und der deutschen Einheitsbewegung,* Vol. 6 (Heidelberg: 1919).

16. The distance between the graduates of the early-nineteenth-century *Burschenschaften* and the later Progress Movement is revealed in the anony-mous memoirs of an older university graduate, *Von 1846 bis 1853, Erinne-rungen aus Verlauf und Folgen einer akademischen und politischen Revo-lution* (Darmstadt: 1875). See also Georg Heer, *Geschichte der deutschen Burschenschaft, Quellen und Darstellungen zur Geschichte der Burschen-schaft,* Vol. 11 (Heidelberg: 1929).

17. Griewank, pp. 8–18; Obermann, pp. 165–90; Heer (cited in preceding note), pp. 125–36. A discussion of the concept of generations and the rela-tionship of age groups to historical change is provided by S. N. Eisenstadt in *From Generation to Generation* (New York: 1966), Chapters 4 and 6; and in Eisenstadt, "Archetypal Patterns of Youth," *The Challenge of Youth,* ed. E. Erikson (New York: 1965), pp. 29–50.

18. Conrad, pp. 27–30; Paulsen, *Geschichte des gelehrten Unterrichts,* Vol. 2, pp. 286–90.

19. Conrad, p. 111. The average age of the administrative Assessoren in the Rhine Province in 1840 was twenty. In 1850 it was twenty-two and a half.

20. Loos, p. 28.

21. Letter of Minister of Interior Westphalen to Oberpräsident Kleist-Retzow, April 20, 1857, replying to the latter's question about the fairness of the seniority system. HA Berlin Rep. 90 No. 2336.

22. *Preussische Staats Zeitung,* No. 341, 1842, Beilage.

23. Loos, p. 92; Heinzen, p. 146; Schorn, Vol. 1, p. 238; Koselleck, *Preus-sen,* pp. 412–13.

24. Frederick William IV to the Staatsministerium, Oct. 14, 1842, BA Ko-blenz P135 6034.

25. O'Boyle; Krieger, Chapter 7.

26. Fann, pp. 246–50.

27. Zunkel, *Rheinisch-Westfälische Unternehmer,* pp. 27, 52; Eichholtz, pp. 150–72.

28. Hamerow, p. 77.

29. *Preussens Beamtentum;* Dronke, pp. 32–33. Documents relating to the problem of indebtedness of officials can be found in BA Koblenz P135 2486.

30. Many of the petitions received during the 1850's refer to 1847 as the worst year for those on fixed salary. BA Koblenz P135 7165. For contem-porary comment, see Diest, p. 242; Heinzen, pp. 189–202; and Dronke, p. 33.

31. Naudé, pp. 11–16; Eberty, p. 385.

32. From an official handbook for judicial officials published in Münster in 1851. BA Koblenz P135 2531.

33. On the changing life-styles in the early nineteenth century, see Boehn, *Die Mode,* Vol. 2, pp. 142–55.

34. Schulze and Ssymank, pp. 281–82, 432–33. Broad trends are discussed in Zorn, pp. 325–32.

35. The size of the families of administrative officials in the Trier district fell from an average of four children in the 1830's to an average of three children in the 1870's. Further evidence of the restriction of family size is provided by Most, pp. 208–9. The famous English social critic Henry Mayhew noted the distress among Rhineland officials because they felt they could not marry their fiancées until they had attained salaried positions. Mayhew, *The Upper Rhine: The Scenery of Its Banks and the Manners of Its People* (London: 1858), p. 239.

36. Marcks, pp. 131–33.

37. Loos, p. 60.

38. Marcks, pp. 133–36.

39. Quoted in Zunkel, *Rheinisch-Westfälische Unternehmer*, p. 101.

40. Jacoby, p. 91.

41. Perthes, p. 46.

42. Hansemann, *Preussen und Frankreich*, pp. 219–35; Heffter, pp. 207–30.

43. Bülow-Cummerow, *Preussen*, pp. 95–137; Sigmund Neumann, *Die Stufen des preussischen Konservatismus* (Berlin: 1930), pp. 21–43.

44. *Neue Preussische Zeitung*, Feb. 12, 1857.

45. Ammon, pp. 46–47, 134–35; Heinzen, pp. 188–92; Riehl, pp. 305–6.

46. The composition of the conservative and highly exclusive corps reflected this change. See lists of members by year in *Kösener Corpslisten*, ed. O. Gerlach (Jever in Oldenburg: 1960).

47. Rudolf von Delbrück, Vol. 1, pp. 62–68; Ernsthausen, p. 80.

48. Lotz, p. 425.

49. Rudolf von Delbrück, Vol. 1, pp. 127–28. For accounts by others with similar experiences, see Justus von Gruner, "Rückblick auf mein Leben," *Deutsche Revue*, Vol. 2 (1901), pp. 25–30; Bismarck, pp. 16–17.

50. Eugen Schiffer, *Rudolf von Gneist* (Berlin: 1929), pp. 1–13.

51. Gneist, *Freie Advocatur*, pp. 33–34; Ferdinand Fischer, p. 149.

52. Gneist, *Berliner Zustände*, p. 52.

53. Jacoby, p. 90.

54. Loos, p. 11.

55. *Ibid.*, p. 56; and various petitions from the 1850's in BA Koblenz P135 7155 and P135 7165.

56. Richard Dietrich, "Von der Residenzstadt zur Weltstadt," *Das Hauptstadtproblem in der Geschichte* (Berlin: 1952), pp. 111–37; Dronke, pp. 12–18, 22–25; Boehn, *Die Mode*, Vol. 3, pp. 60, 147–48; Most, pp. 184–87.

57. Loos, p. 11. For reports on indebtedness, see BA Koblenz P135 2486.

58. Weidemann, p. 47.

59. Riehl, pp. 347–58. Further evidence of the social defensiveness of the middle ranks of German society in the 1840's is provided by recent work on the conditions in the South German states by Edward Shorter, "Middle-

Class Anxiety in the German Revolution of 1848," *Journal of Social History*, No. 3 (1969), pp. 189–215.

60. Riehl, pp. 428, 372, 367.

Chapter Four

1. Koselleck, "Staat und Gesellschaft," pp. 89–93; Engelsing, pp. 337–69.

2. Koselleck, *Preussen*, p. 414; O'Boyle, "The Image of the Journalist in France, Germany, and England, 1815–1848," *Comparative Studies in Society and History*, Vol. 10 (1968), pp. 302–12.

3. Krieger, pp. 278–328; Huber, Vol. 2, pp. 477–500; Koselleck, *Preussen*, Chapter 3, Part 1.

4. R. Hinton Thomas, *Liberalism, Nationalism and the German Intellectuals, 1822–1847* (Cambridge, Eng.: 1951), pp. 86–101.

5. Report on the Soest conference, BA Koblenz P135 5410.

6. Order of Minister of Justice, Feb. 6, 1844, BA Koblenz P135 5410.

7. Order of the king, March 15, 1844, BA Koblenz P135 5410.

8. Weissler, pp. 461–67, 510–21; Eduard Kern, *Geschichte des Gerichtsverfassungsrechts* (Berlin: 1954), pp. 61–66.

9. Details of this movement are found in Jacoby, pp. 161–84; Joseph Wicke, *Heinrich Simons Kampf gegen die Disziplinargesetze vom 19. März 1844* (Breslau: 1912); Plathner, pp. 111–18.

10. Jacoby, p. 166; Heinzen, p. 124.

11. Rudolf von Delbrück, Vol. 1, p. 190.

12. Heinzen, p. 70.

13. Wilhelm, pp. 42ff; Wolfram Fischer, pp. 150–56.

14. Hansemann, *Preussen und Frankreich*, p. 229; Heffter, pp. 310–11.

15. Koselleck, *Preussen*, pp. 364–76; Nathan, pp. 78–86; Heinz Boberach, *Wahlrechtsfragen im Vormärz* (Düsseldorf: 1959), pp. 62–77.

16. The order of Dec. 21, 1834, suspended all trainees with Burschenschaft affiliation. BA Koblenz P135 3140; SA Koblenz Abt. 403 Nr. 2522; Schulze and Ssymank, pp. 234–42.

17. BA Koblenz P135 3140.

18. Memorandum of Nov. 12, 1830, BA Koblenz P135 3140.

19. Rudolf von Delbrück, Vol. 1, p. 38.

20. Frederick William IV to Minister of Justice Mühler, July 18, 1843, BA Koblenz P135 3140; Treitschke, Vol. 5, pp. 255–56.

21. Frederick William IV to Minister of Justice Mühler, July 18, 1843, BA Koblenz P135 3140; Mühler directive to all courts, July 28, 1843, *JMB*, 1843, p. 186.

22. Koselleck, *Preussen*, p. 414.

23. Meyer, pp. 44–45; Engelsing, pp. 345–55.

24. Report of Düsseldorf Regierungspräsident von Spiegel, March 1, 1845, BA Koblenz P135 5410.

25. Report of Düsseldorf State Prosecutor Korkeritz, April 1, 1845, *ibid.*; *Düsseldorf 1848*, p. 12.

26. Oberpräsident Eichmann to Minister of Interior Arnim, Dec. 23, 1845, BA Koblenz P135 5410; Faber, *Rheinlande*, pp. 260–62.

27. Dronke, pp. 50–54.

28. Born, pp. 20–28; Noyes, pp. 48–49.

29. Jacoby, pp. 185–96.

30. Meyer, pp. 40–51; Noyes, pp. 46–50.

31. Erwin H. Ackerknecht, *Rudolf Virchow: Doctor, Statesman, Anthropologist* (Madison, Wis.: 1953), p. 160.

32. Jacoby, pp. 107–12; Eberty, pp. 365–75.

33. Heinzen, pp. 146–71; Ernsthausen, pp. 95–98.

34. Report of the Minister of the Interior to the Minister of Justice, July 15, 1845, BA Koblenz P135 5410.

35. Report on activities of the Cleve *Volksverein*, from the Oberpräsident of the Rhine province to the Minister of the Interior, Dec. 23, 1845, BA Koblenz P135 5410; Haenchen, pp. 97–114; Meyer, pp. 40–47.

36. Haenchen, p. 114.

37. Koselleck, *Preussen*, pp. 414–27.

38. Dronke, pp. 146, 160, 183; Faber, *Rheinlande*, pp. 406–31.

39. Jacoby, pp. 112–16.

40. Koselleck, *Preussen*, pp. 387–97; 694–96.

41. Frederick William IV to Staatsministerium, July 24, 1847, HA Berlin Rep. 90 Nr. 2322.

42. Treitschke, Vol. 5, pp. 629–32.

43. Regierungspräsident of Arnsberg, Graf von Itzenplitz, to the Oberpräsident of Westphalia, Eduard von Flottwell, Sept. 20, 1847, HA Berlin Rep. 90 Nr. 2322.

44. Landrat Georg von Vincke to Staatsministerium, Nov. 30, 1847, *ibid.*

45. Jacoby, p. 170.

46. Frederick William IV to Staatsministerium, Jan. 4, 1848, HA Berlin Rep. 90 Nr. 2322.

47. Huber, Vol. 2, pp. 327–45; Wilhelm, pp. 47–61.

48. Repgen, pp. 328–29; Wilhelm Mommsen, *Deutsche Parteiprogramme* (Munich: 1960), pp. 125–27.

49. Huber, Vol. 2, pp. 374–80.

50. Bülow-Cummerow, *Preussen*, p. 104; Heinzen, pp. 12–13.

51. Nathan, pp. 78–79; Heffter, p. 236.

52. Heffter, pp. 246–67; Koselleck, *Preussen*, pp. 366–81; Faber, *Rheinlande*, pp. 422–31; Reinhard Adam, "Der Liberalismus in der Provinz Preussen zur Zeit der neuen Ära," *Altpreussische Beiträge* (Königsberg: 1933), pp. 151–58.

53. Koselleck, *Preussen*, pp. 392–97; Faber, *Rheinlande*, pp. 419–31; James J. Sheehan, "Political Leadership in the German Reichstag, 1871–1918," *AHR*, Vol. 74 (1968), pp. 511–15.

54. Rudolf von Delbrück, Vol. 1, pp. 190–91; Eberty, pp. 362–63.

55. Rudolf von Delbrück, Vol. 1, p. 190.

56. Koselleck, *Preussen*, pp. 586–87; Rudolf von Delbrück, pp. 116–17, 191.

57. Eberty, p. 367; Bülow-Cummerow, *Preussen*, pp. 218–22.

Chapter Five

1. Unrest within the civil service was a characteristic prelude to revolution in Europe during the second half of the eighteenth century and the first part of the nineteenth. See John R. Gillis, "Political Decay and the European Revolutions, 1789–1848," *World Politics*, Vol. 22 (1970), pp. 344–70.

2. Reichensperger, pp. 23–24.

3. Official report on the investigation of Regierungsrat Scherer, HA Berlin Rep. 90, Abt. 3 Nr. 989.

4. Wolff, pp. 173–75; Valentin, Vol. 2, p. 71.

5. Repgen, pp. 52–58; Dreesen, p. 50.

6. Albert Florschütz, *Die politischen und sozialen Zustände der Provinz Westphalen während der Jahre 1848/49* (Elberfeld: 1861), p. 11; Reichensperger, pp. 28–29. The activities of students and young officials in Berlin are described by Griewank, pp. 18–30; and Holtze, pp. 184–85.

7. Gneist, *Berliner Zustände*, p. 10.

8. Ammon, pp. 169–70; Repgen, pp. 54–55.

9. Ferdinand Fischer, p. 111; Jacoby, p. 211.

10. Petitions on this subject are in HA Berlin Rep. 90 Nr. 984, 989; Jacoby, p. 231.

11. An excellent description of the confusion in the conservative ranks is provided by Alexander Andrae-Roman, *Erinnerungen eines alten Mannes aus dem Jahr 1848* (Bielefeld: 1895), pp. 20–27.

12. Wolff, pp. 277–78; Holtze, p. 185.

13. *Deutsche Arbeiter Zeitung* (Berlin), No. 6, April 19, 1848.

14. Eberty, p. 385.

15. Orders of July 8 and July 20, BA Koblenz P135 5411.

16. Holtze, p. 184.

17. Reichensperger, p. 26; Ammon, pp. 176–77; Kaeber, pp. 115–22.

18. Kaeber, p. 119. The few lists of Bürgerwehr members in the Berlin Ratsbibliothek collection of revolutionary pamphlets and posters indicate that the leadership was uniformly upper-class.

19. Wolff, pp. 147–48; Streckfuss, Vol. 2, pp. 1048, 1071.

20. *Das Volk* (Berlin), No. 6, June 15, 1848.

21. Noyes, pp. 136–45.

22. *Reform* (Berlin), No. 198, Nov. 10, 1848; Noyes, pp. 142–43.

23. Kaeber, p. 155.

24. On the evolution of these terms, see Conze, "Vom 'Pöbel' zum 'Proletariat.'"

25. Bernstein, Vol. 1, p. 121.

26. *Die Contra-Revolution in Berlin, oder Bürger und Arbeiter* (Berlin: 1848), p. 4; Noyes, pp. 21–23.

27. *Der Publicist, Eine Zeitschrift für Freiheit und Gesetz, für öffentliches Rechts- und Gerichtsverfahren* (Berlin), Nos. 72 and 73, Aug. 22 and 24, 1848; *Deutsche Arbeiter Zeitung*, No. 4, April 19, 1848; *Das Volk*, No. 1, March 25, 1848; *Der Demokrat*, No. 1, May 22, 1848.

28. Born, pp. 137–38; Noyes, pp. 34–54.

29. *Feuerbrände*, Nos. 1 and 2, May 16 and 22, 1848.

30. Paul Boerner, *Erinnerungen eines Revolutionärs* (Leipzig: 1920), Vol. 1, pp. 233–38.

31. On Berlin, see Kaeber, pp. 101–14; and *Berlins Gegenwart*. For the Rhine Province, information is supplied by reports on political activity submitted Oct. 1848, SA Koblenz Abt. 403 Nr. 7045. On various towns, see Kersken, p. 37; *Düsseldorf 1848*, pp. 14–16; Dreesen, pp. 50–53.

32. Huber, Vol. 2, pp. 571–86; Rudolf Stadelmann, *Soziale und politische Geschichte der Revolution von 1848* (Munich: 1948), pp. 83–99.

33. *Berlins Gegenwart*, p. 10.

34. Reports on political activity in the Rhineland, submitted Oct. 19 and 26, 1848, SA Koblenz Abt. 403 Nr. 7045.

35. *Ibid.*, report of Oct. 18, 1848; also *Düsseldorf 1848*, p. 14.

36. Report of Oct. 31, 1848, SA Koblenz Abt. 403 Nr. 7045.

37. Kaeber, p. 110; Griewank, pp. 27–30.

38. Kersken, p. 45.

39. Dreesen, p. 50.

40. Jacoby, pp. 210–31.

41. Born, p. 136. On similar generational conflict in Vienna, see R. Lutz, "Fathers and Sons in the Vienna Revolution of 1848," *Journal of Central European Affairs*, Vol. 22, pp. 161–73.

42. *Berlins Gegenwart*, p. 13.

43. Kersken, p. 45.

44. HA Berlin Rep. 90 Abt. 3 Nr. 989. Ernsthausen, who was at first deeply involved in revolutionary activity, went through a similar process (pp. 92–93).

45. Report of Oct. 26, 1848, SA Koblenz Abt. 403 Nr. 7045. On the issue of the army's political role, see Craig, pp. 112–20.

46. Kaeber, p. 111.

47. Typical of these were the cartoons in *Kladderadatsch*, No. 6, Feb. 11, 1849.

48. Streckfuss, Vol. 2, p. 1059.

49. Huber, Vol. 2, 575–86; Repgen, pp. 145–55, 225–308.

50. See Jung; Holtz, p. 184; and Hermann, pp. 265–66.

51. Bergenroth, p. 7; Benedikt Waldeck, *Die constitutionelle Monarchie mit einer Kammer* (Berlin: 1848). These and other campaign pamphlets are available in the Ratsbibliothek collection in East Berlin.

52. Heffter, p. 259.

53. Gneist, *Berliner Zustände*, p. 52.

54. The following table shows in percentages the most important occupa-

tional groups represented among the Prussian membership of the Frankfurt
and Berlin Assemblies:

Occupation	Frankfurt Assembly				Berlin Assembly
Large landowners	10%				6.8%
State administrators	14				9.5
Higher ranks[a]		97%	Higher ranks	87%	
Trainees		3%	Trainees	13%	
State judges	21				24
Higher ranks[b]		64%	Higher ranks	69%	
Trainees		36%	Trainees	31%	
Military officers	3.5				0
Other professionals	22				25.4
Urban businessmen	2.5				2.5
Artisans and peasants	2				22.7

SOURCE: Figures for the Frankfurt Assembly are taken from Schilfert, pp. 402–3;
and Max Schwarz, *MdR, Biographisches Handbuch der Reichstage* (Hannover:
1965). Figures for the Berlin Assembly were compiled from lists in *VCV*.

[a] Landräte and Ministers are included in the higher administration figures; Bur-
germeisters are excluded.

[b] Figures for the higher judiciary include state prosecutors but exclude lawyers.

55. Three-quarters of the Frankfurt deputies had been born in the period
1796–1815, and were thus probably somewhat older than the average Berlin
deputy. On the age of Frankfurt deputies see Eyck, pp. 100–101.

56. Heinrich Abeken, *Ein schlichtes Leben in bewegter Zeit*, 2d ed. (Berlin: 1898), p. 158.

57. Schilfert, p. 401.

58. Heinrich von Poschinger, ed., *Ein Achtundvierziger, Lothar Buchers
Leben und Werke* (Berlin: 1890), Vol. 1, p. 8.

59. For cost-of-living estimates, see Friedrich von Reden, *Erwerbs- und
Verkehrs-Statistik des Königsstaats Preussen* (Darmstadt: 1853), Vol. 1,
pp. 180–81.

60. Bernstein, Vol. 1, p. 123.

61. Hermann, p. 160.

62. Huber, Vol. 2, pp. 576–80, 584–86.

63. The leadership of the parties on the Left was made up of younger men.
Jung was 34, Bucher 31, Schulze-Delitzsch 40, von Kirchmann 46, Waldeck
46; Temme, the oldest, was only 50.

64. A useful classification of deputies by faction is contained in the *Conduiten-Liste*, a pamphlet published in Berlin in late 1848 or early 1849. I
have used it in compiling these figures, since nowhere in the standard litera-

ture could I find a similar list. The *Conduiten-Liste* was compiled according to the way deputies voted on major issues and seems relatively accurate.

65. Included in the category of lower-ranking officials are members of the subaltern bureaucracy and those trainees who had not reached tenure. The Rechtsanwälte are excluded from the category of civil officials.

66. The remainder of the Left were made up of members of traditional lower classes. A very few larger landowners voted left as well.

67. Huber, Vol. 2, p. 726.

68. Craig, pp. 114–16.

69. The tabulation below gives a breakdown of the vote to abolish the legal status of the nobility, taken on October 31, 1848.

Rank	For abolition	Against abolition
Administration		
Regierungsrat and above	1	8
Trainees and subalterns	—	1
Judiciary		
Tenured judges	8	22
Trainees and subalterns	16	11
Vote of total Assembly	200	153

70. On divisions within the Frankfurt Parliament, see Eyck, pp. 94–97.

71. Huber, Vol. 2, pp. 751–66; Kaeber, p. 167.

72. For a list of those who defied the government to remain in Berlin, see *Conduiten-Liste*.

73. Huber, Vol. 2, pp. 755–56.

74. Kersken, p. 88; Streckfuss, Vol. 1, pp. 1186–88; Busch, pp. 53–57.

75. Order issued by Oberpräsident Eichmann, Nov. 17, 1848, SA Koblenz Abt. 403 Nr. 2550.

76. SA Koblenz Abt. 403 Nr. 4148, 2550.

77. Pinder to Graf Brandenburg, Nov. 15, 1848, HA Berlin Rep. 90 Nr. 984.

78. Wegge, pp. 24–26.

79. See Dorn.

80. Kurt Untermann, *Der Kampf um die preussische Selbstverwaltung in Jahre 1848* (Berlin: 1937), p. 54; Alexander Bergengrün, *David Hansemann* (Berlin: 1901), pp. 500–501; Hartung, "Studien," pp. 252–54.

81. Debates of June 28, 1848, *VCV*, Vol. 2, pp. 735–40; *MB*, 1848 p. 250.

82. Hartung, "Studien," p. 253.

83. Temme, pp. 272–84.

84. *Ibid.*, pp. 284–89.

85. Hermann von Peterdorff, *Kleist-Retzow* (Stuttgart: 1907), pp. 133–48.

86. Poschinger, *Unter Friedrich Wilhelm IV,* Vol. 2, p. 15; Hans Walter, *Die Innere Politik des Ministers von Manteuffel und der Ursprung der*

Reaktion in Preussen. Dissertation (University of Berlin, 1911), pp. 40–41.

87. Constitution of Dec. 5, 1848, Articles 77, 96, 97, in Ernst Huber, ed., *Dokumente zur deutschen Verfassungsgeschichte*, Vol. 1 (Stuttgart: 1961), pp. 391–93.

88. Heinemann, pp. 15–23. Circular of Dec. 28, 1848, from Minister of Interior, *MB*, 1848, pp. 363–64.

89. For a comparative view of this problem, see Bendix, pp. 105–42.

90. Karl Mannheim, *Ideology and Utopia* (New York: 1936), p. 118.

Chapter Six

1. Heinemann, p. 19.

2. *Neue Preussische Zeitung*, Jan. 10 and 17, 1849; Leopold von Gerlach, Vol. 1, pp. 258–60.

3. Poschinger, *Unter Friedrich Wilhelm IV*, Vol. 1, p. 134.

4. Dorn, pp. ii-x.

5. *MB*, 1848, pp. 368–69; HA Berlin Rep. 90 Nr. 2322.

6. Wegge, pp. 35–44.

7. Constitution of Dec. 5, Article 67, in *Dokumente* (cited in note 87, Chapter 5), Vol. 1, p. 390.

8. Circular of Dec. 28, 1848, *MB*, 1848, p. 363.

9. The government appears to have kept its pledge of due-process during this period. See the reports on various investigations of officials suspected of having participated in revolution in HA Berlin Rep. 90 Nr. 989.

10. *GS*, 1848, p. 7; Huber, Vol. 3, pp. 121–26.

11. Gneist, *Freie Advocatur*, pp. 20–22.

12. Bülow-Cummerow, *Die Reaktion und ihre Fortschritte* (Berlin: 1850), p. 8.

13. Debates of April 4 and 5, 1851, *SBV*, 1851.

14. Huber, Vol. 3, pp. 121–22.

15. Weissler, pp. 523–35.

16. The Minister of Justice now controlled the appointment of a quarter of the judiciary, mainly the upper ranks. Gneist, *Freie Advocatur*, p. 41.

17. *Ibid.*, pp. 34–35.

18. Ferdinand Fischer, p. 130.

19. *Ibid.*, pp. 131–33, 135–36.

20. In a circular of Aug. 24, 1849, the government urged all administrative personnel to take advantage of their right to sit on juries. *MB*, 1849, p. 189.

21. Ferdinand Fischer, pp. 135–36.

22. Hamerow, pp. 199–237; Paul Geissen, *Die preussische Handwerkerpolitik unter Otto von Manteuffel* (Wupperthal-Elberfeld: 1936).

23. Hansemann, *Verfassungswerk*, pp. 163–64; Wegge, pp. 89–93.

24. Heinemann, p. 30.

25. These figures and subsequent estimates of the composition of factions in the Prussian Lower House are compiled from Lauter.

26. The number of Landräte rose from seven in 1848 to seventeen in the Lower House elected in January 1849. Of these, thirteen were listed by Lauter as loyal to the government.

27. In the opposition stood the Extreme Left, the Left, the Center-Left, and the Polish faction. On the government's side were the Center-Right, the Auerswald-Schwerin faction, and the Extreme Right (*Kreuzzeitungspartei*). The two groups were about evenly divided in numbers.

28. See Table 1, p. 134.

29. Compiled from Lauter.

30. From a flyer published in Jan. 1849, *Enthüllung der Wahl-Operationen der Demokraten*. This listing of democratic leaders, which appears to be accurate, is found in the collection of materials relating to the Revolution of 1848 in the Landesarchiv Berlin Rep. 240 Acc. 685, Vol. 2.

31. Bismarck, p. 61.

32. Ernst von Gerlach, Vol. 2, p. 42.

33. Bülow-Cummerow, *Revolution*, pp. 5–6.

34. *Ibid.*, pp. 33–34.

35. Hansemann, *Verfassungswerk*, pp. 167, 172–73.

36. Frederick William IV was constantly concerned with the discipline within the profession. See his memoranda in HA Berlin Rep. 90 Nr. 2322; and BA Koblenz P135 3140. On the attitude of the Kreuzzeitungspartei, see *Neue Preussische Zeitung*, April 12 and 17, 1849.

37. Pückler-Muskau to Manteuffel, Dec. 27, 1848, in Poschinger, *Unter Friedrich Wilhelm IV*, Vol. 1, pp. 70–71.

38. Bonin to Manteuffel, May 24, 1849, *ibid.*, p. 117.

39. Eichmann to Manteuffel, June 22, 1849, *ibid.*, p. 73.

40. Poschinger, *Preussens Auswärtige Politik*, Vol. 1, p. 141.

41. Poschinger, *Unter Friedrich Wilhelm IV*, Vol. 1, pp. 202–3.

42. From a conversation with Leopold von Gerlach, reported in Leopold von Gerlach, Vol. 1, pp. 706–7.

43. Huber, Vol. 3, pp. 40–44.

44. *Ibid.*, pp. 45–49; Schilfert, pp. 256–59.

45. *GS*, 1849, p. 205.

46. Schilfert, pp. 267–76; Walter Gagel, *Die Wahlrechtsfrage in der Geschichte der deutschen liberalen Parteien 1848–1918* (Düsseldorf: 1958), pp. 8–20.

47. Schilfert, pp. 288–93, 304–6.

48. Rudolf Gneist, *Die nationale Rechtsidee von den Ständen und das preussische Dreiklassenwahlsystem* (Berlin: 1894), pp. 192–94.

49. Louis Rosenbaum, *Beruf und Herkunft der Abgeordneten zu den deutschen und preussischen Parlamenten 1847 bis 1919* (Frankfurt: 1923), pp. 59–63.

50. Compiled from Lauter.

51. Huber, Vol. 3, pp. 49–51.

52. Schilfert, pp. 313–14.

53. *GS*, 1849, pp. 221.
54. Minister von der Heydt's report of Feb. 7, 1849, HA Berlin Rep. 90 Nr. 2322.
55. Quoted in Ferdinand Fischer, p. 112.
56. Frederick William IV to Staatsministerium, June 20, 1849, HA Berlin Rep. 90 Nr. 2322. Reports on renewed radical activity among officials in the Rhineland are to be found in SA Koblenz Abt. 403 Nr. 6568.
57. Circular of June 8, 1849, BA Koblenz P135 3140; Ferdinand Fischer, p. 257.
58. Circular of June 18, 1849, BA Koblenz P135 3140.
59. Petition dated May 30, 1849, BA Koblenz P135 3057.
60. For the government's interpretation of the two discipline regulations, see *MB*, 1849, pp. 119–23; and the report of Staatsministerium to the king, July 9, 1849, in Poschinger, *Unter Friedrich Wilhelm IV*, Vol. 1, pp. 131–32.
61. *MB*, 1849, pp. 119–23.
62. A special Diziplinhof was established on Aug. 22, 1849. *MB*, 1849, p. 160.
63. Hartung, "Studien," pp. 248–53.
64. *Ibid.*, p. 254.
65. BA Koblenz P135 6068 and 6069.
66. Hartung, "Studien," pp. 256–58.
67. *Neue Preussische Zeitung*, July 19, 1849.
68. *SBV*, 1851.
69. I have not found any evidence in the archives of systematic manipulation of officials in the elections of 1849. Whatever interference there was seems to have been of a negative sort: censoring voter lists, numbering the ballots in order to intimidate voters, and so on. For an account of the elections in one district, see Schierbaum, pp. 37–78.
70. Huber, Vol. 3, pp. 161–69.
71. Heinemann, pp. 15–48; Enax, pp. 27–40.
72. *MB*, 1850, pp. 89–91.

Chapter Seven

1. Huber, Vol. 3, p. 160.
2. Poschinger, *Unter Friedrich Wilhelm IV*, Vol. 1, p. 384.
3. *Ibid.* On the Hesse crisis, see Reinhard Höhn, *Verfassungskampf und Heereseid* (Leipzig: 1938), pp. 190–212.
4. Poschinger, *Unter Friedrich Wilhelm IV*, Vol. 3, pp. 104–5; Enax, pp. 12–18.
5. Hartung, "Regierung," pp. 1–17.
6. Huber, Vol. 3, pp. 64–65; Enax, pp. 13–17.
7. On Bismarck's handling of similar problems, consult Hintze, "Bismarcks Stellung."
8. Enax, pp. 12–15.

9. Huber, Vol. 3, pp. 165–67.

10. *Ibid.*, pp. 178–80; Moritz von Bethmann-Hollweg, *Die Reaktivirung der preussischen Provinziallandtage* (Berlin: 1851); Walter Schmidt, *Die Partei Bethmann Hollwegs und die Reaktion in Preussen 1850–1858* (Berlin: 1910). On the individual personalities, see Bunsen and Nippold; and Albert von Mutius, *Graf Albert Pourtalès* (Berlin: 1933).

11. Peter Rassow, "Der Konflict König Friedrich Wilhelms IV mit dem Prinzen von Preussen im Jahre 1854," *Abhandlungen der Geistes- und Sozialwissenschaftlichen Klasse,* No. 9 (1960).

12. *MB,* 1851, p. 1.

13. Heinrichs, pp. 40–48; Herbert Kaltheuner, *Der Freiherr Georg von Vincke und die Liberalen in der preussischen zweiten Kammer 1849–1855* (Münster: 1928), pp. 58–61; Hartung, "Studien," pp. 255–56.

14. Poschinger, *Unter Friedrich Wilhelm IV,* Vol. 2, p. 41; Heinrichs, pp. 40–43.

15. Huber, Vol. 3, pp. 233–37.

16. *Neue Preussische Zeitung,* Jan. 29, 1851.

17. Concerning the membership of officials in the Polish nationalist organization Liga Polska, see BA Koblenz P135 3140. After 1850 membership was banned in even such apparently innocuous organizations as Berlin's Nursing and Health Care Society. BA Koblenz P135 5411; and SA Koblenz Abt. 403 Nr. 7045.

18. Decision of Oct. 13, 1852, HA Berlin Rep. 90 Nr. 1044.

19. Case of two Rhineland Landräte, Delius and von Hilgers, HA Berlin Rep. 90 Nr. 1045; case of Landrat von Hettermann of Pomerania, *ibid.,* Nr. 1035; case of Landrat von Poninski of Posen, *ibid.,* Nr. 2322.

20. Ferdinand Fischer, p. 257.

21. Another ten were brought before this court in 1850, but there is no record of the results of their hearings. HA Berlin Rep. 90 Nr. 661.

22. Order of April 27, 1853, BA Koblenz P135 3140.

23. The list submitted by the Minister of Justice on March 11, 1855, included the names of thirteen Kreisrichter, two Kreisgerichtsräte, and two Obergerichtsassessoren. BA Koblenz P135 3140.

24. These lists included only those recommended for advances in salary and promotion, and therefore we have no record of those who were passed over.

25. *GS,* 1848, p. 20; order of June 7, 1854, HA Berlin Rep. 90 Nr. 2318.

26. Quoted from the report of the President of the Insterberg Court of Appeals, Feb. 25, 1851, and from the report of the President of the Königsberg Court of Appeals, May 30, 1855. BA Koblenz P135 2986.

27. Wagner, pp. 46–47.

28. *Ibid.,* pp. 41–44.

29. Stoelzel, pp. xxxii–xxxv.

30. Huber, Vol. 3, pp. 123–25.

31. Loening, pp. 183–86.

32. Eduard Kern, *Geschichte des Gerichtsverfassungsrechts* (Berlin: 1954), pp. 77–82.

33. Wagner, p. 119.

34. Loening, p. 258. For the opposite view, see Wagner, pp. 109–36.

35. In the vote of the Lower House 45 percent of the higher-ranking judicial officials voted for the bill, but only 17 percent of the lower ranks supported it. Wagner, p. 119.

36. Letter of Dec. 16, 1848, reprinted in Streckfuss, Vol. 2, p. 1206.

37. *Ibid.* A full report of the trial is provided in *Waldeck'sche Prozess.*

38. Bernstein, Vol. 2, p. 120; Temme, pp. 322–37.

39. For the series of negative decisions concerning the admission of Jews to the civil service, see HA Berlin Rep. 90 Nr. 498; Ernest Hamburger, *Juden im öffentlichen Leben Deutschlands* (Tübingen: 1968), pp. 1–27, 40–48.

40. Schön to G. H. Pertz, Nov. 15, 1849, in *Briefwechsel des Ministers und Burggrafen von Marienburg Theodor von Schön mit G. H. Pertz und J. G. Droysen* (Leipzig: 1896), p. 27. Similar comments in Gneist, *Freie Advocatur*, pp. 27–28.

41. Huber, Vol. 3, pp. 172–74.

42. Ferdinand Fischer, p. 138; Streckfuss, Vol. 2, p. 1255.

43. *Waldeck'sche Prozess*; Kurt Koszyk, "Carl D'Ester als Gemeinderat und Parlamentarier 1846–49," *Archiv für Sozialgeschichte*, Vol. 1 (1961), pp. 43–61; Bernstein, Vol. 1, pp. 312–18.

44. See Dorn.

45. Temme, pp. 322–400, 436.

46. Carl Schurz, *The Reminiscences of Carl Schurz*, Vol. 1 (New York: 1917), pp. 246–69, 288–95; Rudolf Herrnstadt, *Die erste Verschwörung gegen das internationale Proletariat* (Berlin: 1958).

47. Bernstein, Vol. 1, p. 324; Ferdinand Fischer, p. 146.

48. August Ladendorf, *Sechs Jahre Gefangenschaft unter den Folgen des Staatsstreichs* (Leipzig: 1862), pp. 144–50; Stieber, pp. 57–58.

49. Stieber, pp. 56–60.

50. Unruh, pp. 142–43; Varnhagen von Ense, Vol. 8, p. 338; Vol. 11, p. 356; Vol. 12, p. 336; Vol. 14, p. 247.

51. Unruh, p. 142; Streckfuss, Vol. 2, pp. 1312–17.

52. Hans Joachim Schoeps, *Das andere Preussen* (Stuttgart: 1952), Chapter 1; Enax, pp. 27–40.

53. Varnhagen von Ense, Vol. 6, p. 8; Unruh, pp. 132–33.

54. Figures from Lette, pp. 80–93.

55. Schierbaum, pp. 69, 229.

56. *Neue Preussiche Zeitung*, July 4, 1850.

57. According to Lauter, ten deputies laid down their mandates between September and the end of December 1850. For evidence of pressure exerted on one official, see Poschinger, *Preussens Auswärtige Politik*, Vol. 3, p. 107.

58. Lauter; Manteuffel's order of Feb. 17, 1851, SA Koblenz Abt. 403 Nr. 8452.

59. Minister of Interior to all Ober- and Regierungspräsidenten, SA Koblenz Abt. 403 Nr. 8452.

60. Huber, Vol. 3, pp. 162–64; and Ludwig von Gerlach's editorial in *Neue Preussische Zeitung*, July 28, 1852.

61. Circular to Oberpräsidenten, Oct. 7, 1852, SA Koblenz Abt. 403 Nr. 8452.

62. Circular to Landräte, Oct. 7, 1852, SA Koblenz Abt. 403 Nr. 8452; Schierbaum, p. 80.

63. Hermann Donner, *Die Katholische Fraktion in Preussen 1852–58,* Dissertation (University of Leipzig: 1909), pp. 1–5.

64. Lauter.

65. Kurt Borries, *Preussen im Krimkrieg 1853–56* (Stuttgart: 1930); Enax, pp. 61–79.

66. Circular of May 18, 1855, SA Koblenz Abt. 403 Nr. 8453.

67. Gerrymandering began in 1852, but apparently was not systematically practiced until the 1855 elections. Schierbaum, pp. 43, 67, 102, 119.

68. Westphalen's report on the results of the 1855 elections, HA Berlin Rep. 90 Nr. 111.

69. Bernstein, Vol. 2, pp. 212–13; Ludwig Pastor, *August Reichensperger,* Vol. 1 (Freiburg: n.d.), pp. 368–69.

70. Circular of Minister of Interior to Landräte, May 18, 1855, SA Koblenz Abt. 403 Nr. 8452.

71. Schierbaum, pp. 98–99.

72. Circular of Minister of Interior to Landräte, Sept. 7 and 15, 1855, SA Koblenz Abt. 403 Nr. 8452.

73. Lette, p. 75.

74. Circular of Minister of Culture, Sept. 19, 1855, and circular of Minister of Trade, Sept. 22, 1855, SA Koblenz Abt. 403 Nr. 8445.

75. Westphalen to Oberpräsident Kleist-Retzow, Sept. 4, 1855, SA Koblenz Abt. 403 Nr. 8452. The Landrat in question, Maximilian Foerster, had been a loyal member of the right-wing faction during the 1849–52 session of the Lower House.

76. Lauter.

77. Westphalen's report on the outcome of the 1855 elections, HA Berlin Rep. 90 Nr. 111.

Chapter Eight

1. Hübner, p. 363. The growth of a conservative critique of bureaucracy is described by Wilhelm, p. 16.

2. Party composition from Lauter; description of parties in Huber, Vol. 3, pp. 178–80.

3. Lauter.

4. Hess, pp. 15–50.

5. *Ibid.,* pp. 73–119.

6. *Ibid.,* pp. 61–72.

7. Hartung, "Studien," pp. 260–61; Hess, pp. 105–6; Anderson, *Social and Political Conflict*, Chapters 11 and 12.

8. Hess, pp. 108–19.

9. The extent of government repression of officials, particularly the numbers disciplined, has often been exaggerated. Hartung, "Studien," pp. 260–63.

10. Hintze, "Bismarcks Stellung," p. 677.

11. Rosenbaum, p. 53; Karl Demeter, "Die soziale Schichtung des deutschen Parlaments seit 1848," *VSWG*, Vol. 39 (1952), pp. 9–11.

12. Sheehan, pp. 518–19; Thomas Nipperdey, *Die Organisation der deutschen Parteien vor 1918* (Düsseldorf: 1961); Peter Molt, *Der Reichstag vor der improvisierten Revolution* (Cologne: 1963).

13. For a comparison of Prussia with other countries, see Finer, pp. 755–904.

14. On the widespread antipathy to party politics, see Theodor Schieder, "Die Theorie der Partei im älteren deutschen Liberalismus," *Staat und Gesellschaft im Wandel unserer Zeit* (Munich: 1958), pp. 110–32.

15. Rudolf von Delbrück, Vol. 2, p. 149; Ernsthausen, p. 92; Lette, p. 35.

16. Temme, p. 436; Unruh, p. 174.

17. Streckfuss, Vol. 2, p. 1311.

18. Minister of Justice Simons to king, Oct. 13, 1853, BA Koblenz P135 3140.

19. Ludwig Dehio, "Benedikt Waldeck," *HZ*, Vol. 136 (1927), pp. 25–26.

20. Unruh, pp. 123–24.

21. Hübner, Vol. 2, p. 639.

22. Varnhagen von Ense, Vol. 8, p. 273.

23. Ludwig von Gerlach's Rundschau, *Neue Preussische Zeitung*, July 28, 1852.

24. Lette, p. 37; Gneist, *Freie Advocatur*, p. 20.

25. Gneist, *Berliner Zustände*, p. 88.

26. Quoted in Varnhagen von Ense, Vol. 8, p. 228.

27. Letter dated April 1851, Bunsen and Nippold, Vol. 3, pp. 104–5.

28. Enax, pp. 27–40.

29. Wolfram Fischer, pp. 113–42.

30. Lette, pp. 96–100.

31. Hintze, "Bismarcks Stellung," p. 653.

32. Hartung, "Regierung," p. 17.

33. Weissler, pp. 467–70; Gneist, *Freie Advocatur*, p. 52.

34. Huber, Vol. 3, pp. 161–62.

35. Stieber, p. 56.

36. Unruh, p. 164.

37. Berthold Schulze, pp. 92–98; Bernstein, Vol. 2, pp. 188–89.

38. Adolf Wermuth, *Ein Beamtenleben* (Berlin: 1922), p. 15.

39. *Ibid.*, p. 14.

40. Berthold Schulze, pp. 82, 92.

41. Streckfuss, Vol. 2, p. 1117; Varnhagen von Ense, Vol. 12, p. 437.

42. Varnhagen von Ense, Vol. 8, pp. 289, 402.

43. Heinrich von Sybel, "Karl Ludwig von Hinckeldey 1852–1856," *HZ*, Vol. 189 (1959), pp. 111–18; Berthold Schulze, p. 101; Kraft Karl Prinz zu Hohenlohe-Ingelfingen, *Aus meinem Leben*, Vol. 1 (Berlin: 1897), pp. 134–37.

44. Berthold Schulze, pp. 101–7.

45. Stieber, pp. 25–30.

46. *Ibid.*, pp. 206–7.

47. Stieber to Minister of Interior Westphalen, March 1857, *ibid.*, p. 83.

48. Westphalen to Berlin Polizeipräsident Sedlitz, May 1857, *ibid.*, p. 83.

49. Huber, Vol. 3, pp. 173, 1017–18.

Chapter Nine

1. Various aspects of this process are described in Demeter; Rosenberg, "Demokratisierung"; and Muncy, pp. 220–34.

2. *JMB*, 1858, pp. 300–304; 1863, pp. 166–68.

3. Circular from Minister of Culture, May 13, 1857, BA Koblenz Abt. 113 Nr. 2652.

4. Circular from Minister of Justice, Jan. 11, 1858, *JMB*, 1858, pp. 18–19.

5. Petition signed by 135 judicial Assessoren to the Judiciary Committee of the Lower House and dated 1860, BA Koblenz P135 3556.

6. Report of the Judiciary Committee of the Lower House, June 1861, *ibid.*

7. Conrad, pp. 105–18.

8. Finer, pp. 794–808; Clemens von Delbrück, pp. 9–14.

9. Kleist-Retzow to Staatsministerium, Feb. 28, 1857, HA Berlin Rep. 90 Nr. 2336.

10. Reply of Minister of Interior to Kleist-Retzow, April 20, 1857, *ibid.*

11. Between 1850 and 1911 the total number of civil officials in Prussia rose from 25,000 to 250,000. The higher administration (including Land-räte) increased from about 1,100 to about 1,850. There are no figures available for the higher judiciary, but it can be supposed that its increase paralleled that of the higher administration. For figures on the total bureaucracy, see Finer, p. 710.

12. On the judiciary, consult Gneist, *Freie Advocatur*, pp. 29–30, 38–39. The trend toward a monocratic system began earlier in the administrative branch, but the full effects were not felt until the second half of the century. Fann, pp. 63–73.

13. Figures compiled from lists to be found in BA Koblenz P135 2792; and *JMB*, 1839, pp. 414–16; 1858, pp. 300–304.

14. Gneist, *Freie Advocatur*, pp. 29–30; Schulze and Ssymank, pp. 430–33.

15. Muncy, pp. 70–71. On the attempts to reverse this situation during the 1880's, see Kehr, "Soziale System," pp. 74–78; and Dahrendorf, "Deutsche Richter," pp. 176–96.

16. Lotz, p. 424; Most, pp. 183–85.

17. Lotz, p. 615; Muncy, pp. 173–74.
18. Ralf Dahrendorf, *Class and Class Conflict in Industrial Society* (Stanford, Calif.: 1959), pp. 6–7.
19. Report of Königsberg Court of Appeals, Sept. 26, 1855; and petition of subaltern officials at Culm, Nov. 7, 1855, BA Koblenz P135 7165.
20. Bodelschwingh to Minister of Justice Simons, Nov. 10, 1855, *ibid.*
21. Most, p. 185.
22. *Preussens Beamtentum; Neue Preussische Zeitung*, Feb. 12, 1857, Beilage.
23. Eichholtz, pp. 159–66.
24. This point is developed in Talcott Parsons, "The Professions and Social Structure," *Essays in Sociological Theory, Pure and Applied* (Glencoe, Ill.: 1949), pp. 185–99; and Lenore O'Boyle, "The Middle Class in Western Europe," *AHR*, Vol. 71 (1966), pp. 826–45.
25. Zunkel, *Rheinisch-Westfälische Unternehmer*, pp. 99–132.
26. *Neue Preussische Zeitung*, Feb. 12, 1857, Beilage.
27. Zunkel, *Rheinisch-Westfälische Unternehmer*, pp. 51–54.
28. Griewank, pp. 38–40; Ringer, pp. 25–28.
29. Conrad, pp. 51–52.
30. Ringer, pp. 40–61; Zorn, pp. 329–32.
31. Friedrich Paulsen, *Die Deutschen Universitäten und das Universitätsstudium* (Berlin: 1902), pp. 137–70.
32. Conrad, pp. 51–52; Ringer, p. 39; Wolfgang Zapf, *Wandlungen der deutschen Elite* (Munich: 1965), pp. 38–43.
33. BA Koblenz P135 2556.
34. The numbers of sons of higher officials studying law dropped from 130 per semester in the early 1850's to 70 in the late 1870's. The proportions dropped from 28 percent to 16 percent in the same period. Conrad, pp. 51–52. On similar patterns at Leipzig University, see Eulenburg, pp. 65–75, 202–3.
35. The average number of children for married officials in the Rhineland administration fell from four plus in the 1840's to three at the end of the century. In the 1850's 22 percent of the regular administrators (including Landräte) were unmarried, but by 1905 this had climbed to 27 percent. This and subsequent figures on the Rhineland administration come from SA Koblenz Abt. 403 Nr. 5292, 14556, 14553, 5308, 5319, 14562, 5320, 14559, 14560, 14565, and 14558. These include data from the years 1875 and 1905.
36. Most, p. 195.
37. Conrad, pp. 51–52; Eulenburg, pp. 65–75; Lenz, p. 522.
38. See various petitions submitted by judicial officials, BA Koblenz P135 7155, 7165.
39. Zunkel, *Rheinisch-Westfälische Unternehmer*, pp. 86–88, 114–15; Demeter, Chapter 1.
40. Demeter, pp. 18, 22, 53, 78; Kehr, "Genesis des Reserveoffiziers," pp. 53–63.

41. Muncy, pp. 104, 107.
42. Personnel records of Rhineland administrators, 1905.
43. Helmuth von Gerlach, *Vom Rechts nach Links* (Zurich: 1937), p. 20; Runge, pp. 169–79; also Richter, p. 114.
44. Muncy, pp. 105–7; Kehr, "Genesis des Reserveoffiziers."
45. Conrad, pp. 51–52; Eulenburg, p. 72; Paulsen, *German Universities*, pp. 122–26; Lenz, p. 522.
46. This is demonstrated by the percentages of sons of businessmen and landowners serving as administration officials in the Rhineland in 1905. See personnel records of 1905; cf. Runge, p. 170. In 1911 the government produced its own survey of the social composition of the total higher administrative bureaucracy. The following table shows the results (taken from *SBV*, 1911 session, Vol. 1, p. 103):

| Rank | Father's profession | | | |
	Military officer or civil official	Free profession (including lawyers)	Land-owner	Business or industry
Regierungspräsident	60%	2%	30%	8%
Regierungsrat	46%	16%	18%	20%
Landrat	48%	6%	32%	14%

47. Compiled from *Personnel Reports* of 1850–58 (cited in note 41, Chapter 2); and personnel records of 1875 and 1905. The small number of Assessoren in each of the three years used may account for the wide variations in the percentages of that particular category.
48. In 1905 20 percent of those who owned land were Landräte.
49. A small number of higher officials sat on the boards of banks, trusts, or public organizations. It appears that the additional incomes derived from these activities amounted, in a very few cases, to as much as half their regular salary. See personnel records of Cologne Regierung, SA Koblenz Abt. 403 Nr. 5320.
50. Personnel reports of 1905. Figures exclude Landräte.
51. The 1905 sample indicates no substantial differences between the wealth of easterners and westerners.
52. Bachem, p. 83; Runge, pp. 172–76.
53. In the Rhineland administration of 1905, Catholic officials were generally wealthier than other officials. On the conservatism of Catholic officials, see Runge, pp. 174–78.
54. In the 1840's the Prussian judiciary was 10 percent Catholic; by 1870 it was 25 percent Catholic. In 1912 only about 18 percent of the administration was Catholic. Figures for judiciary from lists in BA Koblenz P135 2791, 2792, 3258; and Bachem, pp. 74–75. On administration, see Runge, p. 173.

55. From lists dated 1871–72, BA Koblenz P135 3258.
56. Weissler, pp. 600–603.
57. Rosenberg, "Demokratisierung"; Peter Molt, *Der Reichstag vor der improvisierten Revolution*, pp. 83–90; John R. Gillis, "Aristocracy and Bureaucracy in Nineteenth-Century Prussia," *Past and Present*, No. 41 (Dec. 1968), pp. 104–29.
58. Muncy, pp. 100–113; Horn, pp. 273–78; Runge, pp. 171–72.
59. The 1911 report also distinguished between what the government called "old nobility," by which it apparently meant those with attachments to the land, and the "new nobility," aristocrats with service associations. Unfortunately, no further breakdown was given.

Rank	Old (landed) nobility	New (service) nobility	Non-nobles
Regular officials (excluding Landräte)	23%	5%	72%
Landräte	50%	6%	44%

60. Compiled from *HHS*, 1839 and 1914.
61. Demeter, pp. 36–40; Preradovich, pp. 124–53.
62. Kehr, "Soziale System"; Dahrendorf, "Deutsche Richter," p. 185; Muncy, pp. 71–72.
63. Preradovich, pp. 115–17.
64. The following table indicates changes in the estate composition of the total higher administration (compiled from *HHS*, 1820 and 1851; and from 1911 report on social composition of higher administration):

Year	Oberpräsidenten and Regierungspräsidenten		Regierungsräte		Landräte	
	Noble	Non-noble	Noble	Non-noble	Noble	Non-noble
1820	79%	21%	18%	82%	73%	27%
1851	79%	21%	27%	73%	64%	36%
1911	71%	29%	22%	78%	56%	44%

65. Gutsmuth Freimund [pseud.], *Patriotische Untersuchungen bezüglich preussischer Zustände* (Hamburg: 1860), Vol. 1, pp. 20–41; Muncy, pp. 101–4, 180–82; Herbert Jacob, *German Administration Since Bismarck* (New Haven, Conn.: 1963), pp. 11–21.
66. Muncy, pp. 59–60.
67. Runge, pp. 176–78.

68. Leonard D. White, "The British Civil Service," *Civil Service Abroad,* ed. L. D. White (New York: 1935), pp. 1–54; R. K. Kelsall, *Higher Civil Servants in Britain from 1870 to the Present Day* (London: 1955); T. Bottomore, "Higher Civil Servants in France," *Transactions of the Second World Congress of Sociology,* Vol. 2 (1954), pp. 143–51; Walter Sharp, *French Bureaucracy in Transition* (New York: 1931); F. Ridley and J. Blondel, *Public Administration in France* (London: 1964). General comparative treatments of the role of bureaucracies in politics are provided by Thomas I. Emerson and David Helfield, "Loyalty Among Government Employees," *Yale Law Journal,* Vol. 58 (1948), pp. 120–27; Bendix, pp. 116–28; and Anderson and Anderson, pp. 388–93.

Chapter Ten

1. See Most. The emergence of elite studies is discussed in Anthony Oberschall, *Empirical Social Research in Germany, 1848–1914* (The Hague: 1965).

2. The period of depression 1873–97 provided some relief for those on fixed salary, but inflationary prosperity worked more to the advantage of the businessman than the bureaucrat. Hans Rosenberg, *Grosse Depression und Bismarckzeit* (Berlin: 1967), pp. 42–43, 53–55.

3. Rosenberg on the Bismarck period, *ibid.,* pp. 126–32. The internal divisions revealed in the conflict over agrarian issues is treated by Horn; and by J. C. G. Röhl, "Higher Civil Servants in Germany," *Journal of Contemporary History,* Vol. 2 (1967), pp. 101–21. For a brilliant analysis of the position of the bureaucracy at the end of the monarchy, see Max Weber, "Wahlrecht und Demokratie in Deutschland," *Gesammelte politische Schriften,* 2d ed. (Tübingen: 1958), pp. 233–79.

4. Dahrendorf, *Society and Democracy,* pp. 268–69.

5. The English case is carefully analyzed in Henry Parris, *Constitutional Bureaucracy* (London: 1969), pp. 80–106, 134–59; and in George Kitson-Clark, "Statesmen in Disguise: Reflections on the History of the Neutrality of the Civil Service," *Historical Journal,* Vol. 2 (1959), pp. 19–39.

Selected Bibliography

A Note on the Archival Materials and Official Published Sources
Not having access to the East German archives, I have relied on the collections of the Hauptarchiv in Berlin-Dahlem and the Bundesarchiv in Koblenz for the documents of the central government ministries. The Hauptarchiv contains *Akten des Preussischen Staatsministeriums* (Rep. 90) and *Akten des Preussischen Ministeriums des Innern* (Rep. 77), both useful for the history of the administration. The Bundesarchiv contains *Generalakten des preussischen Justizministeriums* (P135), a rich source for the history of the judiciary. The archives of the Rhineland administration were indispensable to this study. The Staatsarchiv at Koblenz contains *Akten des Oberpräsidiums Koblenz* (Abt. 403), as well as *Akten der Regierung Trier* and *Akten der Regierung Köln*. The Staatsarchiv at Düsseldorf contains *Akten der Regierung Düsseldorf* and *Akten der Regierung Aachen*. Most of the pertinent Düsseldorf documents are in Schloss Kalkum, outside Düsseldorf. For contemporary newspapers and pamphlets, I relied on the extensive collections of the Landesarchiv Berlin (West) and the Ratsbibliothek in East Berlin. The Landesarchiv's collection of material relating to the Revolution of 1848–49 is listed as *Erinnerungsblätter 1848* (Rep. 240 Acc. 648); the Ratsbibliothek's collection is filed as *Plakate und Flugschriften zur Revolution 1848–49* (eleven portfolios).

Several publications of the government were also indispensable. These are *Gesetzammlung für die Königlich Preussischen Staaten*; *Handbuch über den Königlich Preussischen Hof und Staat*; *Königlich Preussischer Staatskalender*; *Justizministerialblatt*; *Ministerialblatt für die Innere Verwaltung*; *Stenographische Berichte über die Verhandlungen des Hauses der Abgeordneten* (Lower House), 1849–58; and *Verhandlungen der constituierenden Versammlung für Preussen 1848*, in seven volumes (Berlin, 1848). It would have been impossible to analyze the parliamentary politics of the 1850's without Franz Lauter's semiofficial listing of deputies by party affiliation, *Preussens Volksvertretung in der zweiten Kammer und im Hause der Abgeordneten vom Februar 1849 bis Mai 1877* (Berlin, 1889).

Sources in addition to those listed below may be found in the extensive bibliographies in Theodore S. Hamerow's *Restoration, Revolution, Reaction* and Reinhard Koselleck's *Preussen zwischen Reform und Revolution.*

Ammon, Friedrich von. *Erinnerung an Friedrich von Ammon.* Bonn, 1878.

Anderson, Eugene N. *The Social and Political Conflict in Prussia, 1858–1864.* Lincoln, Nebraska, 1954.

—— and Pauline R. Anderson. *Political Institutions and Social Change in Continental Europe in the Nineteenth Century.* Berkeley and Los Angeles, 1967.

Bachem, Karl. *Vorgeschichte, Geschichte und Politik der Deutschen Zentrums Partei,* Vol. 9. Cologne, 1932.

Bendix, Reinhard. *Nation-Building and Citizenship: Studies in Our Changing Social Order.* New York, 1964.

Bergenroth, Gustav. *Was hat der Landmann bei den bevorstehenden Wahlen zu Thun?* Berlin, 1848.

Berlins Gegenwart und Zukunft. Berlin, 1848.

Bernstein, Aaron. *Revolutions- und Reaktionsgeschichte.* 3 vols. N.p., 1882.

Bismarck, Otto von. *Gedanken und Erinnerungen.* Munich, 1962.

Boehn, Max von. *Biedermeier: Deutschland von 1815 bis 1847.* Berlin, 1911.

——. *Die Mode.* 4 vols. Munich, 1908.

Born, Stephan. *Erinnerungen eines Achtundvierzigers.* Leipzig, 1898.

Brunschwig, Henri. *La crise de l'état prussien à la fin du XVIIIe siècle et la genèse de la mentalité romantique.* Paris, 1947.

Bülow-Cummerow, Ernst von. *Preussen, seine Verfassung, seine Verwaltung, sein Verhältnis zu Deutschland.* 2 parts. Berlin, 1842.

——. *Die Revolution, ihre Früchte, die Politik, die Reform.* Berlin, 1850.

Bunsen, Baroness, and F. Nippold, eds. *Christian Carl Josias Freiherr von Bunsen.* Vol. 3. Leipzig, 1871.

Busch, Alexander. *Die Geschichte des Privatdozenten.* Stuttgart, 1959.

Conduiten-Listen. Berlin, n.d.

Conrad, Johannes. "Das Universitätsstudium in Deutschland während die letzten 50 Jahre," *Sammlung nationalökonomischer und statistischer Abhandlungen,* III (1884).

Conze, Werner. "Spannungsfeld von Staat und Gesellschaft im Vormärz," in *Staat und Gesellschaft im deutschen Vormärz.* Stuttgart, 1962.

——. "Vom 'Pöbel' zum 'Proletariat,'" *Vierteljahrsschrift für Sozial- und Wirtschaftsgeschichte,* XLI (1954), 333–64.

Craig, Gordon A. *The Politics of the Prussian Army.* Oxford, 1956.

Dahrendorf, Ralf. "Deutsche Richter," in *Gesellschaft und Freiheit.* Munich, 1963.

——. *Society and Democracy in Germany.* New York, 1967.

Delbrück, Clemens von. *Die Ausbildung für den höheren Verwaltungsdienst in Preussen.* Jena, 1917.

Delbrück, Rudolf von. *Lebenserinnerungen 1817–1867.* 2 vols. Leipzig, 1905.
Demeter, Karl. *Das deutsche Offizierskorps in Gesellschaft und Staat.* 2d ed. Frankfurt, 1964.
Die Contra-Revolution in Berlin, oder Bürger und Arbeiter. Berlin, 1848.
Diest, Gustav von. *Aus dem Leben eines Glücklichen.* Berlin, 1904.
Dorn, C. *Der Prozess gegen 42 steuerverweigernde, Abgeordnete der Preussischen National-Versammlung.* Berlin, 1850.
Dreesen, Jacob. *Köln im tollen Jahr 1848.* Cologne, 1898.
Dronke, Ernst. *Berlin.* 2d ed. Berlin, 1953.
Düsseldorf 1848. Düsseldorf, 1948.
Eberty, Felix. *Jugenderinnerungen eines alten Berliners.* Berlin, 1878.
Eichholtz, Dietrich. *Junker und Bourgeoisie.* Berlin, 1962.
Enax, Karl. *Otto von Manteuffel und die Reaktion in Preussen.* Dresden, 1907.
Engelsing, Rolf. "Zur politischen Bildung der deutschen Unterschichten 1789–1863," *Historische Zeitschrift,* CCVI (1968).
Epstein, Klaus. *The Genesis of German Conservatism.* Princeton, N.J., 1966.
Ernsthausen, A. Ernst von. *Erinnerungen eines preussischen Beamten.* Bielefeld and Leipzig, 1894.
Eulenburg, Franz. *Die Entwicklung der Universität Leipzig.* Leipzig, 1909.
Eyck, Frank. *The Frankfurt Parliament.* New York, 1968.
Faber, Karl-Georg. *Die Rheinlande zwischen Restauration und Revolution.* Wiesbaden, 1966.
———. "Verwaltungs- und Justizbeamte auf dem linken Rheinufer während der französischen Herrschaft," in *Aus Geschichte und Landeskunde.* Bonn, 1960.
Fann, Willard R. "The Consolidation of Bureaucratic Absolutism in Prussia, 1817–1827." Unpublished Ph.D. diss. University of California at Berkeley, 1965.
Finer, Herman. *Theory and Practice of Modern Government.* New York, 1949.
Fischer, Ferdinand. *Preussen am Abschlusse der ersten Hälfte des neunzehnten Jahrhunderts.* Berlin, 1876.
Fischer, Wolfram. "Staat und Gesellschaft Badens im Vormärz," in *Staat und Gesellschaft im deutschen Vormärz 1815–1848.* Stuttgart, 1962.
Friedrich, Carl J. "The Continental Tradition of Training Administrators in Law and Jurisprudence," *Journal of Modern History,* XII (1939).
Gerlach, Ernst Ludwig von. *Aufzeichnungen aus seinem Leben und Wirken 1795–1877,* ed. J. von Gerlach. 2 vols. Schwerin in Mecklenberg, 1903.
Gerlach, Leopold von. *Denkwürdigkeiten aus dem Leben Leopold von Gerlachs.* 2 vols. Berlin, 1892.
Gerstfeldt, Philip. "Beitrage zur Statistik der Finanzen in Preussen," *Jahrbücher für Nationalökonomie und Statistik,* VII (1883).
Gerth, Hans. *Die sozialgeschichtliche Lage der bürgerlichen Intelligenz um die Wende des 18. Jahrhunderts.* Frankfurt, 1935.

Gneist, Rudolf. *Berliner Zustände, Politische Skizzen aus der Zeit vom 18. März 1848 bis 18. März 1849.* Berlin, 1849.

———. *Freie Advocatur, Die erste Forderung aller Justizreform in Preussen.* Berlin, 1867.

Griewank, Karl. *Deutsche Studenten und Universitäten in der Revolution von 1848.* Wiemar, 1949.

Haenchen, Karl. "Zur revolutionären Unterwühlung Berlins vor den Märztagen des Jahres 1848," *Forschungen zur brandenburgischen und preussischen Geschichte,* XLIV (1943).

Hamerow, Theodore S. *Restoration, Revolution, Reaction.* Princeton, N.J., 1958.

Hansemann, David. *Preussen und Frankreich.* Leipzig, 1834.

———. *Das preussische und deutsche Verfassungswerk.* Berlin, 1850.

Hansen, Joseph, ed. *Rheinische Briefe und Akten zur Geschichte der politischen Bewegung 1830–1850.* 2 vols. Essen, 1919.

Hartung, Fritz. "Studien zur Geschichte der preussischen Verwaltung," in *Staatsbildende Kräfte der Neuzeit.* Berlin, 1961.

———. "Verantwortliche Regierung, Kabinette und Nebenregierungen im konstitutionellen Preussen 1848–1918," *Forschungen zur brandenburgischen und preussischen Geschichte,* XLIV (1932).

Heffter, Heinrich. *Die deutsche Selbstverwaltung im 19. Jahrhundert.* Stuttgart, 1950.

Heinemann, Fritz. *Die Politik des Grafen Brandenburg.* Berlin, 1909.

Heinrichs, Joseph. *Die Reaktivierung der Kreis- und Provinzialstände.* Bonn, 1917.

Heinzen, Karl. *Die preussische Büreaukratie.* Darmstadt, 1845.

Henderson, William O. *The State and the Industrial Revolution in Prussia, 1740–1870.* Liverpool, 1958.

Hermann, Alfred. *Berliner Demokraten.* Berlin, 1948.

Hess, Adalbert. *Das Parlament das Bismarck widerstrebte.* Cologne and Opladen, 1964.

Hintze, Otto. *Der Beamtenstand, Vorträge der Gehe-Stiftung zu Dresden.* Vol. 3. Leipzig, 1911.

———. "Bismarcks Stellung zur Monarchie und zum Beamtentum," in *Geist und Epochen der preussischen Geschichte,* ed. F. Hartung. Leipzig, 1943.

———. "Der oesterreichische und preussische Beamtenstaat im 17. und 18. Jahrhundert," *Historische Zeitschrift,* LXXXVI (1901).

Holborn, Hajo. "Der deutsche Idealismus in sozialgeschichtlicher Beleuchtung," *Historische Zeitschrift,* CLXXIV (1952).

Holtze, Friedrich. *Geschichte des Kammergerichts in Brandenburg-Preussen.* Vol. 4. Berlin, 1904.

Horn, Hannelore. "Die Rolle des Bundes der Landwirte im Kampf um den Bau des Mittellandkanals," *Jahrbuch für die Geschichte Mittel- und Ostdeutschlands,* VII (1958).

Huber, Ernst Rudolf. *Deutsche Verfassungsgeschichte seit 1789.* 3 vols. Stuttgart, 1957–63.

Hübner, Rudolf, ed. *Johann Gustav Droysen Briefwechsel.* Vol. 2. Berlin, 1929.

Jacoby, Johann. *Heinrich Simon.* Berlin, 1865.

Jung, Georg. *Der Berliner Cavaignac.* Berlin, 1848.

Kaeber, Ernst. *Berlin 1848.* Berlin, 1948.

Kehr, Eckart. "Das soziale System der Reaktion in Preussen unter dem Ministerium Puttkamer," in *Primat der Innenpolitik,* ed. Hans-Ulrich Wehler. Berlin, 1965, pp. 64–86.

———. "Zur Genesis der preussischen Bürokratie und des Rechtsstaats," in *Primat der Innenpolitik,* ed. Hans-Ulrich Wehler. Berlin, 1965.

———. "Zur Genesis des Königlich Preussischen Reserveoffiziers," in *Primat der Innenpolitik,* ed. Hans-Ulrich Wehler. Berlin, 1965.

Kersken, Hans. *Stadt und Universität Bonn in den Revolutionsjahren 1848–49.* Bonn, 1931.

Köllmann, Wolfgang. "Die Anfänge der staatlichen Sozialpolitik," *Vierteljahrsschrift für Sozial- und Wirtschaftsgeschichte,* LIII (1966).

Koselleck, Reinhard. *Preussen zwischen Reform und Revolution, Allgemeines Landrecht, Verwaltung und soziale Bewegung von 1791 bis 1848.* Stuttgart, 1967.

———. "Staat und Gesellschaft in Preussen 1815–1848," in *Staat und Gesellschaft im deutschen Vormärz.* Stuttgart, 1962.

Krieger, Leonard. *The German Idea of Freedom.* Boston, 1957.

Lauter, Franz. *Preussens Volksvertretung in der zweiten Kammer und im Hause der Abgeordneten vom Februar 1849 bis Mai 1877.* Berlin, 1889.

Lenz, Max. *Geschichte der Universität Berlin.* Vol. 3. Halle, 1910.

Lette, Wilhelm. *Über die Verfassungzustände in Preussen.* Berlin, 1857.

Loening, Edgar. *Gerichte und Verwaltungsbehörden in Brandenburg-Preussen.* Halle, 1914.

Loos. *Aphorismen über den Rechtszustand in Preussen.* Berlin, 1842.

Lotz, Albert. *Geschichte des deutschen Beamtentums.* Berlin, 1909.

Marcks, Erich. *Bismarck.* Stuttgart, 1909.

Meyer, Dora. *Das öffentliche Leben in Berlin im Jahr vor der Märzrevolution.* Berlin, 1912.

Most, Otto. "Zur Wirtschafts- und Sozialstatistik der höheren Beamten in Preussen," *Schmollers Jahrbuch für Gesetzgebung, Verwaltung und Volkswirtschaft,* XXXIX (1915).

Muncy, Lysbeth Walker. *The Junker in the Prussian Administration under William II, 1888–1914.* Providence, R.I., 1944.

Nathan, Helene. *Preussens Verfassung und Verwaltung im Urteile rheinischer Achtundvierziger.* Bonn, 1912.

Naudé, Wilhelm. "Zur Geschichte des preussischen Subalternbeamtentums," *Forschungen zur brandenburgischen und preussischen Geschichte,* XVIII (1905).

Noyes, Paul. *Organization and Revolution: Working-Class Associations in the German Revolution of 1848–49*. Princeton, N.J., 1966.

Obermann, Karl. "Die Berliner Universität am Vorabend und während der Revolution 1848–49," in *Forschung und Wirkung*. Vol. 1. Berlin, 1960.

O'Boyle, Lenore. "The Democratic Left in Germany, 1848," *Journal of Modern History*, XXXIII (1961).

Paulsen, Friedrich. *The German Universities and University Study*, trans. F. Tilly. New York, 1906.

———. *Geschichte des gelehrten Unterrichts*. Vol. 2. Berlin and Leipzig, 1921.

Perthes, Clemens Theodor. *Der Staatsdienst in Preussen*. Hamburg, 1838.

Plathner, Günther. *Der Kampf um die richterliche Unabhängigkeit bis zum Jahre 1848*. Berlin, 1935.

Poschinger, H. von, ed. *Preussens Auswärtige Politik 1850–58*. 3 vols. Berlin, 1902–3.

———. *Unter Friedrich Wilhelm IV: Denkwürdigkeiten des Ministers Otto Freiherrn von Manteuffel*. 3 vols. Berlin, 1901.

Preradovich, Nicholaus von. *Die Führungsschichten in Österreich und Preussen 1804–1918*. Wiesbaden, 1955.

Preussens Beamtentum und seine Finanzen. Berlin, 1857.

Reichensperger, Peter. *Erlebnisse eines alten Parlamentariers im Revolutionsjahre 1848*. Berlin, 1882.

Repgen, Konrad. *Märzbewegung und Maiwahlen des Revolutionsjahres 1848 im Rheinland*. Bonn, 1955.

Richter, Eugen. *Jugenderinnerungen*. Berlin, 1892.

Riehl, Wilhelm Heinrich. *Die bürgerliche Gesellschaft*. 5th ed. Stuttgart, 1861.

Ringer, Fritz. *The Decline of the German Mandarins: The German Academic Community, 1890–1933*. Cambridge, Mass., 1969.

Rosenbaum, Louis. *Beruf und Herkunft der Abgeordneten zu den deutschen und preussischen Parlamenten 1847 bis 1919*. Frankfurt, 1923.

Rosenberg, Hans. *Bureaucracy, Aristocracy and Autocracy: The Prussian Experience, 1660–1815*. Cambridge, Mass., 1958.

———. "Die 'Demokratisierung' der Rittergutsbesitzerklasse," in *Zur Geschichte und Problematik der Demokratie*. Berlin, 1958.

Runge, Wolfgang. *Politik und Beamtentum in Parteistaat*. Stuttgart, 1965.

Schierbaum, Hansjürgen. *Die politischen Wahlen in den Eifel- und Moselkreisen des Regierungsbezirks Trier 1849–67*. Düsseldorf, 1960.

Schilfert, Gerhard. *Sieg und Niederlage des demokratischen Wahlrechts in der deutschen Revolution 1848–49*. Berlin, 1952.

Schön, Theodor von. *Woher und Wohin?* Strassburg, 1843.

Schorn, Karl. *Lebenserinnerungen*. 2 vols. Bonn, 1898.

Schulze, Berthold. "Polizeipräsident Karl von Hinckeldey," *Jahrbuch für Geschichte Mittel- und Ostdeutschlands*, IV (1955).

Schulze, Friedrich, and Paul Ssymank. *Das deutsche Studententum von den ältesten Zeiten bis zur Gegenwart.* 4th ed. Munich, 1931.

Sheehan, James J. "Political Leadership in the German Reichstag, 1871–1918," *American Historical Review*, LXXIV (1968).

"Statistische Übersicht des öffentlichen Unterrichts im preussischen Staate im Jahre 1816 und im Jahre 1846," in *Mittheilungen des statistischen Bureau's in Berlin*, I (1848).

Stieber, Wilhelm J.C.E. *Denkwürdigkeiten des Geheimen Regierungsrathes Dr. Stieber*, ed. L. Auerbach. Berlin, 1884.

Stoelzel, Adolf. *Brandenburg-Preussens Rechtsverwaltung und Rechtsverfassung.* Vol. 1. Berlin, 1888.

Streckfuss, Adolf. *500 Jahre Berliner Geschichte.* 2 vols. Berlin, 1886.

Temme, Jodocus D.H. *Erinnerungen*, ed. Stephan Born. Leipzig, 1883.

Thiede, Klaus. *Die Staats- und Wirtschaftsauffassung des Freiherrn vom Stein.* Jena, 1927.

Tocqueville, Alexis de. *The Old Regime and the French Revolution.* Garden City, N.Y., 1955.

Treitschke, Heinrich von. *Deutsche Geschichte im neunzehnten Jahrhundert.* 5 vols. Leipzig, 1927.

Unruh, Hans Viktor von. *Erinnerungen aus dem Leben von Hans Viktor von Unruh*, ed. H. von Poschinger. Stuttgart, 1895.

Valentin, Veit. *Die Geschichte der deutschen Revolution von 1848–49.* 2 vols. Berlin, 1930–31.

Varnhagen von Ense, Karl A. *Tagebücher von K. A. Varnhagen von Ense.* 14 vols. Hamburg, 1869.

Wagner, Albrecht. *Der Kampf der Justiz gegen die Verwaltung in Preussen.* Hamburg, 1936.

Der Waldeck'sche Prozess. 2d ed. Berlin, 1849.

Wegge, Hans. *Die Stellung der Öffentlichkeit zur oktroyierten Verfassung und die preussische Parteibildung 1848–49.* Berlin, 1932.

Weidemann. *Oberschlesische Zustände in freien Rasirspiegel Scenen.* Leipzig, 1843.

Weissler, A. *Geschichte der Rechtsanwaltschaft.* Berlin, 1905.

Wilhelm, Theodor. *Die Idee des Berufsbeamtentums, Ein Beitrag zur Staatslehre des deutschen Früh-Konstitutionalismus.* Tübingen, 1933.

Wolff, Adolf. *Berliner Revolutionschronik.* Berlin, 1898.

Zorn, Wolfgang. "Hochschule und höhere Schule in der deutschen Sozialgeschichte der Neuzeit," in *Spiegel der Geschichte*, ed. K. Repgen. Münster, 1964.

Zunkel, Friedrich. "Beamtenschaft und Unternehmertum beim Aufbau der Ruhrindustrie 1849–1880," *Tradition*, IX (1964).

———. *Der Rheinisch-Westfälische Unternehmer 1834–1879.* Cologne and Opladen, 1962.

Index